JAPANESE COUNTERCULTURE

Japanese Counterculture

. . . .

The Antiestablishment Art of Terayama Shūji

Steven C. Ridgely

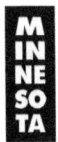

University of Minnesota Press
Minneapolis • London

A subvention for this publication has been awarded through a competitive grant from the University of Wisconsin–Madison Provost's Office and the Graduate School. Graduate School funding has been provided by the Wisconsin Alumni Research Foundation (WARF) with income generated by patents filed through WARF by UW–Madison faculty and staff.

Quotations of poetry throughout the book are reprinted here with permission of Miyoshi Daisuke, Kujō Kyōko and Terayama World, Fukunaga Kayo, Nakamura Yumiko, and Saito Naoki.

Poems by Nakamura Yumiko copyright Nakamura Yumiko

Published by the University of Minnesota Press
111 Third Avenue South, Suite 290
Minneapolis, MN 55401–2520
http://www.upress.umn.edu

Library of Congress Cataloging-in-Publication Data

Ridgely, Steven C.
Japanese counterculture : the antiestablishment art of Terayama Shūji / Steven C. Ridgely.
p. cm.
Includes bibliographical references and index.
ISBN 978-0-8166-6752-9 (hc : alk. paper)—ISBN 978-0-8166-6753-6 (pb : alk. paper)
1. Terayama Shūji, 1935–1983—Criticism and interpretation.
2. Counterculture—Japan. I. Title.
PL862.E7Z82 2011
895.6′8509—dc22
2010028451

Printed in the United States of America on acid-free paper

The University of Minnesota is an equal-opportunity educator and employer.

17 16 15 14 13 12 11 10   10 9 8 7 6 5 4 3 2 1

Contents

Global Counterculture, Visual Counterculture

A JAPANESE EXAMPLE CANNOT PROVE COUNTERCULTURE to have been global. Yet if counterculture was a global phenomenon, then we stand to learn more about it by looking at the work of a Japanese figure like Terayama Shūji (1935–83). While slightly young for the beat generation, Terayama debuted in the mid-1950s, and he was similarly entranced by improvisational jazz (both as music and as a model for writing), similarly scandalous, and similarly positioned by the mid-1960s to be an elder leader (at around age thirty) in youth culture's Great Refusal. Terayama's creative output shifts over time from haiku, tanka (the thirty-one-syllable genre), and free-verse poetry toward radio drama, television scripts, and screenplay writing for early 1960s New Wave films, then on to cultural critique, a novel about boxing, and finally settling from 1967 on underground (*angura*) theater and experimental film, which would occupy him until his death in 1983 at age forty-seven. His work in the 1960s makes a transition from individual toward collaborative production and from verbal toward visual expression—a shift we see in a number of Japanese authors in this period.

Terayama certainly stands out for his contribution to each of these fields but perhaps most importantly for his shifts across media over time and his overtly transmedia projects. He was a decathlete more than a specialist. As such, he is often praised in Japan as being "multi," and it has become standard for any description of Terayama to begin with a long list of his personalities. But this notion of a jack-of-all-trades or a Renaissance man does not do full justice to the significance of Terayama's movement across different cultural forms. He was not working in all fields throughout his career, and so it is important to recognize that Terayama's participation in particular modes typically occurred when something significant was happening in that realm (young poets seizing control of haiku and tanka in the 1950s, radio drama experimenting with form and content after the brain drain to television around 1960, young assistant directors given free rein in the New Wave as cinema combated television, the important boxing discourse in the mid-1960s, underground theater in the politicized late 1960s, and experimental short film through the 1970s after both the studio system and art-house cinema had collapsed). There is an important historical embeddedness in Terayama's work in each field that gets obscured when this movement is painted over with the image of a clever dilettante.

However we want to characterize Terayama Shūji, we can safely claim him to be near the center of Japanese counterculture—he wrote antiestablishment poetry in the imperial court's genre; agitated for sexual revolution; paired velvet platform sandals with suits; put together a theater troupe out of runaways, street musicians, and transvestites who performed rock musicals and guerilla street theater; and directed films that invoke *Flaming Creatures* or some of Andy Warhol's projects. He collaborated in book publishing, theater production, and filmmaking with major countercultural artists like photographer Moriyama Daidō and the graphic designers Yokoo Tadanori, Awazu Kiyoshi, and Uno Akira. There are markings of the 1960s Zeitgeist in Terayama's movement across media as well. This vagabond pose—never getting tied down, staying in motion, rejecting expertise and specialization, and refusing to keep a job past the time it works for you—is central to understanding Terayama Shūji and is the reason treating just one facet of his work (poetry, theater, or film) tends to miss the larger point.

We could also safely claim that Terayama was a participant in the global counterculture—his troupe performed at Ritsaert ten Cate's Mickery Theater in Amsterdam, at Jack Lang's Festival de Nancy in France, and at Ellen Stewart's La Mama in New York; they were a hit in Shiraz; his films were shown in Berkeley; and they toured the European festival circuit. Renate Klett (of *Theatre Heute* in Berlin) said their troupe conveyed the spirit of 1968 better than any of the other performances she saw at the 1972 Olympics.[1] When in Paris, he hung out with Jim Haynes (Edinburgh Fringe Festival cofounder, coeditor of Amsterdam's sexual revolution magazine *Suck*, and core member of Arts Lab in London).[2] He visited Nelson Algren (whom he had hosted for two weeks in Tokyo in 1968) at his apartment in the Polish slums of Chicago, the same apartment Simone de Beauvoire would have gone to during her affair with the "lost generation" author of *The Man with the Golden Arm* and *Never Come Morning*.[3] He interviewed Michel Foucault in Paris and angered him by repeatedly calling him a "structuralist."[4]

If we look for counterculture in Japan, we can find men with long hair who are into psychedelia, young people obsessed with the Stones and Hendrix and Godard films, and wanderers who set out on journeys either across the country, or maybe more often, around the world. Many would see this as imitation. We might try to mitigate discomfort with the notion of imitation by framing this in a globalization–localization paradigm and to start digging around for the particular Japanese inflection of yet another wave of cultural borrowing. This model has serious flaws almost anytime we speak of culture and its movement—naturalizing the logic of imperialism—but counterculture may have developed and flowed in a way that particularly frustrates efforts to see it as motion from center to periphery. Better to conceive counterculture as a rhizomatically structured and globally synchronic mode—a new set of ideas and methods that appeared around the world at roughly the same time. This is not to deny material exchange or origins for these ideas but rather to recognize that the speed with which ideas, information, and even people could move between Paris and Tokyo, say, was functionally equivalent by the 1960s to their velocity between the East Village and Berkeley. Kerouac's road trip from New York to California certainly took him longer than Terayama's flights from Tokyo to Amsterdam—it is this internationality that so many of the clichéd markers of counterculture point toward. The Japanese in bell-bottom blue jeans with a fresh copy of *Sgt. Pepper* and the American in a *shiborizome* (tie-dyed) shirt reading about Eastern spirituality both had abandoned local or national modes of self-understanding in favor of something even beyond cosmopolitanism—a postnational (for some cosmic) state of consciousness. *Counterculture was global from the start.*

If counterculture was always already global—in its mindset, in its geographical distribution, and in its patterns of movement—then the globalization paradigm and the localization-type questions that would generate are not applicable in this case, and all for the better. Imagine trying to sort out what parts of counterculture were Japanese and which were Western when Zen was more fashionable in the West than in Japan. The globalization paradigm would inevitably gravitate toward claims about the enduring nature of Japanese cultural patterns, that against all odds we could still find group orientation, vertical society, minimalist aesthetics, and some hint of the samurai code in as unlikely a place as the "Japanese version" of a hippie. Alternatively, assuming the 1960s youth to still be shell-shocked from the war (over before most of them were born) and somehow resentful of America is a thinly glossed update to the old Orientalism—any resentment toward the United States in the late 1960s had everything to do with Vietnam, and as such was very much in solidarity with the American (and worldwide) student movement. There would be real violence in a localization paradigm—a violence against the project of counterculture itself, the kinds of global solidarity it had developed, and its own break with past practice. Such an approach would serve only to rein in and tame Japanese counterculture, to sever the ties it made, and to undo what it achieved.

We know too much about subcultures now, after Dick Hebdige and cultural studies, to stop short at sketching out the countercultural style—we must analyze this formation as a set of particular relationships. This is not to say that elements of countercultural style cannot be read semiotically—long hair speaks clearly to years *not* spent getting shot at in Vietnam (around six inches per year) just as long hair on men from places other than America or Australia showed solidarity with those nonsoldiers. These communicative elements of style are important, but we stand to learn a great deal more from the structure of counterculture—the specific tactics it used. What I hope to show with this book is how Terayama, as both a practitioner and a theorist of counterculture (he would argue that practice should never follow theory), developed and clarified a set of relations we might understand as the countercultural position. His artistic practices demonstrate the potential of this mode of cultural production, and careful analysis of them reveals a set of core principles used across a range of media and genres.

The cultural studies methodology Hebdige used (and helped to create) was itself a product of the 1960s—a countercultural intervention against the university from within by figures like Richard Hoggart and Stewart Hall. This move to erode the elitism of the university from within the campus parallels efforts in the art world to build up pockets of counterculture within major cosmopolitan centers like London, Paris, and Tokyo. Terayama's closest theatrical rival, Kara Jūrō, refused to take his troupe to these wealthy cities, traveling instead to perform in Okinawa, Bangladesh, and the Palestinian refugee camps. But we would do well to consider the way these two positions, as oppositional as they may seem, actually worked in tandem—Kara creating links of solidarity with the global proletariat while Terayama airlifted cultural sustenance to fifth columns in the finance capitals. Who cared if the art collectives were doomed to collapse; longevity and institutionalization was never the point. This emphasis on the pocket of time-limited freedom—what Hakim Bey would later describe as the temporary autonomous zone—as a viable form of resistance rather than a pointless distraction marks the 1960s as an era in transition from transcendent toward immanent forms of opposition. There was no more time to wait around for the grand-narrative revolution; it had to be created in the gaps. Counterculture should be credited (or discredited?) with a contribution to this shift.

If the now stabilizing field of visual culture is a relative of cultural studies—a corrective of cultural studies' lack of emphasis on the mediated image—then the roughly simultaneous emergence of the field of cultural studies and the rise of counterculture might also be correlated with the "visual turn," a shift from linguistic to visual modes of understanding and models for analysis. It would be difficult to overestimate the role of television in this shift, but we should also consider counterculture's parallel move toward visual (and audio and audiovisual) modes after the text-based beats. The underground theater movement would not have had the force it did without the relationship between actors in the flesh and images on television. This shift from linguistic to visual modes of representation is one we can trace (roughly) in Terayama's career, as he moved from poetry and scripts for radio to the boxing novel and finally settling on directing theater, film, and photography projects. Terayama was certainly not the only Japanese writer to make this transition: Abe Kōbō would move from fiction toward theater in the 1960s, and Tomioka Taeko would shift from poetry toward film collaborations at the end of the decade. The core of literature itself might well be understood to have moved away from the short story or novel and toward writing for film, theater, and television in this period. If the countercultural project was consistently to intervene, we might rightly understand the visual turn we witness at this time as counterculture's effort to stay a step ahead of the mainstream—a set of experiments with the rhetorical power of images to probe the way they manage to generate enough truth value to be viewed as *real*.

Two figures are particularly important in clarifying and popularizing the English term "counterculture," and a brief outline of their work should help position the way the term will be used in this book. The sociologist J. Milton Yinger spent much of his career working out the contours and social function of counterculture (he initially proposed "contraculture" in 1960 but later capitulated to the mass-media preference for "counterculture"

in the 1970s), particularly in contradistinction to the category of "subculture" as used within the field of qualitative sociology. He emphasized that a
conflict element is central in a counterculture and that norms within such
a group "can be understood only by reference to the relationships of the
group to a surrounding dominant culture."[5] This is distinct, then, from a
subculture, which he describes as having a set of common values but not
necessarily ones contradicting the mainstream norms. Yinger credits Talcott Parsons for coining the term and sketching out its parameters briefly in
The Social System of 1951, where he writes of deviant groups, such as gangs
of delinquents, stuck in the primitive stage of a "counter-culture" without a
"counter-ideology" (a term he prefers to Harold Lasswell's still earlier use of
"countermores") that might legitimate them and aid recruitment.[6] Already
in Parsons we find traces of a distinction between a delinquent "counterculture" described as lacking a coherent ideology versus the overtly ideological groups of political revolutionaries in "radical" movements—a
distinction seen again in the 1960s between the politically serious New
Left and the more playful hippie/yippie/tranny/pot-smoking/psyche-
delic/sexual-revolution/electric–rock 'n roll/revolution-of-consciousness
cluster we tend to euphemize as "counterculture."

Theodore Roszak is the other major figure we should credit with popularizing the term "counterculture." Roszak's series of articles for *The Nation*
in March and April 1968 on "The Counter Culture" set out specifically to
look for common threads between "the New Left, flower power, mind
explosion, psychedelia, pot, and Zen." Roszak's definition attempts to mend
the rift (widening by 1968) between the political and psychosexual sides
of the movement.[7] These articles and his expansion of them into his 1969
book on the subject, *The Making of a Counter Culture*, are focused on the
historically embedded late-1960s phenomenon, particularly in the United
States (although he does acknowledge a youth movement in Japan and
Latin America). His core thesis is that counterculture arises as a rejection
of increasingly technocratic tendencies in cold war societies, where "post-
ideological," technologically savvy bureaucracies run by "experts" and
"specialists" seek to expand the common good by eliminating inefficiencies
through rational, objective analysis. Since the trend is found in both major
American political parties and in the Soviet bloc, the dissenting youth had
to search for new alternatives to all existing possibilities.[8] Roszak gives us a
tour of where counterculture has gone to look for these alternatives: R. D.
Laing, Herbert Marcuse, Norman Brown, Paul Goodman, C. Wright Mills,

Allen Ginsberg, Alan Watts, and Timothy Leary. Roszak's book was translated into Japanese and published in 1972, resulting in two new words in the
Japanese language: *taikō-bunka* ("opposition-culture") and *kauntākaruchā*,
the second given as the pronunciation of the first in the Japanese edition of
the book.

Tracing a lineage of these Japanese words for counterculture, we find
a series of articles and roundtables in the 1970s by sociologists like Takahashi Akira, Maekawa Tomokata, and Takada Akihiko, all of whom, in line
with Roszak, use the terms to refer to a primarily American phenomenon
of the late 1960s stretching into the early 1970s. By this time, however, the
moment had passed, and discussion is often focused on what counterculture had morphed into (organic food cooperatives, nonprofit organizations,
citizens' movements). Working back through earlier publications by these
figures, however, reveals Takahashi in particular to have been researching
in real time the development of what would later be called counterculture.
Takahashi writes articles in the 1950s on mass communication and the
political influence of television, translates Beauvoir and Karl Mannheim,
and writes on José Ortega y Gasset before turning his attention almost
exclusively to the American student movement in the early 1960s. He
starts a carefully documented eight-part series of articles on the American
New Left and the student movement in the journal *Sekai* in January 1967,
chairs a roundtable on student movements around the world for *Asahi
jānaru* in April 1968, and publishes a book-length survey of worldwide "student power" in October 1968 ("world" here is the United States, France,
West Germany, Latin America, Eastern Europe, Northern Europe, and
Japan—South Korea, home to the only student movement that success-
fully deposed its head of state, is conspicuously absent). In 1973, Takahashi
releases an anthology of translations covering Tom Hayden and Students
for a Democratic Society (SDS), the Student Nonviolent Coordinat-
ing Committee (SNCC), the Black Panther Party, Timothy Leary, David
Horowitz, and Abbie Hoffman. The term "counter" appears in Takahashi's
writing on the New Left at least as early as January 1967, when he describes
the "new radicalism" as a "movement giving birth to a theory" rather than
as a "movement born of a theory" and one in which the new 1960s activists
take a "counter-stance" (*taikō shisei*) to their more theory-oriented 1950s
forebears.[9] Takahashi is often more thorough than either Yinger or Roszak,
published earlier, and (although an Americanist) tends to treat counterculture as a more fully international phenomenon.

My use of "counterculture" will be closer to Roszak and Takahashi than to Yinger, it will lean more toward the art world and further away from "lifestyles" than any of the three, and I will try to follow as closely as possible Terayama's preferred term, *han-taisei undō* (antiestablishment movement), which for him was typically far to the psychosexual side of the spectrum discussed previously but with the understanding (as with Marcuse) that achievement of the sexual revolution would entail a comprehensive social reconfiguration as a matter of course.

Too much of the existing discourse on counterculture—Yinger, Roszak, and Takahashi included—emphasizes the rebellion against a stagnant, conformist, dull, suffocating mainstream. The assumption is that counterculture was primarily a *reaction* to an unbearable society. We stand to gain better insights, however, with a more autonomist reading of the situation that sees counterculture as an instigating force. Terayama makes particularly important contributions in this vein, which can help us visualize countercultural patterns and sketch out a new theory of counterculture. I propose distilling his artistic and political position into three clusters that clarify the countercultural form, particularly the oppositional tactic of lateral motion, a reorientation toward a synchronic understanding of time, and the recognition of the potential of agnosticism and indeterminacy to break apart static systems.

If we look broadly at resistance in the 1960s, lateral motion stands out as an important shift. We see sidestepping, flanking techniques, and indirect confrontation across guerrilla warfare tactics in Third World liberation movements, in the attention-dodging pose of the hipster (as described in Norman Mailer's 1957 essay "The White Negro"), in civil rights protests at lunch counters instead of courtrooms, in student occupations of university buildings supplanting direct attacks on parliaments, in transmedia motion in the arts, and in the interdisciplinarity of new academic fields like semiotics and cultural studies. The term "counterculture" itself may be misleading, then, since these types of maneuvers might better be visualized as a 90-degree turn away from the square establishment than as a 180-degree reversal, which comes off as a reactionary inversion and is easily dismissed as a childlike rejection of adult society. What we find in this 90-degree, lateral movement is an emphasis on abandonment over destruction, on moving sideways to capture and defend new territory rather than on attempting to seize existing (illusionary) power centers. This visualization is particularly useful in explaining the apparent ambiguousness of counterculture because a 90-degree turn from the mainstream could point in any of 360-degrees as it moves away from that established axis (creating an entirely new plane of heterogeneous existence), whereas a 180-degree turn is limited in movement to the same one-dimensional axis of that which it opposes. It is, in fact, recognition of power's need for opposition to justify its reign that may have led to counterculture's refusal to become that sort of predictable, and welcomed, frontal attack. The 90-degree turn literally turns the tables, and the power center suddenly has to give chase, but by the time they find these pockets of counterculture (now scattered in every direction), it is counterculture that is in the position of defending its own territory against invasion, a useful boost for morale. Terayama visualizes this tactic through the image of aerodynamics, in which an airplane does not confront gravity directly, but rather uses a 90-degree lateral motion to trigger a reaction in the form of air resistance. His specific suggestion was that street theater could similarly utilize opposition from police to help a play "take off" (more on this in chapter 4).

This 90-degree turn from power and the lateral motion we find in countercultural tactics are paralleled by a shift of time orientation, from a diachronic (past-to-present) toward a synchronic (cross-sectional) world-view. It is here that we find the hints of antihistoricism that seem to align counterculture with an adrift postmodernist stance and against rigorous historical consciousness (a tension that seems to have carried through largely unchanged into the 1990s debate on art history vs. "ahistorical" visual culture). Certain elements of this deemphasizing of history probably held true, where historical materialism was seen as too calculating and square by hippies who had already begun living out their version of the liberated, postrevolutionary life. I prefer to see the synchronic turn in counterculture, however, not as a turn *away* from historicity or historical consciousness at all but rather as a shift of orientation *within* a historicized field of consciousness that heightens the sense of interrelation between diachronic strains precisely by focusing on the synchronic connections between them—it is in cross-sections of time that differential development becomes clearest. That "history" was used as shorthand for the diachronic, here, likely confuses the issue, but close attention reveals in countercultural discourse an engagement with, if not a completely synchronic worldview, at least a double-axis version of the times. Terayama addressed this issue in the mid-1960s by using a metaphor of history versus geography, claiming himself to be against "history-ism" and of geographical orientation.[10] His focus is on spatial movement in the present rather than that "which used to be in present-tense" and the set of causalities that have led to conditions of the past shaping the form of the present. Nation-states, he points out, lose their legitimacy when considered synchronically (the "imagined community" is no longer imagined, and therefore ceases to exist). Terayama is most opposed to the general sense of passivity he sees among people overwhelmed by an understanding of existing in a historically determined present, waiting around as observers for history to take its course: "When I say that I hate history, what I basically mean is that I 'dislike returning home.' There's nowhere we can return to. It's meaningless to talk about returning to 'medieval times' or 'primitive psychology' or 'the mainland' or 'religion' or 'hard and fast solutions.' No matter how much Sheckley and Bradbury vex themselves over the creation of a time machine, the past is always our first 'lost home' . . . we can 'go,' but we cannot 'return.'"[11] History functionally comes to represent, in Terayama's formation, either a passivity trap that locks us in stasis with the belief that individual action is fruitless or, worse, a regressive force, a desire to reel back motion against the arrow of time. An image from Terayama's second film project (and the oldest extant), *Kanshū* (Caged prisoner, 1962), illustrates this stance well, with a man immobilized as a human sundial.[12] Diachronic time has him trapped (at least until dusk), and he is less mobile than the dog calmly strolling by in front of him (Figure I.1). The short film is an abstract montage, but images of clocks and time predominate. Several wall clocks are smashed or thrown out of windows as though to liberate their owners. This will become a common theme in Terayama's work, typically with wall clocks linked to the oppression of a central authority versus the liberatory image of a wristwatch, associated with decentralization and autonomy (and a panic-inducing threat to those whose worldview crumbles without an ultimate authority). The focus on synchronic time, on a geographical orientation, and on a liberation from diachronic time aligns counterculture closely, then, with the mindset of Mailer's "hipster," who "exists in the present, in that enormous present which is without past or future."[13]

If there is a "world turned upside down" (to use Yinger's formulation) element to counterculture—a strict inversion of the mainstream, protechnocracy worldview—it may be in assumptions about the effects of knowledge versus agnosticism. If much of the great refusal is against pseudo-science and false rationality being leveraged by the administrators against the administrated, then we might do well to view the clash as one

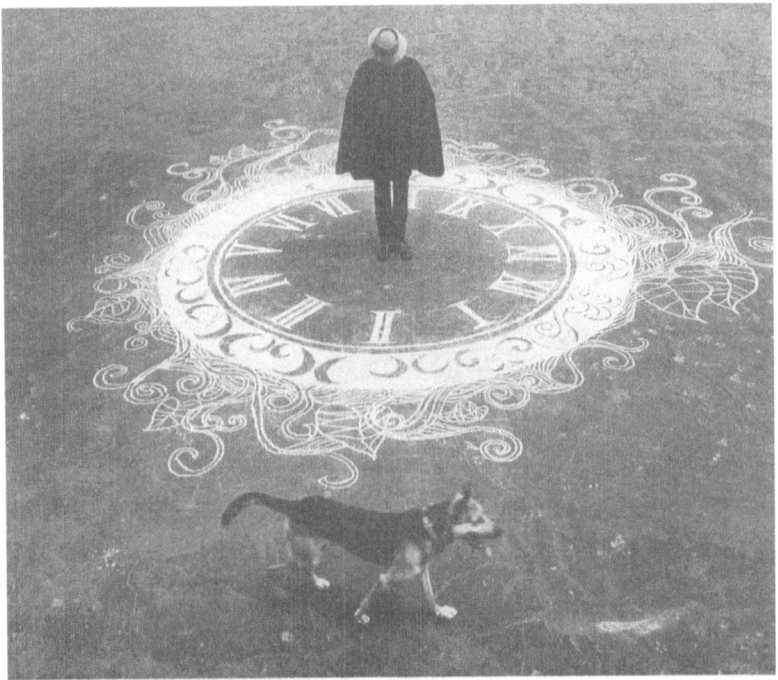

Figure I.1. This human-sundial photograph was taken on the set of Terayama's short film Kanshū *(Caged prisoner, shot in 1962, edited in 1969). Courtesy of Kujō Kyōko and Terayama World.*

between a side that sees increasingly specialized knowledge (faked in times of crisis) as the means toward keeping society moving forward against a side that sees society (particularly social hierarchy) as being detrimentally locked in place exactly by that form of "progress." The refusal, then, might be one not just *against* technocracy but also *for* pockets of unpredictability as useful and necessary. If the establishment wants to stamp out these pockets of unanswered or unanswerable questions (as it sanitizes unregulated segments of urban space), counterculture wants to maintain them and build more, seeing the agnostic pockets not as blockades to progress but as springboards for motion and sources of energy for new ideas. For as much opposition as we find in counterculture to the base-superstructure logic of "vulgar" Marxism, there are plenty of traces not only of political anarchism (mutual aid, classlessness) but also of the vulgar anarchism of bohemian, ungoverned, unpredictable spaces.

This dubiousness toward history (or rather the equation of history with truth) describes a situation we might be tempted to associate with a postmodern cynicism or a poststructuralist entrapment in language. But what Terayama seems to have discovered here was not the problem of alienation from reality but rather the opportunities created when language (or image) has heightened rhetorical power. He finds here a chance to fabricate history—starting with personal history as a test case—and ways to create false realities that function as quasi-independent spaces from which to look back critically at the experience of "reality" as lived in everyday life. Terayama cultivated a reputation as a liar and required the skill of self-fictionalization for entrance into his theater troupe. The film scholar Yomota Inuhiko reports one of Terayama's interview questions (to a fifteen-year-old girl) at a tryout for the troupe: "Please tell us how you felt the last time you had sex with your father."[14] Her ability to transform herself into an incestuous patriphile on the spot got her into the troupe; others too bound to their identities did not make the cut (Yomota included). Yet to read this sort of test as an examination of the ability to ad-lib fiction as an actor does not go quite far enough. The troupe itself might best be understood as a social experiment, an effort to create a different kind of person and an alternative form of being in the young actors recruited into it. The audience, then, was most likely only of secondary importance, serving as a sort of patron or witness to the transformations taking place within these young amateurs thrust onto the stage.

It is tempting to read this self-fictionalization and generation of false history as a border crossing or a blurring of the boundary between fiction and reality. But what Terayama was doing was more radical than that: he was demonstrating that these categories have flexible boundaries, ones we can manipulate. Recognizing that we will never get closer to reality than what we experience as reality (in phenomenological terms), and that fiction and reality as discursive constructs are in a co-determined relationship, Terayama realized that the boundary of reality could be shifted by pushing and pulling on its perceived border within the realm of fiction. It is quite likely that he was much more concerned with reality than with fiction but realized that it would be more effective to expand the reach of reality by drawing back the border of fiction than to simply push reality further into fiction's territory.

Although Terayama would certainly reject a biographical sketch in answer to the question "Who was Terayama Shūji?" a brief tour of his background is in order. His active promotion of self-fictionalization complicates this task, since his commentary on his own history (and repetitions of it elsewhere) is fraught with conspicuously unreliable narration. Nevertheless, the standard narrative on Terayama's biography now reads roughly the following way.[15] He was born on December 10, 1935, in the northern rural town of Hirosaki in Aomori prefecture, the hometown of the novelist Dazai Osamu. Shūji's father, Terayama Hachirō, was a police detective who moved the family often as he was transferred around Aomori in the late 1930s. Hachirō was drafted and left for the front in 1941, leaving Shūji's mother, Hatsu, to care for their son. Hachirō would die on the island of Celebes of dysentery, news of which reached Hatsu after the war in September 1945. During the war, Shūji and Hatsu lived in Aomori City, the metropolitan center of the prefecture, until the air raids that burned the city on July 28, 1945 (about a week before the atomic bomb was dropped on Hiroshima). They escaped and resettled over a restaurant owned by Hachirō's relatives in his hometown of Misawa, the city that is now home to the Terayama Shūji Museum. Hatsu took a job at the U.S. air base in Misawa—a former Japanese Navy installation taken over by the Allied forces after the war—while Shūji attended the local elementary school. His literary aspirations were evident by his first year of middle school, when he edited and published a handwritten and mimeographed weekly newspaper that included his own creative writing.

During the autumn of 1948, when Shūji was halfway through his first year of middle school, Hatsu took a job at another Allied forces base in southern Japan (in Ashiya, near Fukuoka), and Shūji returned to Aomori City to live with his mother's relatives while she worked in Kyūshū, saving money to pay for his college tuition. These relatives, the Sakamoto family, owned and operated an eight-hundred-seat cinema in town called the Kabukiza, which gave Shūji access to a steady stream of films. He continued work on the school newspaper at his new middle school, publishing free-verse poems and a number of tanka. In high school, his interest shifted toward haiku, and his publication activities, in close relationship with his classmate and rival Kyōbu Hisayoshi, would evolve from a high school haiku club called *Yamabiko* (Echo) into a prefecture-wide high school haiku magazine called *Aoi mori* (Green forest, a play on Aomori), and from there into a nationwide teenage haiku magazine launched in February 1954 called *Bokuyōshin* (Pan/Faunus). Both *Aoi mori* and *Bokuyōshin* included contributions from the important modern haiku poet Akimoto Fujio, who served as an advisor to the magazines.

Terayama moved to Tokyo in the spring of 1954 to begin studies at Waseda University. He wasted no time making his move on the poetry world: he applied and was accepted into the free-verse poetry circle Vou, run by Kitazono Katsue (or Kitasono Katué, as preferred by the dadaist poet and publisher of the interwar magazine *Ge.Gjmgjgam.Prrr.Gjmgem*). Terayama published a handful of poems in Vou's coterie journal between July 1954 and June 1956. He continued work on *Bokuyōshin* and on a new youth-poetry journal called *Kōya* (Wilderness), but his formal, national debut occurred in November 1954 (midway through his first year at Waseda), when he won an open contest for tanka composition held by the magazine *Tanka kenkyū*. It was also this fall when he would be first diagnosed with nephritis (inflammation of the kidneys), which would develop into the more serious condition nephrosis and require nearly continuous hospitalization from March 1955 to July 1958 for treatment and monitoring of his kidney condition. The disease kept him on a restricted diet for the rest of his life, but his heavy regimen of diuretic medication to assist kidney function eventually caused the cirrhosis of his liver that would kill him in May 1983. He read and wrote during his three-year stay in the hospital, publishing two volumes of poetry in 1957.

After Terayama's release from the hospital in the summer of 1958, he began writing scripts for radio dramas on the recommendation of fellow poet Tanikawa Shuntarō. The two would cowrite a radio program called *Oshaberi danchi* (The gossipy apartment building), which aired in segments starting in December 1959. Radio was, at the time, one of the few opportunities for young poets to make money.[16] By 1960, the turbulent year of mass protests by the student movement and organized labor against the renewal of the U.S.–Japan Security Treaty (which would extend by ten years the U.S. military presence in Japan at bases such as Misawa, Yokota, Yokosuka, Tachikawa, and Sasebo), Terayama wrote scripts for radio, theater, and film, engaging (often mockingly) the frustration of failed protest. The precedent set by the 1960 extension has been used to grant now-automatic extensions of the treaty every ten years.

Through the early 1960s, Terayama continued writing for radio, started writing for television, and began publishing cultural critique on topics from the beat generation and right- versus left-wing politics to boxing and horse racing. A twenty-four-part series of short essays first published in late 1962 in the *Student Times* (a bilingual newspaper published by the *Japan Times* targeted at high school and university students) established Terayama's reputation as a cultural critic and solidified his alliance with youth culture.[17] The series was known colloquially as *Iede no susume* (In praise of running away from home), a play on nation-builder Fukuzawa Yukichi's *Gakumon no susume* (In praise of learning), but instead encourages severing one's psychological bonds with family and hometown. The topics are eclectic, but much of the book is an argument for relinquishing attachment to the familiar in exchange for the vivacity of the unknown as well as an introduction to critical thinking, as Terayama guides his reader to root out the agenda behind moral guidance narratives.

Terayama's only full-length novel, *Aa, kōya* (Ah, wilderness) was serialized during 1965 and 1966.[18] The main topic is boxing, explored through a frame of violence as communication, and Terayama was drawing partly from jazz as a compositional technique as well as from Nelson Algren's "neighborhood novel," which in Terayama's case explored the seedy Kabukichō district of Shinjuku, Tokyo. This novel pairs nicely with a book of essays Terayama published around the same time called *Bōryoku toshite no gengo* (Violence as language), along with a number of pieces on boxing written in the mid-1960s.

In 1967, Terayama would launch an amateur, underground theater troupe called the Tenjō Sajiki. The plan was to do around six new plays per year with Terayama as playwright, his wife Kujō Eiko (now Kujō Kyōko) as producer, the graphic designer Yokoo Tadanori as artistic director (both sets and posters), and Higashi Yutaka as stage director. The name of the troupe, best left untranslated, literally means the "upper balcony," or the cheap seats in a theater, which was taken from the Japanese title of Marcel Carné's film *Les enfants du paradis* (*Children of paradise*, 1945), released in Japan as *Tenjō sajiki no hitobito* (The people in the upper balcony). Terayama claims in one magazine article from 1967 to have been making a playful inversion of the "underground" by naming his troupe after the ceiling.[19] The subtitle of the troupe's name may be more significant: *engeki jikkenshitsu* (theater laboratory, often in their own materials as "A Laboratory of Play") can be traced back to a sign Terayama posted on the door of his apartment in the early 1960s proclaiming the space his "laboratory," but it would have resonated by 1967 both with Ellen Stewart's literally underground (illegal, and in hiding) "experimental theatre club" (which Terayama first visited in 1966) and the Arts Lab in London, where

Terayama's friend Jim Haynes was doing similar projects. In the context of modern Japanese theater history, this would also invoke the 1924 founding slogan of the Tsukiji Little Theater, "A Laboratory of Theater, A Freak Show for the Masses" (*Engeki no jikkenshitsu, minshū no misemono-koya*), as former Tenjō Sajiki member Takatori Ei points out in his recent book on Terayama.[20] While Yokoo and Higashi would both leave the troupe by 1970, the Tenjō Sajiki would form the base of Terayama's activities from the time of its launch until his death around fifteen years later.

One puzzle regarding Teryama's biography that has not been fully explained is the problem of his birth date. Almost all publications since his death have listed his birth date as December 1935, but several institutions (including the National Diet Library and Waseda University) continue to list his dates as 1936 to 1983. The standard explanation for this is that his mother was late in registering his birth (which occurred at home), and she claims in her 1985 memoir that because she missed the deadline for birth registration, she decided to lie on the paperwork and claim he was born one month later than he had been, thus January 10, 1936.[21] This all seems perfectly rational and there is little reason to doubt the truth of this story, save for Terayama's claims about the malleability of history and the liberatory effect of self-fictionalization. This narrative of the one-month-late birth registration, in fact, first appears in an "autobiography" Terayama began serializing in 1967 called *Tareka kokyō o omowazaru* (Everyone longs for home), which should be treated with extreme skepticism as it is riddled with contradictions, has been shown to be embellished, and revolved around the general theme of the way rhetorical modes (like confession) generate their own truth value and facilitate reception as historical fact. The subtitle of the text signals this clearly, *Jijoden rashiku naku* (Not your typical autobiography), as does his explanation that this autobiography will align itself more with a poetic, metaphorical understanding of history than with a scientific one.[22] One episode, for example, relates details of his first sexual encounter, building and building tension before breaking it with: "This episode, however, is a lie." The first confession is revealed as false here by this second one, which we likely believe. We trust the confession of the lie despite it being in the same rhetorical mode just revealed to have been deceptive. Terayama seems to be leveraging our psychological need to balance the false with the true, to remove the lie and the memory of being deceived by patching over the experience with trust.

With only one exception from 1966, all of Terayama's publications prior to the publication of his "autobiography" list a birth year of 1936.[23] Even the book version of the autobiography itself, in which the narrative of the 1935 birth year first appears, cites 1936 as Terayama's birth year in the biographical information at the end of the book. The two possibilities coexist for several years with the stability of the 1935 birth year not really taking hold until after Terayama's death. Perhaps most interesting is the possibility that Terayama himself did not even learn of his "true" birthday until sometime in the mid-1960s.[24] His date of birth, then, may have functionally shifted back one month around halfway through his life, a perfect example of the malleability of history and a playful undermining of the authority of state bureaucracy. In any case, if we cannot fully trust this "true" birth date narrative, we find ourselves forced into a fittingly agnostic position about the most basic biographical detail of Terayama's life.

The core problem with this birth-date issue and more broadly with Terayama's biography is that the reaction to discoveries of embellishment has typically been either to denounce him as a liar or to support his claims and fill in the details with additional interviews with his acquaintances. But this sort of positivist, scientific relationship with the past is precisely what Terayama's playful manipulation of personal history was mocking. We need a certain amount of data to prevent Terayama's autobiography from being read as fact, certainly, but it seems that the proper response to this sort of text is not so much to fact check as it is to begin the process of liberatory self-fictionalization ourselves or at least to recognize the point of such an exercise. Demythologizing Terayama, or counterculture, or the sixties may actually be a reactionary response, one that serves mainly to assimilate that deviance back into the technocratic establishment.

This book is not a literary biography, but I do take up broad critical problems in Terayama's work roughly in the order they arose before moving back and forth in time as necessary within the chapters to work through those problems and put them in context. As much as I want to resist a developmentalist model, there is an accumulation of experience and production on some issues that make it easier to organize the book as a whole in roughly chronological thematic chapters.

In the first chapter, I analyze Terayama's tanka from the 1950s, paying particular attention to instances of appropriation, quotation, allusion, and especially critique. After an extended analysis of the relationship between Terayama's most famous poem (from 1956) and the film *Casablanca*, I move back to 1954 to look at Terayama's public debut with a set of poems called "Chehofu-sai" (Chekhov festival). These poems sparked a plagiarism controversy when it was discovered that Terayama had appropriated sizable sections of his tanka from both contemporary haiku poets and his own previous haiku compositions. I look at the critical response that followed these accusations, along with Terayama's own response, with the hope of finding a way past the stalemate between those who saw this as unethical and others who saw Terayama leading the charge for making language public property.

In chapter 2, I focus on two simultaneous technological shifts—the introduction of television into mainstream Japanese society and the transition of radio from monaural to stereophonic broadcast—and the ways Terayama engaged with those changes. He, along with other young poets, found work in radio after established writers moved to television, pairing the youngest writers with a medium threatening to become obsolete. The situation led to several experimental radio drama projects designed to hold on to the youth market, often with subtexts reflexive of radio's newly blinded status relative to television. The technology of stereo came first to radio, however, and Terayama was also commissioned to write scripts for radio to showcase stereo technology in ways other than hackneyed footsteps progressing across a room. The result was an extraordinary stereo radio drama called *Kometto Ikeya* (Comet Ikeya), which uses documentary and scripted footage, mono- and stereophonic sound, and a blind narrator whose position relative to the other characters seems ambiguous if not physically impossible. I link the positioning function of stereo to the countercultural politics of decentering and deuniversalizing, so just as universals were revealed as centered particularities and then decentered within political critique, so too does stereo radio seem to reconfigure the universality of monaural sound into an embodied, centered particularity.

Chapter 3 concerns the interaction of violence and language, which Terayama addressed through the themes of boxing (linguistic representations of violence), stuttering (violated language), and graffiti (violating language). Tracing this boxing-stuttering-graffiti discourse through plays, poems, essays, a novel, and finally the performance of a live funeral for the dead antagonist of the wildly popular boxing comic *Ashita no Jō* (Tomorrow's Jō), I work through Terayama's analysis of the reality effect of these forms as well as their potential to revitalize countercultural spontaneity in the face of a trend toward social bureaucratization. By bundling this cluster of language and violence themes to jazz improvisation (both through direct reference to jazz and in using chord sequences as an organizing principle of his boxing novel), Terayama links these ad-libbed forms to a sensation of time-embedded presence—a temporal sensation that compliments the spatial sensation of position discussed in chapter 2. Ultimately, Terayama celebrates these serendipitous formations as resistant to the sterilizing of culture and as a socially positive type of violence, in the sense used by Georges Sorel for the assertion of power by the low upon the high (vs. "force," power working from the high upon the low).

In chapter 4, I move from analysis of violence and language to an analysis of violence and sex. While a broad trend of eroticized violation narratives emerges in Vietnam-era Japan (seen in the work of Mishima, Ōe, Shibusawa, Wakamatsu), the critique of sadism through sadism-themed texts was countered in Terayama's work by alignment with the contractual libidinal economy of nineteenth-century Austrian novelist, Leopold Ritter von Sacher-Masoch, after whom the term masochism derives. Terayama's direct reference to the locus classicus of masochism (*Venus in Furs*) in his best-known play, *Kegawa no Marii* (Marie in furs), leads me to read the play against Gilles Deleuze's essay ("Coldness and Cruelty") on the role of contracts and institutionalism within a masochistic system. The presentation of this play in Shinjuku Bunka Art Theater, the main countercultural cinema of the era, as well as a direct reference to the play in a subsequent Terayama film (shown at the same cinema), calls into question the relationship between live drama, film, and the institutions (both material and discursive) that house them. Terayama has, by this point in the late 1960s, moved toward images and dialogic, collectively produced projects, utilizing the medium of film to (ironically) rehumanize the interaction between actor and audience and the medium of theater to toy with scriptedness and spontaneity.

In the final chapter, I look carefully at a set of Terayama's projects that all share the title *Den'en ni shisu* (Death in the country): a television drama from 1962, a tanka collection from 1965, and a feature film from 1974. In this case, unlike in his debut, he recycled his own material and repeatedly deployed a set of signifiers (clocks, axes, household shrines, red combs, and Mt. Fear) in a way that generated new, mythlike narrative streams. This set, on further analysis, appears to derive from childhood memories of his home province in northern Japan (Aomori) mixed with later news items and tourism campaigns that billed the area as prehistoric and mystical.

As such, the ten-year *Den'en ni shisu* project charts the loss of Terayama's hometown and childhood past and the recreation of it as a knowingly fictional construct. This process parallels his protagonist's attempt to liberate himself from his own history played against the impossibility of history itself, in the sense of a return to a past that no longer exists.

Ultimately, the significance of this book should extend beyond both a case study of counterculture's manifestation in Japan and a text-and-context analysis of the heart of Terayama's transmedia career. My intention has been to demonstrate the intimate connection between transmedia artistic practice and counterculture in order to highlight the way art can function as politics. The driving force behind this project is a search for a methodological approach capable of handling countercultural subject matter in a way that honors the principles of the countercultural position—oblique opposition, synchronic orientation, indeterminacy. Discovering that methodology and embodying a political position that takes full stock of the cleverness of countercultural tactics is, in the end, perhaps the most important impact of an encounter with the ideas of someone like Terayama Shūji.

CHAPTER 1

Poetic Kleptomania and Pseudo-Lyricism

The novel: it's a mirror one carries down a road.

—Saint-Réal
Stendhal, *The Red and the Black*

The green seed is inside the sun.

—Sorel
Terayama, "Chekhov Festival"

F IXED-VERSE POETRY MAY SEEM A strange place to find an avant-garde movement by young Japanese poets. Free verse is intuitively a better fit, or if there was going to be a move toward a rigid form to toy with the Sartrean paradox of freedom experienced as resistance to oppression, then we might expect to see a move toward haiku, the shortest fixed-verse form. And it is this pair, free verse by Ginsberg and haiku by Gary Snyder, that comes to characterize the American beat scene. The shake up in Japanese poetry in the 1950s, however, occurred in the thirty-one syllable genre of tanka (the standard short form, referred to in other eras as *waka* or simply *uta*). In context, however, this makes perfect sense. Haiku, long a comedic form, had already been radicalized, but tanka (despite modern work by Masaoka Shiki, Ishikawa Takuboku, Yosano Akiko, and others) remained the most austere and somber of the poetic genres, the one with the closest relationship to the long tradition of high-brow Japanese literature (*Genji*, the major medieval courtly anthologies), and the imperial flavor of these poems had been restored as the Japanese soldiers of World War II were expected to be uplifted by verses by Emperor Meiji, grandfather of Hirohito. Tanka, then, was the perfect target for an intervention. Akimoto Fujio, a haiku poet partially responsible for radicalizing that genre in the 1930s, sums up the situation in a 1955 essay on the two forms: "I've cried after reading tanka, but never after reading haiku. And I've laughed out loud after reading haiku, but never after reading tanka."[1]

Terayama Shūji leapt from haiku and free-verse poetry into the world of tanka in 1954 to compete in an open contest organized by the young editor of one of the two major national tanka journals, *Tanka kenkyū* (Tanka studies, the other major journal is called simply *Tanka*). Terayama won the contest, the second of its kind, but what this debut is best remembered for is the plagiarism debate that followed. Terayama was quickly discovered to have appropriated large sections, often verbatim, from several contemporary haiku poets and in other cases to have rearranged and lengthened his own haiku by the fourteen syllables necessary to convert them into tanka (a graver crime than plagiarism to several critics). I will retrace highlights from this debate in the course of this chapter with the goal of finding a perspective that breaks the gridlock between defenders of intellectual property and the proto–open source faction (with its strange alliance with the established premodern tradition of literary appropriation). To do so, it will be useful first to break with chronology and look carefully at a slightly later case of poetic allusion (in this case, a scene from *Casablanca*) to gain some insight into the complexities of Terayama's manipulation of a base text, which in this case, I will argue, is deeply analytical. From there I will return to the debut and the plagiarism debate to look at ways Terayama frustrated efforts to maintain separation between genres by moving laterally between them. At the end of the chapter, I will look at a reappropriation of Terayama's *Casablanca* poem, itself critical of the fictional narrator Terayama is credited with adding to the genre of tanka.

Terayama's debut would not be the last time he was charged with plagiarism; these accusations continue throughout his career, and he eventually turns the situation on its head by naming his plays and books after existing works but then altering the content beyond what could be considered adaptation. He also writes a handful of short prose pieces on the problem of plagiarism that clarify his position. One, a 1960 short story called "Tōsaku" (Plagiarism) tells the story of an aging, established writer mentoring a young upstart.[2] The old writer is frustrated at having never produced a masterpiece (despite his rank within the literary establishment), whereas the young student is now becoming cocky about his talents, having just completed a piece he expects will win him the coveted Akutagawa Prize. The old writer tires of the student's boasting and decides to falsely accuse the student of plagiarizing a French story he claims to have read in the past. The student then commits suicide, driving the old writer, in his guilt, to promote the story as a masterpiece. This, I think, is where a typical parable of this type would end and we would ponder the ethics of plagiarism relative to the impact of an accusation of plagiarism. But Terayama adds one final paragraph, in which the old writer receives a letter from the translator of a story that the student had indeed plagiarized, word for word. This changes things considerably. Either the old writer's clouded memory had served him in the initial accusation but he suppressed it in his guilt, or this was just a lucky guess that helps explain why the student would have been grief stricken enough to kill himself instead of holding his ground. But the larger suggestion, which Terayama will clarify later, is that the accusation of plagiarism is so elastic that it could be used against anyone, since we all do it all the time (and should).

That we are all already plagiarists is the gist of a short essay called "Tōsaku-byō" (Literary kleptomania) that Terayama would write in 1961: "The first symptom of the disease is showing interest in what other people are doing."[3] As the condition grows more serious, the individual starts to be conceived as a part of broader society and (gasp) begins interacting with it. Terayama notes that since we are the authors of our own everyday lives, it follows that brushing one's teeth in the morning, reading the newspaper, eating food in a particular way, walking with a certain gait, and choosing appropriate clothing are all plagiarized from a set of notions of normal behavior. Communication itself is necessarily plagiaristic, and artistic experimentation with a ban on appropriation would find itself in a barren wasteland, in Terayama's vision, looking like "Wyatt Earp and Billy the Kid in a showdown over some little potato patch."[4] As much as he might envy the antisocial lunatic hiding away in a corner somewhere, Terayama claims that his social tendencies, diseased though they may be, pull the kleptomaniac in him back into a system of give and take. Looking closely at some examples of Terayama's use of appropriation in his early tanka will reveal the charge of plagiarism to be overly simplistic.

Reading *Casablanca*

Terayama's most famous poem was first published in April 1956 and has since been printed and reprinted in at least five of his works, is now on the cover of several anthologies, and has become standard reading in literature classes for first-year high school students throughout Japan. It reads,

> matchi suru tsukanoma umi ni kiri fukashi misutsuru hodo no sokoku
>   wa ariya
> In the moment of match-strike, with fog thick on the sea—
>   how could any homeland be worth throwing away my life?[5]

With four images of ephemerality in a row—the match, the moment, the fog, and the disposable human life—this poem at first seems to be a relatively conventional expression of either Buddhist notions of transience or a comment on the brevity of tanka itself. There is one use of wordplay: the word *misutsuru* spoken aloud would normally be understood as "to forsake," written as a compound of the characters "to see" and "to throw away," but here Terayama has replaced "to see" with "body." An alternative meaning of the second half of the poem, then, might be rendered as follows: "Is there any homeland worth forsaking?" Any full reading of the poem will have to integrate both of these meanings, as antithetical as they may appear: one possibility is that this is an image of someone making the decision between dying for country and abandoning that country in the brief moment of striking a match to light a cigarette. The phrasing, however, suggests yet another possibility. *Sokoku wa ariya* (Is there a country?) is a rhetorical question, implying that there are no nations for which it is even worth bothering to decide between these two options. Pushing the grammar to its limit, *sokoku wa ariya* could also be read as a question regarding the very existence of that homeland itself—"*Is* there even a homeland at all?" That is, the poem may be asking whether the "homeland" is an artificial construct and therefore not something concrete enough to even begin considering whether to defend or abandon, as it is certainly not real enough to die for.

In Japanese, *kuni* (country) is both a nation and a part of a "land"; *wagakuni*, then, can refer either to one's nation (Japan) or to the rural area one considers to be home. As such, it shares the possibility of representing a part of the whole nation with the English word "country."[6] Yet it is different in one important regard: *kuni* cannot refer generally to the whole of rural regions as "the country" can in English—the term still carries some flavor of a feudal domain—and so it is always constituted as a part of some whole and one that assumes the existence of other *kuni* making up the rest of that whole. The various domestic *kuni* constitute Japan just as the various global *kuni* constitute the world, and much of the project of national unification after 1868 (by Fukuzawa Yukichi and others) might then be understood as an effort to redefine *kuni* not as a term for the provinces of Japan but rather for the modern nation-states of the world—a process simplified by using the same term as had been used much longer for provinces under the shogunate. The divisions between domestic districts and all their claims to local autonomy dissolve as the word for the autonomous governmental unit slips from this local level to the level of the nation. Terayama makes direct reference to this slippage in a haiku first published in 1953:

kusamochi ya kuni ideshi tomo no uwasa mo nashi
Chrysanthemum rice cake—
   not even a rumor of my friend who left our hometown[7]

The word *kuni* in this poem is a gloss of the compound normally read *kokyō*, or hometown. By glossing the term, Terayama is pointing back to that forgotten transitional moment when the word was redefined—without the gloss, a reader would not have read the compound *kuni*, but if Terayama had used the character for *kuni*, most readers would have understood that to denote the entire nation-state rather than the regional hometown. The disappearance of the friend in the haiku, then, is paralleled by a disappearance of the *kuni* understood as regional hometown. The subtle reference to this chrysanthemum, the symbol of the imperial line, draws the emperor and the militarist state into association with these disappearances as well, which would have been particularly resonant during the early postwar years. *Sokoku* in the tanka above may not go so far as to suggest the disappearance of the nation itself, but Terayama could have been suggesting that the "country of the ancestors" (*sokoku*) had changed so much in modern times that the term's referent lacked enough consistency over time to retain a useful meaning.

Returning to the match-strike poem, we may conclude that it stands well on its own, particularly as an expression representative of the generation who concluded that Japan's effort to unify Asia by force had been criminal or at least fated to fail. However, several poems and a few films have been cited as possible sources for its content. Nagao Saburō, in his 1997 study of Terayama, points out two haiku by Tomizawa Kakio from 1940 and 1941, when Japan's war with China was well under way:

ippon no matchi o sureba mizuumi wa kiri
When I strike one match—fog on the lake[8]
metsumureba sokoku wa aoki umi no ue
If I shut my eyes, my homeland is just over the blue sea[9]

Yet another possibility is a tanka from Ishikawa Takuboku's *Ichiaku no suna* (A fistful of sand, 1910) collection:

machi sureba
nishaku bakari no akarusa no
naka o yogireru shiroki ari no ari
When I struck a match
there was a white ant crossing
inside those two feet of light[10]

None of these poems, however, use the notion of *misutsuru*, which is of central importance to Terayama's poem. Yamada Taichi, a scenarist for radio and television and one of Terayama's oldest friends, writes that the poem might be a reference to the ending of one of the actor Kobayashi Akira's films.[11] But since Kobayashi's first film, *Ueru tamashii* (Hungry ghosts) opened on October 31, 1956, roughly five months after the publication of Terayama's poem, such a connection is chronologically impossible.

All of these possible references help to place particular images from the poem, but the most important may be Nagao's brief comment, almost in passing, that the poem resonates somewhat with the end of *Casablanca*. Nagao points out the fog in both scenes, the common theme of the lost homeland, and the fact that Terayama wrote a fan letter to Humphrey Bogart while in high school.[12] Picking up where Nagao left off, it will be useful to look carefully at Bogart's striking of a match and the link between that match strike and the forsaking of one's nation. That link is at the crux of the poem and worth further attention.

Terayama probably saw *Casablanca* at his uncle's cinema, the Kabuki-za in Aomori City. He had moved in with his aunt and uncle during his middle and high school years (1948–54). There would have been an opportunity for him to see the film ten times or more, especially considering his habit of returning home from school to read in the cinema as films were screened. Terayama's fan letter to Bogart, written during his first year of high school, coincides well with *Casablanca*'s release in Japan around 1949. So if the poem describes the end of the film, then Terayama has obviously changed the airport to a harbor, but the fog and the tension over the decision of whether to defend or forsake one's nation are certainly present. But where does this match strike fit in?

Casablanca balances a shifting web of allegiance, duty, desire, trust, and risk among five characters: Rick Blaine, the suave American bar owner who fought against Franco in the Spanish Civil War and who has two exit visas to leave French Morocco; Louis Renault, the French officer appointed by the Vichy government as police prefect in Casablanca but who consistently hints at his sympathy for the anti-Nazi rebels; Victor Laszlo, the Czechoslovakian leader of the resistance who is attempting to flee to America before the Nazis incarcerate or kill him; Ilsa Lund, Laszlo's wife who had an affair with Rick in Paris while under the impression that Laszlo had been killed; and Heinrich Strasser, the Nazi officer sent to recover the missing exit visas and monitor the movements of Laszlo.

In the final scene, Renault and Ilsa both assume that it will be she and Rick who will get on the airplane with the visas, fulfilling the passion rekindled between them the previous night. Rick turns the tables, though, when he hands the visa papers to Renault and has him fill in Laszlo and Ilsa's names. Renault is impressed by Rick's political idealism and his cool savvy in tidying up a potential mess—with just a few words he had convinced both Ilsa and Laszlo that the old flame from Paris had burned itself out. Having sent them off, Rick has only a few seconds in which to confirm that Renault has committed to the resistance with him, a confirmation requiring more communication than words alone can offer—Rick operates at critical moments primarily with eye contact. The sequence is worth close analysis with Terayama's poem in mind (see Figure 1.1).

RENAULT: What you just did for Laszlo, and that fairy tale you invented to send Ilsa away with him. I know a little about women, my friend. She went, but she knew you were lying.[13]

Notice Rick moving to light his cigarette, the shot carefully framed so that the "Absolutely No Smoking" sign in the background is perfectly aligned with the line of sight between Rick and Renault, punctuating Rick's renegade character:

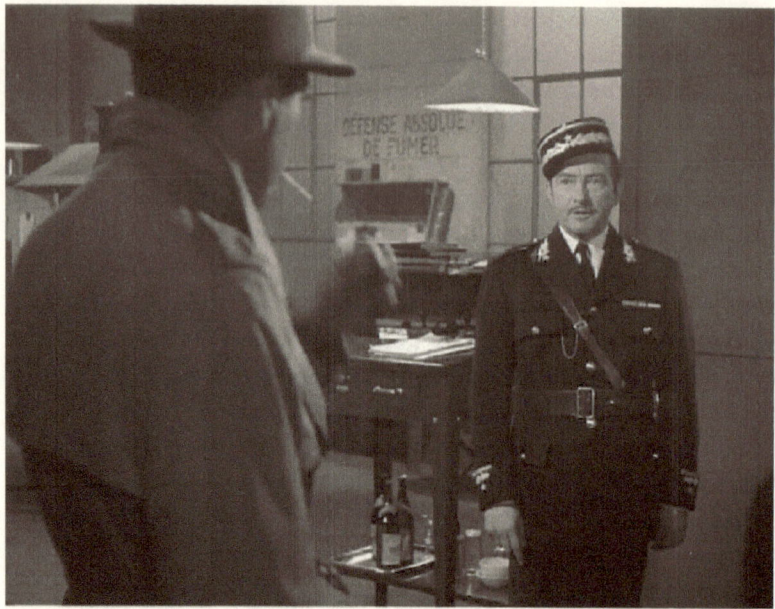

Figure 1.1. Rick on the verge of lighting a cigarette directly under a sign reading "Absolutely No Smoking" in the final sequence of Casablanca *(1942)*

RICK: (*Smoking*) Anyway, thanks for helping me out.
(RICK'*s face reveals nothing.*)
RENAULT: I suppose you know this isn't going to be very pleas-
ant for either of us, especially for you. I'll have to arrest you, of
course.

Rick has lit his cigarette during the quick cut to the shot of Renault. By the time the camera returns to Rick, he is already smoking, but it is precisely during that brief gap that eye contact with Renault has guaranteed his safe escape, along with that of Laszlo and Ilsa. The "moment it takes to strike a match" in Terayama's poem, then, may have been pointing to this critical turning point in the film, a moment the film does not actually allow us to see. The precise instant the Franco–American alliance against the Nazis is formed is simultaneous with this invisible match strike. Confident that Renault is on his side, Rick is now free to challenge Strasser when he shows up seconds later to prevent Laszlo's escape. Strasser moves to telephone the radio tower, Rick threatens to shoot him, and Strasser takes a hasty first shot. It misses, Rick returns fire, and his bullet connects. The flash of Rick striking the match has, in effect, been displaced for a few cuts and transferred from the tip of his cigarette to the tip of his gun (Figure 1.2). Terayama may have hinted at such a connection by titling the set of poems in which *matchi suru* was first published "Shotgun Blast" (*Ryōjū-on*). In front of several witnesses, Renault turns to his men and says, "Round up the usual suspects." Rick's intuition had, of course, been correct. He was finally back in the fight but had managed not to show his cards until the last possible moment, maximizing his ability to operate under the cover of his reputation as the disinterested American—the propagandistic elements here are obvious: the United States' delayed entry into the war was part of a savvy plan to maximize potency by playing neutral until the moment was right. Rick finishes his cigarette, Renault offers to arrange passage to a free French garrison outside of Casablanca, and they walk off together into the thick fog (*kiri fukashi*): "Louis, I think this is the beginning of a beautiful friendship" (Figure 1.3).

If the *Casablanca* connection is a strong one, then the term Terayama has chosen for "homeland" may also have a link to the film. *Sokoku*

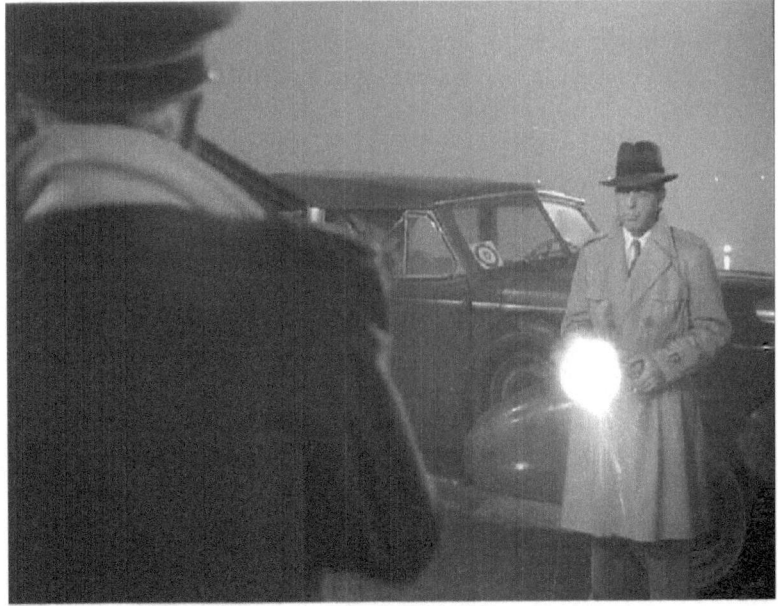

Figure 1.2. Rick fires a shot at Strasser, the Nazi.

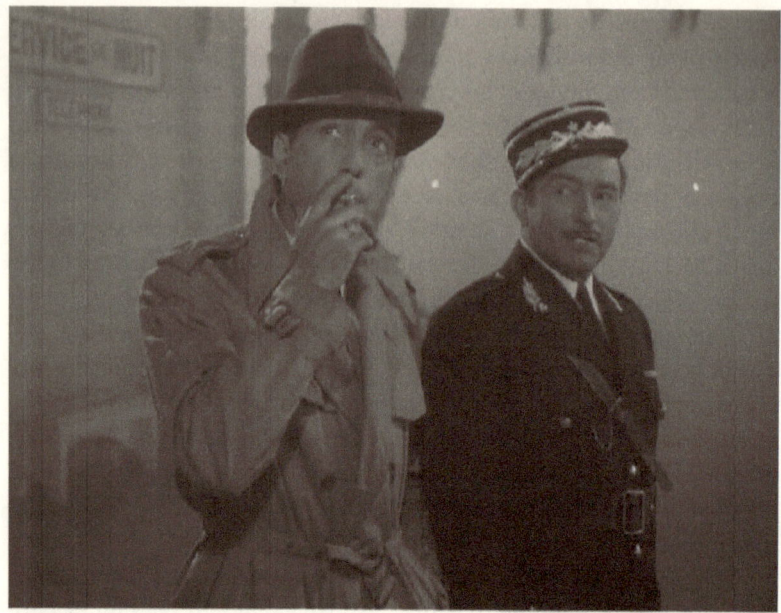

Figure 1.3. Rick and Louis, now allies, walk off into the thick fog and plan for Rick's escape.

literally means "the land of one's ancestors" and was likely chosen over other options with similar meanings such as *bokoku* ("motherland") or *wagakuni* ("our nation"). *Sokoku* is conspicuously patriotic and resonates closest with the showdown of patriotic songs sung in Rick's Place, started by the German soldiers but quickly overtaken by a group singing in French, led by Laszlo. Both *Vaterland*, from the chorus of "Die Wacht am Rhein"—*Lieb Vaterland, machst ruhig sein*—and *patrie* from the first line of "La Marseillaise"—*Allons, enfants de la patrie*—are rendered into Japanese as *sokoku* in the script.[14] This battle of patriotisms—in Japanese not *Vaterland* against *patrie*, but *sokoku* against *sokoku*—reveals its arbitrary nature more clearly in translation. Both sides end up fighting for country in the abstract, and they are all dissolved into a single team of patriots.

To the possible referents for *sokoku*, then, we should add France, Germany, and the United States to the assumed referent of Japan. To the possible meanings of *misutsuru*, we should add "throw down *another's* life" to "throw down one's life" and "forsake." *Casablanca* has expanded as well in its interaction with Terayama's poem. The final scene becomes a play of light layered over the rapid shift of alliances so carefully plotted by Rick.

The displaced match strike might in fact be seen as split in two—half is displaced forward to the gunshot that kills Strasser, and half moved back to the carefully timed glint off Ilsa's tear as she walks to the airplane with Laszlo (Figure 1.4). The dead Nazi and lost love are held in balance as the tradeoffs of war. But read against the poem—against the dilemma of killing or dying for country—we might also recognize just how close Rick may have been to killing Renault in the moment of that match strike. By then he had committed himself to seeing Laszlo and Ilsa off to safety, so if the eye contact made with Renault had not fully convinced him that they would join forces, then Rick likely would have shot both Strasser *and* Renault, which would have meant almost certain death for himself. Was Rick prepared to die? Without that nonverbal assurance (transcending the babel of Casablanca) at the precise moment of the lighting of his cigarette, Rick may have chosen not *between* killing or dying for country but *both* killing and dying for country. The wordplay in the poem certainly allows for such a play of meaning, and it may be that the full potential of the poem is realized only when read in relation to this film.

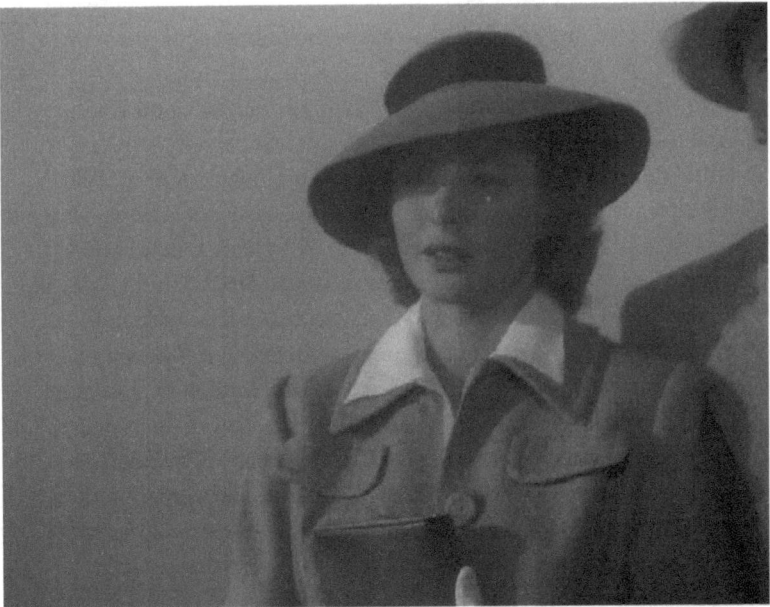

Figure 1.4. *Ilsa, having rekindled her romance with Rick just the previous night, sheds a tear as she walks toward the airplane with her husband Laszlo, the resistance organizer.*

"Chekhov Festival" and the Plagiarism Controversy

Terayama made his public debut in 1954, at age eighteen, by winning a poetry contest run by the journal *Tanka kenkyū*. The submission was a set of thirty-one-syllable poems composed mainly on the theme of a war orphan's coming of age. His was the second such award given for the competition, which was designed largely in response to the deaths in 1953 of two of the genre's great modern masters—Saitō Mokichi and Shaku Chōkū (the tanka pen name of Orikuchi Shinobu)—and to the launch of a rival magazine by the Kadokawa company in January 1954 devoted to preserving their legacy. After their deaths, the future of tanka seemed destined to pass into the hands of their students, many of whom were already in their sixties. The editors at *Tanka kenkyū*, however, were at the time mostly in their twenties, if that. Sugiyama Seiju, for one, began copyediting for *Tanka kenkyū* directly after high school at age nineteen. His head editor, Nakai Hideo, took his position at age twenty-six. From the late 1940s and into the early 1950s, the young editorial staff had almost no control over content and was instructed to publish in accordance to a ranked chart of the various tanka coteries.[15] Things were extraordinarily bureaucratic, mechanical, safe, and stable. Nakai recalls the following circumstances:

> Two stars of the Romantic period, Kitahara Hakushū and Yosano Akiko, had passed away in 1943, so when I first became involved in editing during 1949, poets still active today [in 1971] such as Toki Zenmaro and Tsuchiya Bunmei, as well as Sasaki Nobutsuna, who was born in 1882, were the eldest group. They were followed by Saitō Mokichi, Kubota Utsubo, Yoshii Isamu, Shaku Chōkū, Maeda Yūgure, as well as Onoe Saishū, Ōta Mizuho, and Kawada Jun—all of whom were well-loved major poets with tanka in the primers, and they were all still healthy and active. Under them the forty and fifty year old layer was still thicker and wider, so even poets near forty years old with a great deal of experience like Miya Shūji and Kondō Yoshimi were being treated as absolute newcomers—there was simply no space at all for those in their teens or twenties to emerge. If there were space it would be in a coterie association where they would write poems under the direction of a master, as if they were pruning bonsai trees. Being in my twenties at the time I felt that the situation was very odd and it frustrated me.[16]

Nakai decided to intervene. He wrote anonymously for his own magazine denouncing the absence of space for poets in their teens, twenties, and thirties to publish. Were not younger poets best suited to express the concerns and emotions of an adolescent mind?[17] When Nakai was given more control over content in late 1953, the first thing he did was to announce an open contest in which anyone was welcome to submit fifty tanka to the magazine. The winner of the first contest was announced in April 1954. Nakai selected thirty-two-year-old Nakajō Fumiko, who composed vividly on her experience of mastectomy after being diagnosed with breast cancer. The initial response was negative—her poems were sensationalist and melodramatic—but praise from the novelist Kawabata Yasunari quieted her critics and affirmed Nakai's selection.[18]

Terayama read Nakajō's poems, and he cites them as his inspiration to switch from writing haiku to tanka.[19] He submitted fifty poems to the next contest and won with a set he called "Chichi kaese" (Give me back my father), but that was published as "Chehofu-sai," or "The Chekhov Festival." Nakai drew the title from the following set of verses:

> *tabakobi o yuka ni fumikeshite tachiagaru Chehofu-sai no wakaki haiyū*
> He stomps out his cigarette on the floor and stands up—
>   a young actor in the Chekhov Festival
> *Chehofu-sai no bira no harareshi ringo no ki kasuka ni yururu kisha tōru tabi*
> A Chekhov Festival poster hung on an apple tree—
>   it sways gently with each passing steam rain
> *kago no momo ni hoho itaki made oshitsukete Chehofu no hi no densha ni yuraru*
> My cheek pressed against crated peaches until it hurts—
>   swaying in the electric train on Chekhov Day[20]

The critical response to Terayama's poems followed a path opposite Nakajō's case. The initial reaction was positive, claiming that he had captured the exaggerated emotions of adolescence and that the poems were fresh and exuberant.[21] Several of the tanka mark themselves as youth poems directly:

> *bansei o agete kugatsu no mori ni ireri Haine no tame ni gaku o azamuki*
> I let out a barbaric roar and enter the September forest—
>   forsaking my studies for Heine

tabako kusaki kokugo kyōshi ga iu toki ni asu to iu go wa mottomo
    kanashi
When my cigarette-smelling language teacher says it
    "tomorrow" is the saddest word of all
kubikazari wa mozō naran to hitorigime ni onore nagusamu aware na
    Romio
Now convinced the necklace he bought was a fake—
    self-consolation for a pathetic Romeo[22]

Such praise lasted only a few weeks, however, until several critics pointed out the excessive borrowing from recently published haiku by Nakamura Kusatao and a few others, as well as cases in which Terayama had simply lengthened his own haiku into tanka.

Nakai himself may have been the most frustrated by Terayama's apparent plagiarism. It was he, after all, who had selected the poems, which meant that his qualifications as judge of his own contest were now suspect. Not only that, but the premise of his greater cause—creating space for young poets—had been discredited. Could these poets really be trusted to contribute to the genre? Yet the heated debates that arose in the wake of Terayama's award did not end up hurting tanka as a genre or as a business. The opposite was more likely the case. Suddenly "avant-garde tanka" (*zen'ei tanka*) became a catchphrase that a broad range of authors wrote about, including practicing tanka poets like Tsukamoto Kunio and Okai Takashi, but extending even to the cultural critic Yoshimoto Takaaki.[23]

Those involved in the plagiarism debate over Terayama's poems quickly settled into two camps. On one side were the haiku critics, who were still stinging from an essay by Kuwabara Takeo called "Daini geijutsu: Gendai haiku ni tsuite" (A second-rate art: On contemporary haiku, 1946). In the essay, he claimed to have proven that the so-called contemporary haiku masters were no more talented than high school students by asking the master poets to rank poems by both groups without knowing who had written them.[24] The inconsistency of the results seemed to prove his point, and it sent shock waves through the haiku world, threatening the legitimacy of the entire enterprise. While generally assumed to be an attack on a lack of talent in the master poets, Kuwabara's survey could also be taken as proof *of* talented teenagers. In either case, the logic of the existing gerontocracy had been undermined.

Established haiku critics were the most critical of Terayama, accusing him not only of the ethical breach of stealing phrases but also of undermining the separate identities of tanka and haiku. Haiku critic Kusamoto Kenkichi explicitly scolded him: "I will say it again to this teenager, Mr. Terayama. As I stated, haiku is not a formula or a cipher, let alone a crossword puzzle for emotive language. When a form exists over a long period of time there arises a sort of formulaic convenience in it—as well as a mechanistic laziness, certainly. But taking advantage of this convenient inertia and indulging in crossword puzzles is the 'forbidden game.' It is one which you should restrict yourself from doing, particularly in order to discover the hidden, luxurious, uncultivated realms through which your path may travel."[25] Another critic, Wakatsuki Akira, acknowledges that Terayama had stepped beyond tactful allusion but praises him for reintegrating some sense of social connection into what had become a bleak and lonesome pair of genres. He claims the limited length of the forms had too long been used to excuse solipsistic verse: "The position of tanka and haiku within contemporary life depends on whether or not ideas with social universality are used 'as elements' in the poems themselves. Too often poets (of both tanka and haiku) satisfy themselves by expressing egoistic solitude. Admittedly, it is particularly difficult in the case of short-form poetry such as tanka and haiku to incorporate a sense of social connection into that solitude—and so we find no shortage in the documentation of the unbridgeable psychological rift between the personal solitude of the author and the currency of ideas shared among the masses."[26]

On the other side of the debate were a group of young tanka poets who saw Terayama as a hero in the fight against language conceived as an individual possession. To them, Terayama was a leader in the movement to return language to its rightful place in the public sphere—they argued that criticizing Terayama for quoting phrases required the erroneous step of assuming that he was taking something privately owned away from one person and claiming it for himself. Saitō Shōji, for one, writes that "these were never anyone's possessions from the start, and Terayama is not assuming them to be his own."[27] Rather, he celebrates Terayama's poems as representative of a break from "a Romantic ethic that claims a poem to be private property."[28] Language, Saitō's side argues, ought to be one realm preserved for the public domain, where words and phrases are duplicated and reused but never qualify as legal possessions. One of the poems in Terayama's debut seems, in fact, to touch on this very theme of the conversion of the commons to private property:

> *hitotsubu no himawari no tane makishi nomi ni kōya o ware no shōjochi*
>   *to yobiki*
> Planting a single sunflower seed
>   I pronounce the wilderness my maiden land[29]

Hishikawa Yoshio was the most outspoken in his defense of Terayama's poems:

> At present, when the younger generation's rise to power is increas-
> ing with tangible energy, it seems inevitable that a generational
> shift must soon occur. As for the entrenched poetry establishment
> [*kadan*], one can easily expect the authority of "elders" to result in
> friction and opposition. Yet the younger generation is level-headed.
> Even if we hold the authority of these elders in contempt for the
> weakness of their intellect and lack of creativity—for their over-
> generous opinion of their own lukewarm adolescence—we still have
> not used unrestrained, brutal criticism as a weapon. If there were an
> all-out battle between these opposing generations it is clearer than
> the light of day that we would completely conquer them.[30]

This plagiarism debate quickly settled into a stalemate. Both sides agreed that Terayama conspicuously borrowed considerably more from the poems of others than would usually be expected even in a deliberately allusive composition. Then critics split into camps to either praise or condemn Terayama on ethical grounds. What is missing from the discussion, however, is attention to what Terayama actually *does* with the quotations—what exactly he adds to them and how, but most importantly what kinds of interactions he sets up between his source materials and the additions to them.

The most-often cited example of excessive quotation was a poem that borrowed from a haiku by Nakamura Kusatao. Terayama's tanka reads,

> *himawari no shita ni jōzetsu takaki kana hito o towazuba jiko naki otoko*
> Quite a chatterbox there under the sunflower—
>   without engaging others, a man without a self[31]

Compare it with the haiku by Kusatao:

hito o towazuba jiko naki otoko tsukimigusa
Without engaging others, a man without a self—evening primrose[32]

Terayama has quoted fourteen syllables from Nakamura's haiku, which makes up nearly all of the haiku but less than half of the new tanka. What existing scholarship has seemed to miss about Terayama's poem, however, is that he has left himself exactly seventeen syllables for his addition—precisely the length of a new haiku. Terayama is not just mixing quotation from haiku in his tanka, then, but literally composing haiku within the genre of tanka. This quotation may seem excessively long, but it is still within the guidelines set by the early thirteenth-century poet Fujiwara no Teika's for the maximum permissible length of quotation in *waka*—fifteen or sixteen syllables, or essentially half of the poem.[33] Leaving sufficient space for additional composition is the governing principle here—there is no consideration of an ethical limit to appropriation—and the clear assumption is that knowledge of the quoted poem is expected of the reader (making attribution unnecessary and patronizing). This poem is best understood, then, as a collage comprising the quotation from Kusatao and the following new, original haiku by Terayama:

himawari no shita ni jōzetsu takaki kana
Quite a chatterbox there under the sunflower

Alternatively, we could focus on the strongest image in Terayama's addition, the "chatterbox" (*jōzetsu*). By adding a negative term, he may not so much be embellishing Kusatao's haiku as attacking it. Looking closely at the strong images added to the other poems cited as plagiaristic reveals this type of addition to be a consistent pattern. In one case, Terayama shifts the image of a cigarette toward a more optimistic tone by ironically having it snubbed out. Kusatao's haiku reads,

tomoshibi no hi o tabakobi to shitsu Chehofu-ki
Lighting a cigarette with the lamp—requiem for Chekhov[34]

Terayama lengthens and reworks this into his tanka:

tabakobi o yuka ni fumikeshite tachiagaru Chehofu-sai no wakaki haiyū
He stomps out a cigarette on the floor and stands up—
a young actor at the Chekhov Festival[35]

Maintaining this reference to Chekhov may seem excessive, but Teraya-ma's shift from Kusatao's "requiem" (*ki*) to "festival" (*sai*) is significant. A "requiem," for Chekhov, mourns his loss in a nostalgic mode—the time orientation is toward the past. Kusatao's poetic voice longs, here, to be in a past when Chekhov was still alive. Terayama's "festival," however, is a celebration in the present of the still-living version of Chekhov (as texts, brought alive by theatrical performance). The Chekhov Festival is synchronically oriented, and if there is diachronic motion, it is to pull Chekhov forward into the present tense. This small, but critical, variation is in fact thrown into relief by Terayama's reuse of "Chekhov"—without this level of sameness we would likely not pause here to contemplate the slight difference.

In another case, Terayama adds the stench of manure and removes an origami flower. The resulting image is extraordinary: blues music (*hika*, lit., "sad song" in the poems) from U.S. Army barracks in remote northern Japan during the Allied occupation (1945–51), where a young Japanese boy is in earshot and curious. But recognizing the roots of blues in black culture, the protagonist of this poem makes an associative leap over the military occupation to link himself and his fertilizing chores back to African American slaves and forty-acre farmers. Saitō Sanki's haiku reads,

> *kami no sakura kokujin hika wa ji ni shizumu*
> Paper cherry blossoms—
>   the black man's blues song sinks into the ground[36]

Terayama's tanka reworks the poem into the following:

> *kawakitaru oke ni koyashi o mitasu toki kokujin hika wa daichi ni shizumu*
> As I fill a dry bucket with manure
>   the black man's blues song sinks into the earth[37]

The clearest example of an attack may be the following, in which a bird, an image from another of Sanki's haiku, is shot and killed. Sanki's poem reads,

> *waga tenshi naru ya mo ononoku kansuzume*
> Might be my angel—a winter sparrow shudders[38]

Terayama reworks this into a tanka that reads,

> *waga tenshi naru ya mo shirenu kosuzume o uchite shōen kagitsutsu kaeru*

Having shot the little sparrow that may have been my angel
  I return home smelling the gunsmoke[39]

A pattern forms among these poems, in which Terayama's tanka mock (*jōzetsu*), defile (*koyashi*), crush (*fumikeshite*), and kill (*uchite*) elements within the haiku that they invoke. This is certainly not the standard allusive practice within the *waka* and tanka genres.

Here it becomes clear that categorizing these poems as "avant-garde tanka" (*zen'ei tanka*) is not only taxonomic but can be a useful tool for analysis. If we compare Terayama's poems to a classic from the historical avant-garde, such as Duchamp's mustachioed Mona Lisa painting, for example, several things become clearer. The first is that the quoted text is not the ultimate target of the mockery—Duchamp was not ridiculing either the Mona Lisa or Da Vinci, but rather those who take the painting too seriously. It is, along with being a joke, a jab at the polite culture of museums—what Peter Bürger writes of as the avant-garde's attack on "the status of art in bourgeois society" and the "distribution apparatus on which the work of art depends."[40] No one would bother to call Duchamp a plagiarist because his use of the Mona Lisa is so conspicuous and because it is so clear that the Mona Lisa is merely background to his flourish, the mustache, which is the part of the work that we rightly understand to be his, and which we also rightly understand to be largely meaningless outside the context of the replica of the Mona Lisa onto which it is painted. The base text and the flourish cannot be separated here—they are symbiotic. Assuming Terayama's poems to operate in a similar way might get us a bit further toward understanding how they function.

Read as avant-gardist poems, these tanka begin to resonate closely with a photograph that appears repeatedly across Terayama's work. The image is a simple black-and-white portrait of Terayama's mother, but the photograph has been torn into several pieces, sewn back together, and reframed (Figure 1.5). A narrative develops across these torn fragments, the thread, and the reframing—we imagine a son's passionate moment of anger, followed by his regret for the attack, and finally a recuperation of affection. Terayama has shifted the static image into a realm of narrative potential far more present and tangible than would be possible with a clean photograph. And it is precisely because the base object here, the original untorn photograph itself, is culturally understood to be so *objective*—in contradistinction to composition, choice of content, or any other product of

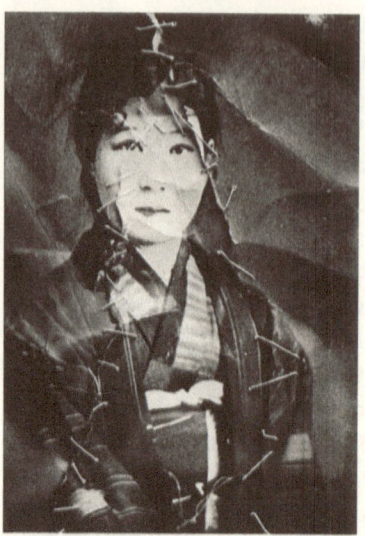

Figure 1.5. This torn-and-stitched-back-together photograph of Terayama's mother appears in the film Den'en ni shisu *(Death in the country, 1974) and Terayama's photography collection,* Terayama Shūji gensōshashinkan: Inugami-ke no hitobito *(Terayama Shūji's fantasy photo studio: Members of the Inugami clan, 1975). Courtesy of Kujō Kyōko and Terayama World*

the photographer's expressive mind—that the hand of the author and the subjectivity of the narrator are thrown into such clear relief by these rips and the thread. Terayama's conflicted narrator is hyperpresent in the sewn photo. Similarly, by attacking other poets' haiku—tearing off a piece of a poem and sewing it together with a piece of his own—Terayama's poetic narrator becomes hyperpresent in his tanka as well.

The satirical appropriation of the classics may be avant-gardist here, but appropriation itself has a long and distinguished history specific to the genre in which Terayama wrote these poems. Quotation in the thirty-one-syllable form traces back at least to Fujiwara no Teika's formulation of *honkadori,* the *waka* practice of "borrowing from the original poem." As Edward Kamens has argued, *honkadori* might best be understood as a quasi-religious rite in which the spirits of the dead poets of the past are kept alive while reaffirming and regenerating the practice of *waka* composition itself.[41] If this is the case, then Terayama may have inverted the devotional nature of such quotation—it is as though he is performing some kind of black-magic curse on the *honka* (original poem). Yet, since he admitted elsewhere that the haiku poets from whom he borrowed were his favorites, it might be most accurate to look at these attacks on the original poems as fundamentally Oedipal—these are the poetic fathers Terayama both idolizes and seeks to overcome.[42]

Terayama's use of quotation compares in an interesting way to a descriptive model of *honkadori* practice suggested by the critic Asanuma Keiji: "An endless play of sending and receiving arises between the *honka* and the poem. It is similar to the play of reflected images that emerge between two facing mirrors. This play is *limited* to the space between these two texts (mirrors)—unable to escape and touch anything in the real world but also incapable of rising above to move toward any sort of Ideal. A limitless play emerging within limitation, an endless cycle of play, which has in some way severed its connection to 'that which exists as itself'—it is play esthétique."[43] Asanuma describes Teika's method as one that breaks down the idealization of canonical poems by playfully quoting, manipulating, and rewriting them. The act of *honkadori*, then, forcibly shifts the classic poem from a "work" to a "text"—the process of quotation denies generation of the symbolic aura of the idealized "poem." But in Terayama's case, the *honka* were published just a year or two before his own. Teika, conversely, would only use poems that were already several hundred years old as *honka* in his work. There are a few important implications in such a difference.

First, no one except perhaps young Terayama himself would have considered Kusatao's haiku to be a classic by 1954 (particularly the "man without a self" poem, released earlier that same year), so if we choose to call this *honkadori*, then we might also have to recognize that Terayama has radically adjusted literary time—the category of the "classic" here signifies any poem of the past. In a separate haiku collection, for instance, he categorizes the early twentieth-century poet Ishikawa Takuboku as part of the classics (*koten*): his collection *Kafun kōkai* (Pollen voyage) includes a chapter called "Migite no koten" (Right-hand classics), which opens with a section titled "Takuboku kashū" (Poems by Takuboku).[44] Then, if we maintain Asanuma's analogy, the mirrors have been pushed very close together in Terayama's debut. By squeezing the infinite play between *honka* and poem into a smaller and smaller space, these poems have been compressed—as though to force them to burst from the limitations of the form.

The mirrors are almost touching, then, quickening and intensifying the reflection between them. It is not just the *honka* that is getting attacked and crushed—the entire poem is being compressed in the vise of these mirrors. So is this radically new? Surely in this particular manifestation, but taken broadly, the practice lines up nicely with the entire repertoire of *waka* techniques, all of which seem, at their core, to be designed to compress more information into the genre's fixed length of thirty-one syllables. *Mitate* (elegant confusion), where one image is aesthetically confused with another—as in falling cherry blossoms and snow—allows for a reuse, and thereby a doubling, of information. *Utamakura* (pillow words) tap an entire lineage of associations with a location or an object with a single word. *Kakekotoba* (pivot words) operate like an overlapping hinge in the poem, functioning once for what comes before it and again, in a different way, for what follows—effectively extending the poem by the length of the pivot. These are all technologies of compression in their most basic form, and in that sense, Terayama's compression of the *honka-dori* mirrors fittingly extends this aspect of the classical tradition.

Shifting from diachronic to synchronic analysis allows us to recognize that Terayama's use of a compression device was as much a timely technique embedded in its postwar moment as it was a continuation of classical method. In 1948, the abstract painter and sculptor Okamoto Tarō published an explanation of his aesthetic theory of *taikyoku-shugi*, or "polar-oppositionalism."[45] The goal under his system was to isolate representations of absolute opposites—rationality and absurdity, or materialism and idealism—and then push them as closely together as possible, but without allowing them to merge. This was thesis and antithesis without synthesis in Okamoto's mind—synthesis being the trap the avant-garde had fallen into in the 1930s that led to its staleness. Okamoto suggests that this antisynthetic compression of opposites generates an outflow of energy the artist can harness and use to drive a creative explosion that will manifest itself as a piece of art. This period also sees the shift from fission to fusion-based nuclear weapons—from split-explosion to *compression*-explosion—as well as the polarization of power during the cold war between the United States and the Soviet Union, politically compressing other nations into allegiance to one or the other power.

The intertextual links in Terayama's poems, however, extend beyond just the set of poems from which he borrowed. A number of the debut tanka allude to literary works but then inflect the original text slightly. A careful look at a few of these instances turns up several interesting new connections not explored in existing criticism, possibly due to the distraction of the plagiarism controversy. One of Terayama's debut tanka evokes Poe's "The Premature Burial":

> *oto tatete hakaana fukaku chichi no kan orosaruru toki chichi*
> *mezamezuya*

My father's casket dropped loudly into its deep grave—
   what if it wakes him up?[46]

Poe's story is an account of several cases of such live burial: "To be buried while alive is, beyond question, the most terrific of these extremes which has ever fallen to the lot of mere mortality."[47] However, while the piece does take live burial as its general topic, it is much more keenly focused on the relationship between belief in the truthfulness of a piece of writing and its potential for emotional effect, pointing out fiction's relative inability to horrify. As such, the story is primarily a study of the rhetorical production of truth value. It opens in the following way: "There are certain themes of which the interest is all-absorbing, but which are too entirely horrible for the purposes of legitimate fiction. These the mere romanticist must eschew, if he do not wish to offend, or to disgust. They are with propriety handled only when the severity and majesty of truth sanctify and sustain them . . . it is the fact—it is the reality—it is the history which excites. As inventions, we should regard them with simple abhorrence."[48] The crime, then, which Poe ultimately invites us to question, is not so much live burial as the artificial production of truth value through linguistic devices, and he gives readers a grand tour. He opens with a straightforward claim of legitimacy: "We have the direct testimony of medical and ordinary experience to prove that a vast number of such interments have actually taken place."[49] Then, he continues with an appeal to probability: "When we reflect how very rarely, from the nature of the case, we have it in our power to detect them, we must admit that they may *frequently* occur without our cognizance."[50] He then ends with a confessional account: "And thus all narratives upon this topic have an interest profound; an interest, nevertheless, which through the sacred awe of the topic itself, very properly and very peculiarly depends upon our conviction of the *truth* of the matter narrated. What I have now to tell is of my own actual knowledge—of my own positive and personal experience."[51] Terayama, through his reference to live burial, may have been alluding to this sort of manipulation of truth as a study in fictionality. Here fiction is a literary lie that momentarily convinces us of its truth but then reveals itself to be false—enabling in readers a keener awareness of our vulnerability to the power of rhetoric.

   If Terayama was referring not only to the horrific image in Poe's story but also to the study of the production of false understanding through the exploitation of assumptions bundled with particular rhetorical modes, then

we might expect other, similar cases. There are at least two more important references to texts focused on truth value. The following poem uses an
image from a children's story by Tsubota Jōji called "Mahō" (Magic):

> kono ie mo dareka ga dōkemono naran takaki hei yori koeideshi ageha
> Is there a prankster in this house, too?
>   A swallowtail butterfly flies out over the tall hedge[52]

The story is of a boy, Zenta, attempting to convince his younger brother,
Sanpei, that he has magical powers. Zenta's claims fail to convince Sanpei until a monk passes by the garden where they are playing and Zenta
announces that he will change the monk into a butterfly:

> A monk passed by outside the hedge. He wore a yellow surplice
> over his black kimono. Seeing him, Zenta said in a quiet voice,
> "Sanpei, look! See that monk there. I'll turn him into a butterfly for
> you."
>   "Yeah! Quick, turn him into a butterfly!"
>   "Wait, wait."
>   "No, Zenta! Hurry up or he'll get away!"
>   Just then the monk passed the house.
>   "Now he's gone! You let him get away! I wanted to see a person
> change into a butterfly."
>   "It wouldn't have worked. He'd have gotten mad if I'd have
> changed him right then. You've got to be careful so they don't
> know. I can do it no matter where he is, so it's better to wait until
> he's not right in front of us."
>   Then it happened. A black swallowtail butterfly flitted over on
> the wind.
>   "There! He's here, he's here!"
>   Zenta looked at it and said in a loud outburst, "Look, it's the
> monk from just now! He turned into a butterfly and flew over to
> us. Quick, huh?"
>   Sanpei got a strange feeling. The butterfly and the monk really
> did look similar.[53]

Terayama's poem is not a simple retelling of Tsubota's story. By adding
mo ("also") after kono ie ("this house"), the image is shifted a degree away

from the original. We imagine someone walking down the street, seeing a butterfly rising over the hedge of someone's garden, and at that moment recalling Tsubota's story. The poem, then, documents the way the experience of reading literature interacts with everyday life—one's knowledge of the Zenta and Sanpei story conditions the response to seeing a real butterfly float over a hedge. There is a revealing and important comment in the story itself, however, immediately following the previous scene:

"Wow, Zenta. Did you really use magic?"
"Yeah. I really did."
"Really? But when?"
"Just now."
"Now? But you didn't do anything."
"I did, but secretly so you wouldn't see. That's why it's called magic."[54]

That's why it's called magic. Zenta's trick would lose its charm if it operated in clear view with its mechanism exposed. Fictionality in Terayama's poems can be seen, initially at least, to work in the same way—these quotations are tricks that slip quotation in where lyrical expression should be. Keeping this in mind, there is one final allusion that helps to fully contextualize this kind of play with quotation.

Tracing out the intertextual play at work in these poems provides a number of hints as to Terayama's poetics and the sensibility toward fiction driving his project. But one seemingly minor line in the debut poems is essential to understanding exactly how quotation functioned in this set. After the title of the poems that won the *Tanka kenkyū* award, "Chekhov Festival," but before Terayama's name or any of the poems, there is a single line printed in a font slightly smaller than that used for the poems:

aoi shushi wa taiyō no naka ni aru	*Soreru*
The green seed is inside the sun.	Sorel[55]

Convention signals this to be a typical epigraph—a direct quotation. With no more information, we are left to decide whether this is from Julien Sorel, the romantic protagonist of Stendhal's *Le rouge et le noir,* or the political philosopher Georges Sorel (whose work on violence Terayama admired). Both were available in translation by the time Terayama debuted and he makes reference to both in his later writings. When the Chekhov poems were reprinted in Terayama's first book of tanka, however, *Soreru* was expanded to *Jurian Soreru*, so we must assume this to be from Stendhal. But, as several critics have pointed out and as Terayama finally admitted, this line is simply not in Stendhal's novel,[56] which in a way—especially in the context of the other quotations—makes perfect sense. These poems are first a study in rhetorical conventions and assumptions about genre. The quotations in the poems, what get cited as plagiarism, are part of a larger project of putting certain types of language in places that they do not belong. There is quotation where lyricism should be, but there is *also* lyricism where quotation should be.[57] Terayama is playing, like Poe, with truth value by exploiting the reader's exaggerated trust in certain types of rhetorical formations—the quotation-shaped expression that creates its own validity, as well as lyrically shaped expression that generates its own honesty. And, like Zenta, he does not reveal the apparatus behind the trick, choosing instead to leave it in the open unexplained. And yet what none of the critics mention about this epigraph is that Stendhal himself did precisely the same thing throughout his novel. Nearly every chapter of *The Red and the Black* opens with an epigraph either completely fictional or misattributed.[58] What this means is that Terayama's epigraph is a direct quotation of Stendhal's *technique*—an appropriation of method masked as a reproduction of content.

Under a strict definition of plagiarism as an unattributed quotation used without permission, there is certainly plagiarism in Terayama's debut poems—maybe twice as much as was first apparent. Using that definition, however, Duchamp and Eliot would be just as guilty. The alternative is to recognize that the charge of plagiarism requires a dubious claim of access to authorial intent—that the unattributed quotation was used with the hope that readers would not discover the source. However, the way the response to Terayama's debut moved so quickly to a debate on the ethical use of other writer's language—particularly in a genre histori- cally so open source in its promotion of borrowing—may speak more to the times than specifically to Terayama. The attack on poetic quotation here exceeds the notion of copyright as a time-limited monopoly, mov- ing much closer to the contemporary concept of intellectual property, a more robust and permanent ownership of ideas. And for professional writers emerging from war-torn Japan, the quick reestablishment of a via- ble market for literature and a strong defense of their right to profit from writing were critical. Terayama's intervention here may have served as a reminder regarding the costs of moving writing toward this kind of legalistic model. The accusation of plagiarism may operate most fundamentally as an excuse to abandon analysis of a text prematurely. This may have been the process through which the analysis of Terayama's first poems were cut short by both his critics, to write him off as a hack amateur, and his admirers, to paint him as a rebel genius. Terayama's own response to the debate he sparked broke apart this stalemate and suggested a new technique for combining emotional authenticity and imaginative creativity.[59]

Neolyricism and Fiction of Possibility

Frustrated with the shallowness of the debate that followed his debut, Terayama wrote to explain the methods he used in the Chekhov poems in an essay titled "Romii no daiben: Tankeishi ni tsuite no echūdo" (Romy's proxy: An étude on short-form poetry). He opens the essay, which goes on to spell out some of his specific techniques and objectives, with the following:

> Where shall I begin? Right, I should first announce my name. I am a third-party, commonly known as a fictional character—one that exists within my author, Terayama Shūji.
>
> Let's assign me a temporary name, say, "Romy." It's actually quite obvious why my author chose to have me, rather than himself, deliver this deceptively simple argument about commonality between the two genres of short-form poetry, tanka and haiku. I have already experienced his Romantic future, and yet we are not one in the same. It looks like my existence won't be recognized by the tanka and haiku establishment, though, consisting as it does only of memorialists like Ishida Hakyō with his claim that "haiku is confessional fiction [shishōsetsu]."
>
> And yet, the very fact that I'm speaking right now proves my existence—and we ought to assume that many more like me will appear. My author, out of sympathy and desire to protect me, takes full responsibility and writes for me by proxy.[60]

This opening is a clever retort. In essence, it reveals the mode of lyricism to be necessarily one not of writerly method but of readerly interpretation—an analytic framework applied to a text—that too easily exposes itself to being duped. By excluding the possibility of fantasy, embellishment, or any other fictional elements, it also imposes severe limitations on the range of forms compatible with it. The assumption that the genres of tanka and the critical essay have some sort of natural link to direct expression by an author is exposed here as absurd by capsizing the logic of the assumption on its own terms: rather than the author (Terayama) producing the confessional text, the confessional text here has created its author (Romy). The rhetoric of lyricism gives life to this narrational voice. This one-to-one correlation of life and art, borrowed for effect from the "memorialists," paradoxically embodies Terayama's fictional narrator here, so much so in this case that it is Romy who becomes the author and Terayama who becomes the stand-in for him, his narrator. Romy writes, therefore he is— or, rather, Romy, having written in the past, comes to be in the present.

The tanka and haiku circles of the moment may have been dominated by a lingering attachment to confessional forms, but as a teenage poet from one of the most traditionally impoverished areas in Japan, Aomori prefecture, Terayama became the perfect target for a renewed and intensified search for the authenticity of lyrical expression. It may not be particularly surprising that urban critics and editors would search for that authenticity in someone from such a doubly naïve category as the rural schoolboy. Nakai Hideo himself was clearly taken with what he perceived to be the pure lyricism of a young, unscathed rustic. He writes the following on Terayama's haiku:

> These poems, composed during high school when he was fifteen or sixteen years old, are the best of the collection in terms of their innocent beauty—they are dream-lamps that cast a faint light onto the childhood of the reader. They possess the freshness of fruit that will never rot. The apple orchards of the north country where Terayama Shūji was born and raised expand within the author, the boy playing there just as he likes, grabbing a piece of fruit the color of women's skin in a Renoir and biting gently into it with his white teeth. The teenage author transmits the psychology of love with exquisiteness unreachable by an adult—we may have examples of elegant expression in symbolist poems, but not the insides of a teenage boy reflected with this degree of clarity and nostalgia.[61]

Terayama himself considered his experiments with artifice to be faithful to a different type of authenticity, that he tries "to compose on what

Nerval called, 'that which is seen, without concern for whether it was or was not a real event—that which has been clearly perceived.'"[62] Objective faithfulness to the subject's imagination may, in this system, qualify as a new type of lyricism. In a twist on phenomenology's removal of the distinction between objective reality and subjective response, Nerval may have moved toward reportage of all sensations, but Terayama, working from the same premise, seems to have begun examining the creation of an authenticity effect within himself, which then generated seemingly lyrical poems. He expresses frustration, for example, that so many people asked if he had ever actually sold the communist newspaper *Akahata* (Red flag) after reading the first poem in his debut:

> *Akahata uru ware o natsuchō koeyukeri haha wa kokyō no ta o uchite imu*
> A summer butterfly passes over me as I sell copies of *Red Flag*—
>   Mother is back home hoeing the fields[63]

The poem summarizes an ethical problem at the heart of left-wing politics: who will bear the labor burden on the road to social change? Yet the typical reaction to the poem was not to consider such a dilemma or the image of the butterfly that transcends and bridges mother and child but to want to know whether Terayama is really a communist. He addresses the problem at a published round table shortly after his debut:

> I'd like to unravel one more thing: the problem of fiction. It seems that until now whenever people say fiction they only ever mean absolute fantasy. I feel that we've got to integrate something else we might call "the fiction of possibility" [*kanōsei fikushon*] into our work. For example, when I composed the poem, "A summer butterfly passes over me as I sell *Red Flag*," everyone instantly started saying: "You sold *Red Flag*?" or "stop lying" or "you're dishonest." Kitamura and I had a long debate about this the other day, and it's true, I have never sold *Red Flag*, but I know a lot of people who do, and when I muster up my empathy for those people I feel justified in saying "*I* sell *Red Flag*." By giving tanka primary significance and subordinating everyday life to the poem, I was able to live within a consciousness that was selling *Red Flag*, even if I hadn't physically stood there selling it. We've got to start using this type of fiction of possibility.[64]

By "fiction of possibility," Terayama seems to claim the potential of fiction to create a legitimate reality (one in which Terayama himself truly possessed a consciousness that sold *Red Flag*)—which is a very different claim than the more familiar insistence that author and narrator (even in first person) are fully separate entities. Terayama is arguing for a rational acceptance of the reality of his fictionalized and fictionalizing poet self—a loyalty (shared with his reader) to the veracity of imagination, which trumps the typical bindings of factual experience.

The frustration Terayama describes here parallels contemporaneous commentary by Alain Robbe-Grillet on his *nouveau roman*. Labeled "antinovels," the type of writing Robbe-Grillet was doing was considered a direct attack on narrative itself—an attempt to destroy the tradition of the novel. He responded to critics by explaining that his project was to describe contemporary reality with greater precision in order to be accurate to a lived experience that did not fit into smoothly flowing prose. This was accuracy to experience operating with recognition that "objectivity in the ordinary sense of the word—total impersonality of observation—is all too obviously an illusion."[65] The period of the *nouveau roman* immediately follows the period of neorealism in film, which might be described in a similar way. Relative to earlier films, they may appear clumsy and disjointed, but it was a willful roughness that recognizes that using the earlier realist mode would come off as forced—previous patterns had become incapable of producing the immediacy of neorealist looseness. Film critic André Bazin describes the genre in the following terms: "In Roberto Rossellini's *Paisà* and *Allemania Anno Zero* and Vittorio de Sica's *Ladri di Biciclette*, Italian neorealism contrasts with previous forms of film realism in its stripping away of all expressionism and in particular in the total absence of the effects of montage. As in the films of Welles and in spite of conflicts of style, neorealism tends to give back to the cinema a sense of the ambiguity of reality."[66] Terayama writes directly of neorealism after winning the tanka contest: "In terms of method, I am attempting to grasp the point of contact between neorealism and emotion."[67] Yet his insistence that this new "fiction of possibility" maintains a form of authenticity and a legitimate sincerity implies that he is still committed to the principle of lyricism, albeit in some kind of new inflection—thinking of this as pseudo-lyricism may in fact fall into the trap Terayama was arguing against here. Given the cluster of similar updates to realism across several cultural forms during the 1940s and 1950s, signaling Terayama's style with something like "neolyricism" might help to accentuate the link to these other cultural forms. In this context, we are also better situated to recognize Terayama's extension of the classic poetic emotional outburst to include contemporary neorealist experience, one that recognizes the constructedness of all things experienced as "true." Such a term would be most effectively understood not as a list of traits but as a new set of problems concerning the nature of expression: Can quotation function as a tool of expression? Do we have any other option? Has there ever been a purer form of lyricism—one that had a somehow more unmediated access to life devoid of reference to other things?

Liberational Self-Fictionalization or Alienation?

Terayama's match-strike poem, in turn, served as the base text, a *honka*, for a tanka by a young political poet named Kishigami Daisaku. The interaction between these two young poets, including Kishigami's critique of Terayama and Terayama's critique of Kishigami (and others like him), offers an opportunity to explore the ways in which Terayama's political thinking around 1960 interacted with his writing. In April 1960, at age twenty, Kishigami published the following tanka:

> *ishi hyōjii semarigoe nakigoe o se ni tada tanagokoro no naka ni*
> *matchi suru nomi*
> He turns his back on expressions of will, on voices trapped by poverty, on weeping voices, and just lights a match in the palm of his hand[68]

This poem is a play off of Terayama's best-known tanka as well as an indictment of his lack of support for the protests against the renewal of the U.S.–Japan Security Treaty, which would be renewed about a month after the poem's publication (allowing a continued U.S. military presence in Japan). Kishigami and Terayama had met briefly in the run-up to the renewal, when Kishigami invited Terayama to speak at a poetry event at his university. During that meeting, Kishigami asked Terayama what he thought of the demonstrations, and to his disappointment, Terayama told him that they had little chance of changing national or U.S. policy and that a mass movement of young people running away from home or dismantling the universities would have a much greater impact on society. Both remarks turned out to be prescient for events in the late 1960s when runaways would join Terayama's theater troupe and when student radicals barricaded themselves in campus buildings, functionally shutting down most of the Japanese university system. When Kishigami asked if he wrote agitation poems, Terayama replied, "Is there any type of poetry *other* than agitation? [*sendō de nai shi nado sonzai suru mono darō ka?*]"[69] The encounter sparked essays from both sides that provide a window into Terayama's politics at the time as well as a strong critique of both his politics and his poetics.

Kishigami's analysis of the fictionalized first-person narrational voice in Terayama's tanka, which had by that time been recognized to be his main contribution to the genre, was neither to celebrate the division of author and narrator nor to denounce it but rather to historicize it as the type of subjectivity needed to cope with the contradiction between celebrations of postwar democracy and the reality of individual (and collective) agency crushed under the 1950s Japanese economic machine.[70] Freedom is to be found in one's imagination and not in real life. Kishigami argues that Terayama chose to simply document his own self-alienated response to the era, a choice made to the exclusion of developing some form of resistance to the social order that had forced fictionalization of the self. Here we finally see a more grounded challenge to Terayama's neolyricism—not one that challenges the possibility of fictionalizing the narrational voice in a poem (which Terayama addressed in "Romy's Proxy"), but one that takes on the core psychological origin for making that choice: alienation as a result of unacceptable social conditions, that is, democracy in name only that refused demands for a referendum on the continued presence of U.S. troops within Japanese borders. Kishigami's essay on Terayama was published in September 1960, just months after the controversial renewal of the security treaty. In December of that year, he would hang himself, leaving suicide notes to friends claiming that he felt trapped by unrequited love, as well as a longer final statement in which he directly addresses the important poet-turned-philosopher Yoshimoto Takaaki: "Mr. Yoshimoto, I am going to die clutching a collection of your poems. Before my hand stiffens this book of poems will probably fall to the floor and be soaked with rain. You were the only one I cared about losing to!"[71] Had Terayama been more supportive of Kishigami's political position, these final words would likely have been addressed to him.

Part of what Kishigami may have been reacting to was a short essay Terayama had published in August, a month before Kishigami's critique was released, which attacked the lemming-like mood of the antitreaty demonstrations with less restraint than he had shown in their personal exchange. Terayama begins the essay by reporting on his own experience of marching in a demonstration where he was frustrated by how somnambulant the protests had become. He recounts wanting to scream out, "Long live Prime Minister Kishi!" or "Come on in, Ike!" just to wake people up from their daze. Midway through the essay he states, more clearly than anywhere else, his personal political stance at the time:

> Maybe it's that I don't have any desire for a "good" government. I might have caused a misunderstanding by saying that I'd rather be the protesters' flag or that I look forward to anarchy, but my hunch is that socialism would be unfit for self-discovery. It is precisely because Japan and I are not unified under a "good government" that these times feel so alive and fresh. But if a socialist nation would be an unfit location for the discovery of the self and for my artistic acts then a monopoly structure under capitalism would be no better. It is when a single ideology matures and comes to unify an entire nation that our decline as humans begins and when we will begin losing sight of the objective of the artist's mission, which must always be oppositional.[72]

Terayama attempts to set up a third position within the struggle—one he addresses more specifically in another article published during the same month: "I wanted to write about a young person who dwells in this politicized era and yet feels completely disconnected from it. The invisible burden these young people bear is that directionless and illusionary causality called 'history.' I believe that the ones who make history are neither the state oppressors or the revolutionaries, but rather a third zone of people who resist the revolutionaries with an invisible form of power—I have often felt that the potential for unleashing passion rests only in the vitality of young people in that third zone."[73] At the time of writing these pieces, Terayama had just been released from the hospital where he had spent over three years, time he would have spent at university had he not dropped out, while being treated for nephrosis (the kidney condition that would eventually kill him). He was bedridden but alert enough to read, and the Spanish Civil War was one of the topics he studied—so the third position of anarcho-syndicalists pinched between Franco's army and communists demanding consolidation of the resistance was a likely model for his thinking.[74] Terayama's position could also be compared to that of the New Left (then just forming), and its third position against both Stalinism and the military-backed expansion of market economies. Terayama's political thinking shifts somewhat from before his time in the hospital—when his poems were dotted with references to adolescent communists and seemed to delight primarily in the rebelliousness of that category—toward a more clearly anarchist stance that denounced any desire for centralized political power. A thread through much of Terayama's subsequent work is satire of the will to power and especially of the desire to be ruled, the main obstacles to classlessness.[75]

In conclusion, a close look at Terayama's debut reveals a clever manipulation of the genre-based expectation for lyricism and prohibition of fiction hidden beneath the plagiarism controversy for which he is still remembered. A core element of Terayama's fiction-making method is clear here—the opportunistic use of his reader's assumptions to generate an impossibility or a truly fictional situation (e.g., the existence of Romy). What is critical here, however, is that this method is more than a simple attack on literary orthodoxy. Slipping plagiarized poems under the nose of a young editor is one thing, but transposing quotation for lyrical expression and lyrical expression for quotation in a way that exposes the rhetorical function of both is quite another. Compressing a subtle reading of the end of *Casablanca* into thirty-one syllables is a still greater feat. What seems to drive this entire process is surprisingly not a critique of the constructedness of authenticity or the limitations on our access to the real but rather a claim that a clear distinction between fiction and reality is itself a distortion of everyday lived experience. The incorporation of imaginative self-fictionalization, of popular culture, and of lies in Terayama's understanding of authenticity is, then, simply a consequence of the inclusive stance he has taken on the process of literary production itself.

· CHAPTER 2 ·

Radio Drama in the Age of Television

THE TRANSISTOR RADIO, THE STEREO phonograph, and the television were all introduced to the Japanese public at about the same
time at the end of the 1950s. Tokyo Tsūshin Kōgyō (later Sony) would
release their TR-55 pocket-sized transistor radio to the Japanese market
in 1955.[1] The first stereo records were released in 1958 and could be played
first on the new Victor STL-1S "Stereophonic Sound System."[2] Television
broadcasting, which had begun on a small scale in 1953, was popularized
by the completion of Tokyo Tower in December 1958 and the scramble
to buy sets to watch the imperial wedding in April 1959 between current
emperor Akihito and the former commoner Michiko.

Sound was suddenly on the move—down the street, back and forth
across a room, and in danger of being chased out of the marketplace and
culture itself by television's new combination of sound and moving images delivered directly to living rooms. Established radio drama scenarists
began moving from radio to television, throwing the new commercial
radio networks (legalized in June 1950) into a minor crisis and marking for
some the end of the "Golden Age of Radio Dramas."[3] Listener- and viewership numbers moved dramatically between 1959 and 1963, with television
use overtaking use of radio midway through 1961 according to surveys
done by the Cabinet Ministry (Figure 2.1). Radio stations, much like the
film studios, addressed the threat of television by recruiting young writing talent to create fresh material—programs targeted at the demographic
of the scenarists themselves. At the moment when assistant directors like
Ōshima Nagisa, Shinoda Masahiro, and Yoshida Kijū were being invited
to direct their own features to revitalize the film studios (and capture the
leading edge of the baby-boomer market), Nippon Hōsō Kyōkai (NHK)
and various regional commercial radio broadcasters also began airing
radio dramas written by young authors and poets. Abe Kōbō and Tanikawa Shuntarō wrote scripts, and Terayama began writing for radio in 1958
on Tanikawa's recommendation. Writing for radio paid well, and as such

· 35 ·

it helped this young poet (fresh out of a three-year stay in the hospital) launch a professional writing career that would have been impossible had he limited himself to publishing poetry.

If photography can be credited not only with pushing painting away from portraiture toward abstraction but also with forcing a reconceptualization of painting as something intimately tied to the brush stroke, to the canvas, to color, and to the texture of paint—that is, if the foregrounded material properties of the medium shifted, or were even discovered, as a result of an interaction with the development and popularization of another visual medium—then we should expect that something similar probably happened to radio through its relationship to television. Did this retroactive production of "essence" effectively create features experienced as core to, or at least intimately related to, broadcast radio? Does radio's "blindness" relative to the visual media (a problem we can trace back at least to Rudolph Arnheim's mid-1930s "In Praise of Blindness" in his book on radio) shift in a significant way during the transition from film to television?[4]

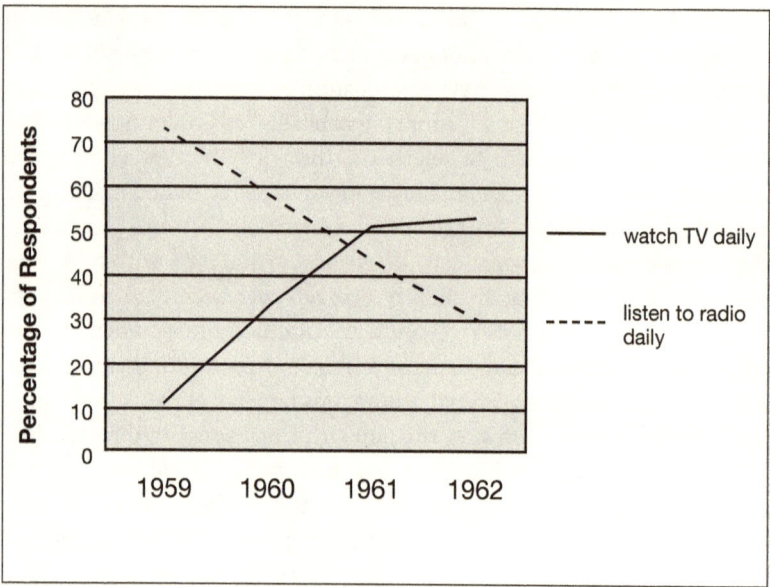

Figure 2.1. Radio listenership versus television viewership rates according to surveys done by the cabinet ministry of around three thousand citizens. Data from Hōsō ni kan suru yoron chōsa *(Tokyo: Naikaku Sōridaijin Kanbō Kōhōshitsu, 1962).*

If we look toward television as one of the forces mediating and conditioning our reception of radio, and particularly as a force that would have been in a listener's mind as television was rapidly spreading through consumer culture, an apt approach to the radio dramas of that era might parallel visual culture's emphasis on the mediation and regulation of images—an "audio culture" methodology. Following Irit Rogoff's suggestion that a critical theorization of visual culture would focus on images (and their contested histories), viewing apparatuses (and their cultural narratives and technologies), and subjectivities of identification (the positions from which and through which we view), we could then, in the case of audio culture, develop a "curious ear" as we work to theorize the contested histories of sounds, the cultural narratives and technologies of listening apparatuses, and the positions from which and through which we hear.[5] My particular interest in this case will be in historicizing these sounds, listening apparatuses, and positions of hearing to try to get a sense of what these radio dramas might have "sounded like" in the context of their historical moment. In this way, we may be able to tweak Walter Benjamin's claim that "during long historical periods the mode of sense perception of human collectivities changes with their entire mode of existence" toward recognizing that a broad shift in perception (e.g., radio as "lacking" visuality) could occur over short historical periods as well, keeping pace with the rapid dissemination of technology like television.[6]

Terayama's Debut(s) in Radio

Yamada Taichi, a scenarist for radio and television and a college friend of Terayama, goes to great lengths to point out that, despite Terayama's own claims to the contrary, the 1958 radio drama *Jiono* was in fact Terayama's debut, not *Nakamura Ichirō*, which would come out the following year in 1959.[7] *Jiono, tobanakatta otoko* (Giono, the man who didn't fly) first aired in October 1958 on Fukuoka's Radio Kyūshū Broadcasting–Mainichi channel. Radio Kyūshū Broadcasting (RKB) was the fourth national commercial radio station, established in 1951, and had just merged with Mainichi Television (connected to Mainichi Newspapers) earlier in 1958.[8] There is a good chance the Giono of the title refers to Jean Giono, the French author of the "Pan" trilogy" that had been translated into Japanese in 1941 as *Bokuyōshin* (Pan/Faunus), which was also the title Terayama and his co-editors had chosen for their national teenage haiku journal.[9]

The narrative of *Jiono, tobanakatta otoko* is fairly straightforward: Giono and his three friends (Gigalo, Ace, and Loner) break out of prison, but Giono's friends are quickly caught. Giono is less interested in the money they buried than in getting back together with his old flame, Mari. He asks about her at a bar where she used to work:

GIONO: I waited for her like a squirrel waits for dusk.

WOMAN: Well, I guess dark got here before dusk, wearing a bow-tie. He was a sailor.

GIONO: No!

WOMAN: She wasn't selling much after the guitarist died. She was like a tree without roots.

GIONO: Mari.

WOMAN: That sailor caught the tree you let fall. Mari can't get by without a man.[10]

Giono wanders off in search of Mari but stumbles into a "forest of forgetfulness" in which memories do not exist. This leads to a utopic sociality, since there is no memory of the distinction between self and other, not to mention personal names, social roles, or any kind of authority structure. Giono asks for Mari, but he is told that anyone in the forest can become Mari; all he has to do is address someone as such. In fact, he could have as many Maris as he desires.[11] This is the purely synchronic paradise Terayama will write more about later in terms of "geographical" orientation versus "historical" orientation.

Giono finally does find Mari, but she has been assimilated into this group. She cannot remember Giono but tells him that memories are filled with envy and that if she tries to remember him "the past will come back for revenge."[12] A police officer finally catches up to Giono and offers to let him escape if he is willing to lose all of his memories—this is his chance to "fly away." But Giono chooses to keep his memories of the Mari who could remember him and to go back to jail rather than to stay with Mari (and forget his years of longing for her). It is with Terayama's second aired radio drama that he shifts toward a more direct engagement with television, which may have been part of the reason *Nakamura Ichirō* would be awarded a major prize, launching Terayama's career in radio and leading him to claim it as his "debut."

Terayama's second radio drama played in February 1959, also on Fuku-oka's RKB-Mainichi, and would later win the chair's prize (Kaichōshō) at the annual commercial radio awards ceremony (Minpōsai). Terayama writes that he intended *Nakamura Ichirō* to be the story of someone who "wanted to disappear, but ended up becoming famous." This, he writes, could be seen as the inverse of an incident at the televised imperial wedding. A young man charged the procession of the royal wedding between Prince Akihito and the commoner Shōda Michiko—the young man had "wanted to become famous, but ending up disappearing," as the police quickly captured him and escorted him away. As a minor (nineteen at the time), his name was withheld from the press, but he was nicknamed the "stone-thrower boy" (*tōseki shōnen*) because he threw a baseball-sized rock at the couple before dashing out of the crowd and trying to climb onto their carriage. Guards captured him before he reached the procession, and the entire event was over in seconds.[13]

The stone-thrower boy explained his motivation for the attack on the imperial wedding: "I am against the Emperor System [*tennōsei*]. I heard that they used 230,000,000 yen [$639,000 in 1959] of tax-money on the newly constructed Crown Prince's palace and it threw me into a rage. My plan was to drag them out of the horse-carriage."[14] After the incident, he was dubiously diagnosed as a schizophrenic and institutionalized. The novelist (and later governor of Tokyo) Ishihara Shintarō interviewed him two months after the incident, sympathizing in an article in the journal *Bungei shunjū* with the stone-thrower's claim that it is the "normal" people who are crazy not to be rising up against the emperor system.[15]

Terayama's radio drama shares little else in common with the incident, however. It was written as a mock news flash (in the style of *War of the Worlds*), reporting "on the scene" about a man walking across the sky, several stories above the traffic. His name, Nakamura Ichirō, was chosen because it is the most common name in the Tokyo telephone book, and he is portrayed as almost perfectly average: a door-to-door insurance salesman in his midthirties who decided to jump off a building after being dumped by his girlfriend.[16] But gravity did not take effect: "I completely lost confidence in myself and jumped off the top of a building, but I didn't fall. All of a sudden, without really realizing it, I was staggering across the sky."[17] After his failed suicide (the pinnacle of despair Terayama's fellow Aomori-born writer Dazai Osamu and his protagonists so often experienced) and the backfiring of his effort to erase his existence, he is propelled into the news headlines, flooded with requests for product endorsements (of shoes, balloons, toys, and clothing), and becomes the subject of the hit song of the week, a new tune called "Skywalker."

What is noteworthy about the piece is its steady reference to television. The first instance comes in a list of caricatured headlines from the major newspapers:

ASAHI: A Man Strolls across the First Sky of Summer, A Land-
scape Sketch from the Nakagawa Region
MAINICHI: A Miracle in the Age of Television, What Did the
Sky-Man See? A Bird's Eye View of the Realities of Urban Life
among the Masses
AKAHATA: Bad Politics Drove Him to the Sky. There Will Be No
Arcadia for Humanity without a Revolution[18]

Standing out among the mockery of the *Asahi*'s artsy flourish, the *Mainichi*'s fetishistic populism, and *Akahata*'s spin of anything and everything into another cause for insurrection is this strange line about a "Miracle in the Age of Television." Is the implication that a new, seeing-is-believing rationality ushered in by television should have demystified the news? By pointing out what was now seemingly impossible on television (realistic reporting of false events), Terayama demonstrates how the new technology created a small window of opportunity for fiction within a medium that appeared destined for obsolescence.

Reference within this radio drama to *Gekkō kamen* (Moonbeam mask) by a group of Nakamura's youngest fans is another nod to this new "age of television." *Gekkō kamen* was Japan's first domestic television superhero, star of a series that aired on Tokyo TV between February 1958 and July 1959, so it would have been at the peak of its popularity when Terayama's radio drama was aired in February 1959. The point is likely a simple one: the reality of Nakamura (within the narrative) is processed by these children through the filter of a visual text—in parallel to the way radio, by the late 1950s, would forever be experienced through the filter of its relationship to television.

The "miracle" of Nakamura's antigravity moment comes up once more in the drama as part of a conversation between two puzzled academics:

SCHOLAR 1: Levitation? Even if we were to posit him as nearly empty, Professor, it's just not possible, is it?

SCHOLAR 2: I saw the miracle myself.

SCHOLAR 1: Scientists mustn't believe in miracles.

SCHOLAR 2: Nevertheless, Professor, I did see it. And seeing it is rational positivism, you see.

SCHOLAR 1: I hear Nakamura Ichirō refused a physical examination.

SCHOLAR 2: What? He refused to cooperate with science?

SCHOLAR 1: He must be up to something, no doubt about it.[19]

The satire here is only partially about the intellect of "intellectuals"—the rest is better read as a critique of the hype about television. Optimists may have hoped for more reliable news reporting, with visual evidence backing up the stories. But the perceptive link between vision and authenticity also sets up new opportunities for exploitation, both by the arbiters of truth (on television), and the creators of fiction (on radio). Terayama seems to be suggesting that the shift of truth value toward television at this moment may have opened up an opportunity for radio to benefit from its relative reduction in truth value in the wake of the transition—this may have been radio's opportunity to exploit its medium in that particular cultural moment as a new space for fictionality and imagination.

Adult Hunting and Emperor Tomato Ketchup

Radio's potential for fictionality, for fake truth, would be pushed further with Terayama's most notorious radio drama about a revolution against adult society by elementary school children. *Otona-gari* (Adult hunting) was broadcast in February 1960 by RKB in Fukuoka.[20] This project would develop into a scandal involving the radio station, a local school from which child actors were recruited, two teacher's unions, and prefectural government. Terayama would later rewrite this narrative a number of times in the mid-1960s for production as a television program or a film, but it was not until 1970 that the film version, *Tomato Kechappu Kōtei* (*Emperor Tomato Ketchup*), would be shot. It opened as part of a Terayama and Jean-Luc Godard series at the Sōgetsu Art Center in June of that year.[21] Tracing out some key features of both of these projects and the transition from radio to film should prove useful in making sense of the media consciousness underscoring these projects.

The frame used in *Otona-gari* is similar to *Nakamura Ichirō*: both are comical, mock news stories, but in *Otona-gari*, the live reports are of an insurrection in progress by elementary school students who have taken up arms and are rounding up all the adults. In this sense, the precedent invoked here is less the radio version of *War of the Worlds* (1938) than the earlier *Broadcasting the Barricades* by Ronald Knox, a 1926 British Broadcasting Corporation radio drama presented as breaking news from a riot in downtown London, where the unemployed marched and the "National Movement for Abolishing Theatre Queues" was leading an attack on the National Gallery, eventually toppling Big Ben with trench mortars.[22]

The revolution in Terayama's drama is sparked by a boy fed up with his father, who had locked the boy in a shed for failing to complete his science homework. This Mr. Kaneda returned to the shed to find a sign reading, "Revolution! Everyone wake up!" shortly before being assaulted by his son. The narrative proceeds with councils of the revolutionary children formulating policy for dealing with the captured adults, reconfiguring society "of, by, and for the children," and eventually creating an independent republic out of the southern Japanese island of Kyūshū, where the radio drama broadcast occurred. A segment from one of the children's council meetings should clarify the type of parody Terayama was using for this project:

CHILD 6: So, first, our next move.

CHILD 3: I think we should start by seizing all the adults' property.

CHILD 7: No, first we need to shore up our own organization.

CHILD 3: We should value most those furthest from the adults.

CHILD 6: You mean by age?

CHILD 7: But the organizational superstructure may not function due to ignorance.

CHILD 3: Adult hunting is a child's right. There's no need to value the voice of superstructure like the adults do in our organization.

CHILD 9: According to Marx's *German Ideology* . . .

CHILD 3: Marx is an adult!

CHILD 10: Yeah, we're not communists, we're child-ists.

CHILD 3: I think we should blow up some statues, incinerate some books, at least get the fairytales.

CHILD 7: Fairytales and textbooks. It's those textbooks that are the source of all our misery.

CHILD 3: But sometimes there's something interesting in the textbooks. The cooking sections at least. But those fairytales, they always treat us like idiots.

CHILD 11: Getting the adults' property is fine, but in due time. The important thing is what we're *imagining*.

CHILD 7: Like Robinson Crusoe.

CHILD 3: Robinson Crusoe is an adult![23]

Whereas Knox's drama was a fairly straightforward attack on revolutionaries as being as petty as impatient theater-goers, the mode of parody in Terayama's project is more ambiguous—it is difficult to parse whether this is a mockery of the student movement (which was in full force at the time of release in opposition to the U.S–Japan Security Treaty up for extension in June 1960 and again in 1970 at the release of *Tomato Kechappu Kōtei*) or agitation for that struggle to radicalize beyond peaceful marches through the streets.

The core flaw of *Otona-gari*, likely there by design, is that the children simply cannot muster enough menace to frighten their audience. It is this gap between the written word and the spoken performance that creates the joke, and our consideration of the potential of the young to accomplish an insurrection is where the comedy moves into critique. The disparity between the written plan and the spoken performance is doubled in the later film version, particularly when these elementary school guerillas are supposed to not only round up the adults and shoot the resisters but also rape their women. The Emperor Tomato Ketchup himself, given this task and a harem for it, clearly has no idea how to perform a sexual assault (thankfully) and quickly transforms the scene into a playful episode one might expect to see in a public bathhouse anywhere in Japan, patting his "victim's" breasts like they were drums.

There is a double alibi set up in this structure. The first is for Terayama himself, who uses this parodic form to deflect criticism of the piece as agitational. He would use this alibi in the controversy following the broadcast, which would move through local media into a flare-up in an existing Left–Right battle between two teachers' unions, and eventually into a review by committees in both the prefectural legislature and RKB.[24] Terayama was interviewed by the weekly magazine *Shūkan bunshun* in the midst of the turmoil where he claimed the project was "a satire of people who support a romantic revolution without any clear vision" and that it was "both a satire of the Zengakuren [student movement] and sympathy toward them." Letters were sent to RKB complaining that the radio drama was "*tero, ero, guro*" ("terrorism, eroticism, grotesque," a play on the ero-guro-nonsense of the 1920s and 1930s), to which Terayama responds, claiming the drama was a simple parable in which "the romantic revolutionaries are 'children,' the sympathizers who are unable to act are 'teenagers,' and those who try to preserve the status quo are 'adults.'"[25] Conservative groups wanted someone punished for allowing local elementary school students to participate in the recording, and they were successful in causing enough of a stir that a manager at the radio station was fired, but the groups seem to have been after an authority from the students' school. Judging from Terayama's remarks after things settled, he seemed regretful that *Otona-gari* had not been *more* agitational than it had been, claiming that it had ended up a "charming trifle" (*aikyō aru adabana*).[26]

The other alibi, however, is for the student movement of 1960, as well as any other insurrection by the young. Youth use this alibi as a shield under which to undermine the ageist hierarchy (which had originally created the protective umbrella of "childhood" now being turned against them). The patriarchy is forced into a corner here: it must either maintain its elevated position and protect the children from harm by not fighting back (but therefore risk losing in a violent struggle) or concede its higher position and take up arms against the young, treating them as equals (by redefining them as adults). Either way the hierarchy collapses at, importantly, the hands of the young.

The problem these young revolutionaries face in *Otona-gari* is ultimately their own inevitable aging into the adults they oppose. This develops gradually over the course of the drama—first in a reluctance to incarcerate their favorite sports heroes, then in a confrontation between a father and son (a child called Freckles tries to help his father escape by boat, but another child guerilla guns him down), and on to the final scene in which one of the boys notices that he has begun growing facial hair. The narrative needs to stop here, effectively, because the project short-circuits at precisely this moment—a critique Terayama was likely leveling at the student movement, which in both 1960 and again in 1970 risked losing ground by staking too much in toppling the security treaty and in marking the movement as one of students. What was the plan after graduation? *Tomato Kechappu Kōtei*, too, concludes with a shot of the newly bearded and mustachioed boy tyrant and his lieutenants—once they manage to adjust these props correctly, the film seizes up in a freeze frame (along with the logic of their project) until the final credits roll (Figure 2.2).

The thematic breach of trust between parent and child in the narrative of *Otona-gari* is paralleled by a breach of trust between broadcaster and listener in the medium of radio. This format of the simulated news broadcast, in fact, poses a greater threat to the public order than any agitational content within the narrative of this drama. We see hints of reaction to this threat in reports that the initial response from the public to this broadcast was concerned not with the impact on young listeners or the treatment of child voice actors but with the use of actual place names within the city of Fukuoka in the broadcast.[27] That is, the radio drama was not marked as sufficiently fictional to reassure its audience of its parodic, and therefore benign, status. As a not-quite-fictional text, *Otona-gari* picks up some

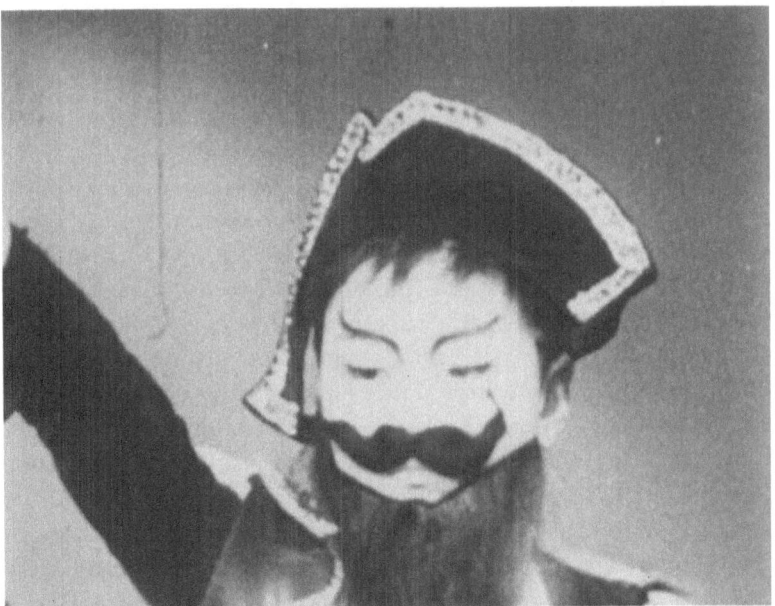

Figure 2.2. Emperor Tomato Ketchup, now bearded and mustachioed, has outgrown his children's empire in the freeze frame that ends the 1970 film.

additional truth value by appropriating rhetorical tactics from the news media, but more importantly, the fake-news style simultaneously exposes and erodes some of the truth effect of the standard news broadcast as a form. When we become conscious of the layers of rhetorical markers used to brand the news as news, those markers not only lose their impact but also begin to erode our confidence in these sources—why should they need to trump up their reports with so much flourish if not to deceive?

The opening sequence of *Otona-gari* is a veritable tour of rhetorical markings of the "news." First is the "special report" music, coded to standard news bulletins and dramatizing the breaking story. Next, a classic, interrupted broadcast line: "We had planned to broadcast 'Love Song on the Horizon' this evening, but due to breaking events, we will now turn to news and live coverage."[28] The news is the news here because it is *not* a fictional drama. Next comes a retrofitted authenticity, leveraging guilt on an audience not quite up to date on events (which they will sublimate beneath belief): "You must have already heard by now, but a group of children are rioting in the Nishijinmachi District of Fukuoka City."[29] The concrete place names enhance our trust with their scientific precision, which will continue as the announcer tracks the group's movement across major landmarks in the city in which this drama was broadcast. This trust is facilitated by radio because the geographical precision is paired with a lack of visual confirmation—our imagination of these scenes will inevitably be more potent than any broadcasted image could be.

This rhetorical play with genre markings and the signifying system that makes a set of statements "news" is peppered here with comic asides about a slogan of "hunting adults" and organizers wearing straw hats, part of a child's school uniform. After this newslike opening, the mode shifts toward a more straightforward drama, but the reflexivity regarding radio, and particularly commercial radio, continues throughout the program. The revolutionary children turn to their own radio to gauge reaction to the revolution around the country, checking a number of channels (expanded by the legalization and promotion of commercial radio after the war). We hear an ironic advertisement for baby powder followed by a news bulletin, and then a conspicuous channel change to coverage of a baseball game, then another change to more news. This is a condensed summary of the trade-offs of allowing for-profit broadcasting: plenty of channels and plenty of repetition. The advertisements are important here, too, since they function much like fictional radio dramas to provide a necessary foil for the news: the news becomes nonfictional when juxtaposed with fiction, just as it becomes noncommercial and objective (and thereby ripe for product placement) when juxtaposed with advertising.

The revelation of the need news has for advertising may get too clear in a later section—cut from the broadcast—in which "Hinomaru-ya" candies are plugged in the script immediately after a list of directives from the police:

- Do not allow children access to radios, television, or newspapers.
- Do not allow children access to sharp objects, even for craft projects.
- Increase their intake of sweets.
- Be as friendly as possible.

Tone shifts suddenly.
- Need a treat? Try Hinomaru Lackerbies, Lackerbies make kids happy!

Tone returns to normal.
- Do not allow children to assemble, even siblings.
- Do not be too strict about discipline and allow them as much freedom as you can.[30]

The problem of product tie-ins with whatever new crisis the news is announcing and the production of a listenership scared into consumption is perhaps too clumsy here, so the producers may have been trying to be helpful. But as one of only a few lines cut from the script, and certainly not in interest of time, it does seem likely that this jab at commercial radio practice was redacted in this case.

The flap over *Otona-gari* was tidied up in the end by declaring the radio drama to be a "fairytale for adults"—that it took the form of a children's story but was broadcast at a time intended for an older audience.[31] We often find claims that Terayama loved reading *Shōnen kurabu* (Boy's club) during the war years and that his style well into the 1970s was in a mode nostalgic for those adventure tales aimed at stoking bravery in young Japanese boys.[32] But if Terayama is invoking the children's fiction of wartime, those stories were anything but innocent. Take the work of Minami Yōichirō, for example, who wrote regularly for *Shōnen kurabu* during the

1930s before moving exclusively toward publishing books for young boys from 1939 until after the war. In the introduction to his early 1941 *Soromon-tō tanken* (Expedition to the Solomon Islands), he explains clearly to his young readers that

> they say "a drop of gasoline is equal to a drop of blood." That gasoline comes from oil. Airplanes, tanks, and armored vehicles all move using gasoline as fuel. Even submarines use heavy oil, which is taken from naturally occurring oil.
>
> Lots of other machines run on crude or gasoline, which is so important that it must never run out. With a shortage of oil we could never win a war.[33]

The expedition, then, is explicitly to discover oil in the Solomon Islands for the benefit of the Japanese war machine. Minami, a globetrotting boy scout, would publish a youth-targeted hagiography of Hitler with the same publisher later that year, in August 1941, under his real name, Ikeda Nobu-masa: "I tried in this book to trace the Führer's path from impoverished orphan to ruler of Germany, and further on to his spectacular victories in the war . . . You, my readers, are the second citizenry that will now deter-mine the fate of the nation. You are the adoration and the treasure of your homeland. With a taste of the attitude and spirit that saw young Hitler become Hitler the Führer, I believe you will be moved and you will learn a great deal."[34] The Hitler and Nazi references in *Otona-gari*, with its round-ing up of adults in hiding—which expand in to more direct references to incinerating humans in *Tomato Kechappu Kōtei*—may have been linked to a particular, time-bound formation of childhood, that is, the young Japanese boy fed "adventures" and biographies of "heroes" from a world that (by age ten in Terayama's case) would have become categorically evil. If Terayama's fictional world was fairytale-like, then it was this kind of tainted, saccharine, sinister sort of fairytale, and particularly the revolt against it, that interested him.

There is a brief reference to ketchup in an earlier Terayama short story from 1960 that might shed some additional light on the film version. "Ningen-jikkenshitsu" (Human laboratory) is one of Terayama's only full-fledged short stories and concerns the life of Kita Kiyoshi, a hyperrich, Wagner-obsessed son of a war criminal. He enjoys imagining himself as a young Hitler, and nicknames his Korean friend "Kubizek" after Hitler's

childhood friend and fellow fan of Wagner operas. Proclaiming the pleasure of Auschwitz to have been a matter of kind, and not of number,
Kiyoshi hatches a plan to capture and slowly starve a prisoner:

> "Hey, Kubizek!" said Kiyoshi, "I'm serious!"
> "Heil" responded Yi earnestly, drawing his hand away from his
> tomato sauce stained trousers. "Heil, Hitler!"[35]

The "tomato sauce" here is from the hot dogs these two enjoy eating,
a likely candidate for the origin of the title of *Tomato Kechappu Kōtei*
(which also includes a human "pet"). They then capture an unlucky Mr.
Nakamura, who is slowly starved and made to do useless tasks on the
Kita property. Nakamura resists at first but eventually realizes that this
situation is no more absurd than his office job, and he begins asking for
more strenuous tasks. This erodes Kiyoshi's pleasure, as his domination
is assimilated by Nakamura's emerging masochism. The story, and this
unsustainable system, ends with Kiyoshi forcing Nakamura to join a mara-
thon passing by outside the Kita home, with the implication that he will
be released into an entire group of likeminded people who are willfully
doing gratuitous labor. This study in the psychology of the domination
fetish is paired with a second narrative about a gang of delinquents who do
drugs, listen to jazz, and take road trips on a whim, living in the moment
and for serendipity, and for whom pleasure has no relationship at all with
power hierarchies—they are the bohemian, beat generation alternative to
struggles on the power ladder.

Tomato Kechappu Kōtei draws, then, both from *Otona-gari* and "Ningen-
jikkenshitsu" but refuses to allow any sort of flowing narrative to develop.
There is no dialogue, but instead intertitles and voiceover are used to list
articles from the new "Tomato Ketchup Constitution" and to read aloud
letters from children to their parents.[36] What might be most significant
about this film is not its content but rather the way it was made, that is,
the counterproposal it suggests to film's reaction to the threat of television in the 1960s. If film's reaction was first to go bigger, with widescreen
formats like Cinemascope, and later to go artsier and more contempla-
tive—in the case of Japan with the Art Theater Guild (ATG) films—then
Terayama's suggestion with *Tomato Kechappu Kōtei* seems to have been
to scale down rather than up. The ATG films were already famously low
budget at ten million yen, but *Tomato Kechappu Kōtei* was completed for

about one-tenth that figure, 1.3 million yen (or roughly US$3,500 in 1970), which made independent financing possible.[37] At around seventy-five minutes, it was essentially a feature-length film shot on 16mm, breaking away from both the experimental short-film model as well as the trappings of commercial financing and distribution. These circumstances allowed Terayama to assemble an unusual group: camerawork was done by the art photographer Sawatari Hajime and the two assistant directors (both in their midtwenties) were Kawakita Kiyomasa, a radical in the Zenkyōtō movement at Nihon University, and Matsuzawa Yao, a woman involved with avant-garde theater. As such, Terayama drew together the politically radical and artistically vanguard elements of counterculture to make a first stab at a more substantively independent cinema. The do-it-yourself aesthetic and wry sense of humor driving *Tomato Kechappu Kōtei* is slightly ambiguous in the film, where the children are almost alarmingly able to deadpan their way through a game of table tennis, for instance, in which a bound, naked adult woman is used in place of a net. It is considerably clearer in a photograph of Terayama himself on the set, posing on a mash-up of bicycle and mannequin parts they called "the pleasure machine" (*kairaku-kikai*; Figure 2.3). After *Otona-gari*, Terayama would continue to write for radio at a pace of about three new scripts per year until 1969, when *Mokush-iroku* (Apocalypse) would mark the end of his steady output. There would be one last radio drama in 1980, an adaptation of an Izumi Kyōka short story called "Tsume no namida" (Fingernail's tears). Noteworthy among Terayama's 1960s radio drama work is the March 1961 *Itsumo uraguchi de utatta* (Always sang at the backdoor), a quasi-documentary about Teraya-ma's courtship with Kujō Eiko (now Kujō Kyōko). *Mō yobu na yo, umi yo* (Stop calling to me, ocean), from August 1961, traces the development of a friendship between a Japanese boy named Shunta and a black Ameri-can soldier named Bobby. This friendship is broken up by protesters of the security treaty, and a suggestion is made in passing that it may actually be more "democratic" (on a global scale) to have the U.S. bases in Japan so that the different races have more chance to interact. Terayama also does a series of folktale style dramas during the years 1962 through 1964, including *Osorezan* (Mt. Osore, lit. "Mt. Fear"), based on the mountain in Terayama's home prefecture of Aomori associated with Buddhist hell; *Inugami aruki* (Dog spirit walking), about the belief of a dog curse on par-ticular families that ostracizes them; and *Yamanba* (Mountain witch), long a figure of the noh and kabuki stages, this first commission from NHK would win Terayama a grand prize in the radio division of the Prix Italia contest for broadcasting.

Positioning the Narrator in Stereophonic Space

Radio surpassed television in the material progress of its sound technology with the advent of stereo radio broadcasting in Japan, the most primitive form of which occurred in 1952, the year *before* NHK began its first television broadcasts.[38] It may have been in this early era of the technology that scenarists were most conscious of radio's material properties. Terayama's first experiment with stereo was a collaboration in 1966 with NHK radio producer Sasaki Shōichirō on an hour-long radio drama called *Kometto Ikeya* (*Comet Ikeya*).[39] Building off of a set of Sasaki's interviews with a young stargazer named Ikeya Kaoru, who had just discovered a new comet in 1963, Terayama added a fictional narrative to complement the documentary elements.[40] In his notes to the script, he describes the project in the following way: "When creating this piece I thought up a method in which one would feel their way through a mental labyrinth as reality and non-reality (fiction and documentary in content; monaural and stereo in technological form) criss-crossed through layers of the three-dimensional

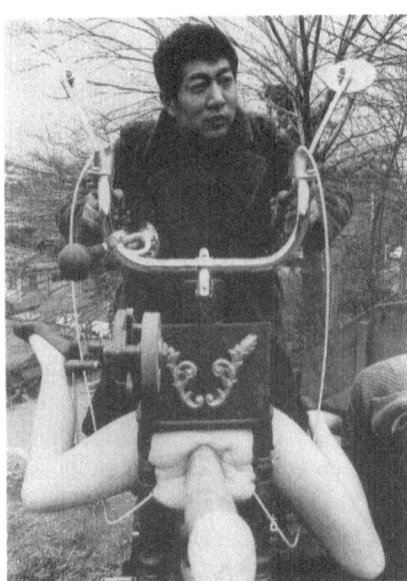

Figure 2.3. Terayama blithely mounts a "pleasure machine" on the first day of shooting for the 1970 film Tomato kechappu kōtei (Emperor Tomato Ketchup). *Courtesy of Kujō Kyōko and Terayama World. Photograph by Sawatari Hajime.*

stereo space."[41] In preparing this nonvisual radio drama, then, Terayama visualized a sound space in which document and fiction are mapped onto multidimensional sound fields and unidimensional sound layers within three-dimensional space.

The decision to use both stereophonic and monaural sound in one composition sets up several interesting, and difficult, analytical puzzles. First, once a sound field is established as stereophonic (which happens from the start in this case), can listeners distinguish between monaural sound and stereo sound centered between the left and right channels? Imagine a conversation between A, B, and C, for example. If A is placed to the left, B in the center, and C to the right, is there any material difference between a conversation recorded in stereo and one in which only B's lines have been replaced by a mono recording? In both cases, the amplitude of B's voice would be evenly balanced between the two speakers, creating the effect of centering within a space conceived of as multidimensional but that could easily slip into sounding like an unpositioned, monaural voice if the space were reconceived of as nonstereo. The next question that arises, then, is whether mono can be established in contradistinction to stereo, or whether the establishment of stereo space conditions the reception of mono voices, bending them into centered voices between the speakers.

Before stereo broadcasting was possible over a single FM channel, the creation of a stereophonic sound field with broadcast radio required two receivers (very rare for families at the time, so the second set was typically borrowed from a neighbor). One was tuned to NHK 1 (594 kHz) and the other to NHK 2 (693 kHz)—the method itself was called *rittai hōsō* (lit., "three-dimensional broadcasting"). The announcer would ask listeners to adjust the volume on both sets until his voice became centered between the two radios. What is critical here is that the announcer's voice started as an unpositioned, ethereal, narrational, ubiquitous, monaural, universal sound emanating from two speakers at the same time. It was then conceptually shifted into a positioned, concrete (but absent), and particularized presence centered within the stereophonic space *before the stereophonic broadcast even began*. This shift was importantly discursive, enabled by the slippage structure inherent in centered particularities—the centered particularity can slip into a universal, but a universal can also be slipped into a centered and particular position. The nature of the sonic space went through three stages of mental preparation: deliberately setting up the stereo apparatus, listening to the announcer "announce" the establishment of the stereo space, and then finally the modulated broadcast producing the effect of a spatialized sound field—but the transition had to be coached. Language here is performing the action of creating stereo from monaural space.[42] Having calibrated the apparatus, NHK would then broadcast a series of stereo sounds such as a train passing from left to right, which must have been an extraordinary experience at the time—particularly for the living room.[43] The earliest of these broadcasts was done on December 20, 1952, when NHK broadcast a stereo version of Wagner's *Tannhäuser* as part of their Saturday concert series.[44] During 1953 and 1954, NHK would use the technology for nine programs, the third of which was Japan's first stereo radio drama—a recording of a *shinpa* performance called *Musuko no seishun* (My son's adolescence) by the Meijiza troupe. It was broadcast on March 22, 1953, just one and a half months after television broadcasting began on February 1.[45]

Considered broadly, then, the two new additions to the simple, monaural radio broadcasting of the past were split between the media of television and radio in 1953—television added moving visual images, and radio added stereo. Starting in November 1954, stereo broadcasting through the *rittai hōsō* system was fully integrated into NHK's weekly radio programming with a show called *Rittai ongakudō* (Stereo music hall), which aired for thirty minutes each Saturday afternoon.[46] These broadcasts became such a regular feature that by 1958 Columbia released a single "stereo set" system, Model 31, with both a turntable and two receivers (one for each speaker) to better facilitate NHK's three-dimensional programming.[47] The artistic potential surrounding slippage between mono and stereo space at this hinge of centered voices is a material property of the medium that Terayama would playfully exploit in *Kometto Ikeya*, adding a degree of reflexivity that likely contributed to it winning the Prix Italia for radio drama in the second year that the contest included a category specifically for stereo dramas.[48] *Kometto Ikeya* became a poster child project for early FM stereo broadcasting. Those who had upgraded their stereo equipment were privy to a sneak preview of the drama via NHK-FM on August 31, 1966 (when it had been nominated for a Prix Italia award).[49] After receiving the award on September 26, encore broadcasts were done via the *rittai hōsō* system of NHK-1 and NHK-2 on October 2.[50]

These problems of distinguishing between stereo and monaural sound are particularly fascinating when they are considered as metaphors for the relationship between the particular and the universal. As such, this experimentation with stereo may help us think through issues of the slippage of power from a centered particularity to a universal or from a universal to a centered particularity. Can we hear any difference between a centered voice of power and a "universal truth," a "universal human right," or an "international standard"? Is the struggle to maintain the concept of universality waged, then, primarily by attempting to center the ideas that compete for universality and allowing the automatic mechanism of slippage between centered particularities and universals to do the rest of the work? If a universality is then positioned within a three-dimensional space (e.g., by the presence of another voice to the side), then does that centered voice lose its authoritative aura?

Slippage between a positioned stereo voice and an ethereal monaural voice is one of several types of slippage in the drama—the main type being quick shifts between initially unrelated narratives. Clips from the documentary-style interview with Ikeya Kaoru about his discovery of the comet are intercut with a fictional drama about a runaway businessman, Hasegawa Tadashi, in such a way as to willfully confuse the audience. For example, both events were reported in the newspaper on the same day, and the naïve narrator of the drama insists on a causal relationship between them. Later, a man visits Mrs. Hasegawa to ask about her missing husband. Just after he knocks on the door and asks, "Is this the Hasegawa residence?" the drama cuts to the recording of the Ikeya interview, where Ikeya is being asked about the moment he found the comet as well as metaphysical questions about what he thinks it all might mean. At the end of the Ikeya interview, the man asks, "Where do you think it's going?" (*Doko e iku to omoimasu ka?*). The question is left unanswered, and then repeated, but it is Hasegawa's wife who answers it. She would have heard the same line as "Where do you think *he's* going?" effectively setting up an extended pivot word (*kakekotoba*), a standard technique of the tanka genre in which Terayama started his literary career. There is a note in the script at this point that reads, "This question will act as a bridge crossing. Ikeya's response and Mrs. Hasegawa's response must transition smoothly and within the same space."[51] That transition is paralleled by a shift in action from the left channel to the right speaker. Ikeya's interview took place only on the left speaker (technically mono, but positioned as "left" within the stereo space), but the dialogue with Mrs. Hasagawa occurs on the right. The audio jump cut from the left to the right channel that links these narratives parallels the earlier conceptual leap that the narrator underwent to link the two newspaper articles (one about Ikeya's discovery and another about Hasegawa's disappearance).

What Terayama is toying with here is an exaggerated version of the implied connection between conspicuously disparate items in newspapers, which Benedict Anderson famously described as one way that disparate groups of people under the umbrella of a nation are unified through the construction of "imagined communities":

> What is the essential literary convention of the newspaper? If we were to look at a sample front page of, say, *The New York Times*, we might find there stories about Soviet dissidents, famine in Mali, a gruesome murder, a coup in Iraq, the discovery of a rare fossil in Zimbabwe, and a speech by Mitterrand. Why are these events so juxtaposed? What connects them to each other? Not sheer caprice. Yet obviously most of them happen independently, without the actors being aware of each other or of what the others are up to. The arbitrariness of their inclusion and juxtaposition (a later edition will substitute a baseball triumph for Mitterrand) shows that the linkage between them is imagined.[52]

The newspaper, by Anderson's explanation, operates like a classic novel plot to imply (and often fulfill an expectation for) an interconnectivity between otherwise independent lives—the novel is "a device for the presentation of simultaneity in 'homogeneous, empty time'" and, as such, is "a precise analogue of the idea of the nation, which also is conceived as a solid community moving steadily down (or up) history."[53]

In *Kometto Ikeya*, Terayama exaggerates the community-generating function of the newspaper format—extended to the extreme of direct and monolinear causality. The drama opens with its narrator (a naïve, blind, adolescent girl) reading separate articles about Ikeya's comet and Hasegawa's disappearance in her Braille newspaper. She then becomes convinced that some form of the law of conservation of matter (or maybe reincarnation) was operating on a cosmic scale, such that the runaway salaryman, Mr. Hasegawa, would transform into the comet that Ikeya discovered: "Why would a new star appear? Maybe something old disappeared from this world in exchange."[54] This mockery of overapplication of the conservation principle shows up often in Terayama's work and might best be understood as a critique of zero-sum logic. In his 1964 radio drama

Yamanba, the protagonist is faced with his limited food supply and is told that in order to marry a wife, he must first kill his mother.[55] Later, in a 1973 play called *Mōjin shokan* (Letter on the blind), a group of magicians have the following conversation:

> MAGICIAN 2: Hey, keep your eyes shut!
> MAGICIAN 1: Me?
> MAGICIAN 2: I told you to keep them shut!
> MAGICIAN 1: What for?
> MAGICIAN 2: I can't see when you open your eyes.
> MAGICIAN 1: You can't be serious.
> MAGICIAN 2: The number of eyes in the world is a set quantity,
>   you know. So if one person opens their eyes, someone else has
>   to close theirs.
> MAGICIAN 1: But there are lots more people who can see than who
>   are blind, your calculation must be off.
> MAGICIAN 2: Idiot! That's why you'll never land a leading role.
>   The balance of open eyes and closed eyes is all well regulated by
>   night and day. When it's day in Shanghai, it's night in England.
>   When we've got our eyes open the people on the other side of
>   the ocean have theirs closed.[56]

In the case of the blind narrator of *Kometto Ikeya,* there is more driving her to conclude that these events are linked than simply their rough simultaneity or an exaggerated faith in karmic balance. After learning of both stories and knowing that both occurred on the same day, she says in a loose and speculative tone, "There's a connection, there must be a connection. Even the smallest events in back alleys could all be connected to me. The song I sang today might have cheered someone up on the street, and the delayed train I rode today may have reminded someone else of a suicide on the tracks and made them sad. But, [*suddenly lucid*] the day will surely come when I meet those strangers."[57] It seems to be the desire for community, in this case, that drives her overreading of the possible connections between stories in the newspaper—that is, the potential for expanding her community underwrites this bridging of disparate events. Terayama's contribution to Anderson's analysis, then, might be to look at the micromechanics driving the maintenance of an individual's desire for social connectivity. What is critical here is the timing: the blind narrator's expectation of balance and her desire to find some kind of absence to match the appearance of the comet comes *before* she learns of Hasegawa's disappearance—she learns of the new existence and then searches for what may have been lost in order to even the scales.

Terayama is also invoking a line of mythology in this narrative found at least as far back as Cicero—one that explains that the spirits of the dead become stars in the night sky. Cicero's comments on the topic in his *Tusculan Disputations* draw on the Pythagorean notion of the permanence of souls, adding,

> If the soul, as we regard it, belongs to the four classes of elements of which all things are said to consist, it consists of kindled air . . . and such a soul necessarily strives to reach higher regions . . . If it survives unadulterated and unchanged in substance, it is of necessity carried away so rapidly as to pierce and part asunder all this atmosphere of ours . . . When the soul has passed this tract and reaches to and recognizes a substance resembling its own, it stops amongst the fires which are formed of rarefied air and the modified glow of the sun and ceases to make higher ascent. For when it has reached conditions of lightness and heat resembling its own, it becomes quite motionless, as though in a state of equilibrium with its surroundings, and then, and not before, finds its natural home, when it has pierced to conditions resembling its own, and there, with all its needs satisfied, it will be nourished and maintained on the same food which maintains and nourishes the stars.[58]

Tracing the lineage of these ideas helps make sense of why the interview of Mrs. Hasegawa might focus not only on her husband's disappearance but also on the possibility of his death, as well as why the interview of Ikeya challenges him on metaphysical questions regarding the ultimate origin of the comet he discovers. Here, we are being asked to consider the possibility of a human soul transforming itself into a star—that Mr. Hasegawa has literally become Comet Ikeya.

Stranger than the slippage between two narratives in the drama is another slippage between the narrator and other characters. Their relationship—specifically, their awareness of each other—is never made fully clear, or perhaps more accurately, it is put into an ambiguous, perplexing state from the start and then consciously and cleverly maintained in that state of indeterminacy until the end. All of this is complicated by the narrator's blindness and the additional possibilities that generates—others could be in the same room, but she might not know it. The drama begins with the narrator reading aloud from a Braille newspaper about Ikeya's discovery of this new comet. She then speculates that something else must have disappeared to balance out its appearance and concludes her monologue by asking if anything has in fact disappeared. Then, the man who will later interview Ikeya and Mrs. Hasegawa asks a question that at first seems to be directed at her. Next, we jump to small talk among "voices" in a café, which seems to respond to this man's question. Although it initially seems as though all four of these characters are in a single space and speaking to each other, it turns out that this is logically impossible and that there must in fact be three layers of independent dialogue intercut in a deliberately confusing arrangement:

> BLIND GIRL: Somebody . . . somebody tell me. What was it that
>   disappeared?
> MAN: Wha? Did you just say something?
> VOICE 1: I didn't say a thing.
> VOICE 2: You must be hearing things.[59]

This conversation in the café moves to headlines from the newspaper and eventually remarks on the oddness of a comet's discovery and the disappearance of a businessman occurring on the same day, apparently answering the girl's original question. Where at first it seemed that the man and the girl are in conversation, we quickly correct that to assume that the man is speaking with the "voices" in the café. In other words, we assume for a moment that the girl has become a participating character within the story, but then she is just as quickly withdrawn back to her position as the disconnected narrator.[60] Yet, following the dialogue carefully, we notice that the man never speaks again in the café scene among these "voices," and even after the voices in the café have discovered and read aloud the two headlines (which the man must have heard if he had been there with them), the man credits not the voices from the café but the blind girl with conveying the news to him: "The words of that blind girl from this morning are still in my ears: Is there a connection between the new comet Ikeya Kaoru discovered and the businessman who disappeared?"[61] So the man seems not to have been in the café at all. And yet now he credits the girl, meaning that information is flowing from her to him, but earlier lines had demonstrated that the girl learned of the missing businessman from the voices in the café. There is a time-violating flow of information here from the voices to the girl to the man, then, that never seems to develop into actual dialogue (despite our instinct to hear it as such). While the girl is the blind one, no one else seems to notice her in the café (if she was actually there), and the audience of the drama struggles to visualize her position among the other characters—she is both present and absent simultaneously, much the same way as her voice (centered between the speakers, or in mono, we cannot know) is both there and not there.

At this point, the girl delivers the lines "There's a connection, there must be a connection," mentioned previously, as though she has just found the disappearance she was searching for at the moment the men in the café read the headlines. Of course, this could be another trick—the note preceding her line says that it is to sound "like a voice from a different dimension"[62]—she could just as easily have read the same story in her own Braille newspaper, with the two independent discoveries juxtaposed for effect. Or Terayama could be playing a bit more here with the creation of an imaginary community of fellow newspaper readers. The point is that we, as the audience, are led to create the causality between characters and events first (and search for proof of that link later) within the radio drama in exactly the same way that the blind narrator links disparate events in the course of the drama itself.

Notes in the script regarding the use of monaural voices within this otherwise stereo production begin in the second of four segments. The interviewer from the first scene has two monaural monologues overlaid onto a conversation among Hasegawa's friends, who are playing a game of go. The narrative returns to the go players and then shifts to a representation of the merging of stars and humans that forms the central theme. Terayama's note reads, "From another dimension, a child's voice reading out the names of the constellations draws gradually nearer, starting with Andromeda and continuing in alphabetical order. This should express the Milky Way galaxy. Then, using a piano, another celestial body expands in the form of a celesta. A man begins apathetically reading names from the telephone book in alphabetical order. It should feel forlorn like counting stars in the vast night sky. The two voices move toward the center, merge together, then are blown away by the wind and disappear."[63] This is the confluence of two voices: one associated with Ikeya's comet, as a celestial body among the constellations, and the other associated with Hasegawa, as one of many anonymous names from the telephone book (Hasegawa Tadashi was selected as one of the most common names after Nakamura Ichirō).[64] They have moved from their discrete positions within the stereo field (i.e., one left, one right) and merged at the critical point at the center where sound can slip from a centered presence into being an ethereal, monaural, universalized narrational voice. Most critically, it is at this center point where the voices risk losing their position-based presence and disappear. The false universals, once exposed, can no longer exist within this stereoized, particularized space.

Ikeya Kaoru was not the only one gazing at the night sky to look for new stars in January 1963; his discovery came at a time of broad popular interest in outer space. The combination of *Sputnik* (1957), the U.S. response with *Explorer I* (1958), and Kennedy's May 1961 announcement that a man would walk on the moon by the end of the decade laid the foundation for a new fascination with outer space. The landscape of the heavens was suddenly transformed into a potential destination. But it may have been the launch of the *Telstar* communications satellite, and the first successful transatlantic transmissions of television using the new transceiver in June 1962, which fully activated public interest. Catching a glimpse of *Telstar* in the night sky must have seemed a rite of passage at the time. *Telstar* was one of the first artificial "stars" in the heavens—one could no longer even look straight up at night without the risk of seeing traces of human intervention. Anticipation was particularly high in Japan because the promise of live satellite broadcasts of the 1964 Tokyo Olympics was well positioned to be the space age's first global television event and would have been so had Kennedy not been assassinated. The first experiment to test the satellite relay system between Japan and the United States was scheduled well in advance for November 23, 1963, and a recorded address from Kennedy to the Japanese public was planned using the new technology.[65] The *Asahi*'s front-page headlines on the morning of November 20 included an announcement of the upcoming historical broadcast, "First TV Broadcasts over the Pacific, Ten Experiments Starting the 23rd": "The first experiment is planned to run from 5:26 to 5:46 A.M. on the 23rd, and the second from 8:58 to 9:15 A.M. the same day. If reception is good, plans include the broadcast of a taped message from President Kennedy. A live broadcast would be impossible because the transmitter, which is in the Mojave desert south of Los Angeles, is not linked to Washington."[66] The Japanese public awoke on November 23 and turned on their sets hoping to see Kennedy's greeting but instead learned of his assassination, which had happened just a few hours earlier (Kennedy was shot at 3:30 A.M. Japan time on November 23).[67] The satellite broadcast of the Olympics was accomplished, although only to the United States (with a special announcement by President Johnson in 1964), and only in short bursts. Since the satellites were not yet positioned in higher, stationary orbits, they only provided about a twenty-minute window for linking the continents.

Ikeya Kaoru's comet discovery on January 3, 1963, occurred during the hopeful expectation following *Sputnik* and *Telstar* and was not yet marred by Kennedy's death announced by early satellite television. The space theme was in the midst of an optimistic peak in January 1963. Most of the major papers ran a small piece announcing Ikeya's discovery by January 8 or 9, often embedded in a cluster of outer-space articles. The *Asahi*, for example, writes of his discovery on a page facing installment number seven of a fifteen-part series called *Chikyū no nakama-tachi* (Friends of Earth), which had been running since the first of the month with boxed pieces on topics like Mars and the *Mariner 2* satellite. The *Mainichi* essentially announces 1963 to be the year of the *Telstar* with a half-page photo of its transceiver radar dome on January 1's front page: "The *Telstar* Base—A huge white dome sits in a clearing of pines in the city of Andover, Maine in the northeastern United States. Since the launch of the *Telstar* satellite on July 10, 1962, which announced the dawn of a communications revolution, this transceiver of continent-linking outer space television has been letting out its high pitched hum. We are not far from the day when the entire world can enjoy the same TV programs."[68] Under the photo is a poem by Japan's postwar bard, Tanikawa Shuntarō, comparing the new radar domes to Mongolian yurts and Eskimo igloos and diffusing anxiety about a potential intercontinental ballistic missile function in the cold war by noting that humans make yurts, igloos, and radar domes, and that our human curiosity about outer space will never cease.[69] On the same day, in the *Asahi*, the Nippon Electric Company (NEC) ran a full page advertisement dominated by an image of the *Telstar* circling the Earth that announced their production of a thirty-meter-wide parabolic antenna that was capable of receiving signals as weak as one ten-quadrillionth of a watt, that the majority of the microwave transceivers for television around the country were NEC products, and that their "television and radio broadcasting equipment is used not just domestically but has been exported abroad, and has come to play a leading role in the acquisition of foreign capital."[70] On January 6, the *Asahi* ran a short article on that same NEC antenna titled "Rushing Construction for the Olympics: The Outer Space Transmission Center—First, the Completion of the Parabolic Antenna," which detailed some of the struggle between the Ministry of Posts and Telecommunications and the Finance Ministry to approve accelerated funding for the remaining equipment needed to have the transmission center in Kagoshima up and running by the Olympics in 1964.[71]

If *Nakamura Ichirō*, the 1959 radio drama, operated in a relationship with the first wave of television to hit Japan in time for the imperial wedding, then *Kometto Ikeya* was set against the second wave, often characterized as the color-television boom immediately preceding the Tokyo Olympics (which was much more significantly the advent of global television through the use of satellite transmission). Rather than sitting at the breakfast table reading the *Asahi* and (perhaps subconsciously) imagining a nation of other Japanese reading the same newspaper, television audiences could watch the Olympics in 1964 and imagine the growing community of television-owning global citizens who were watching exactly the same images at essentially the same moment—satellite television stood to synchronize a global collectivity through simultaneous and instantaneous access to the news.

There are two moments in *Kometto Ikeya* that suggest Terayama may have been considering the clustering of the Olympics, new celestial bodies (a conflation of comet discovery and artificial satellites), and an emergent form of globalism. The first is a direct reference to the 1964 Tokyo Olympics. The Olympic theme song is played to introduce a scene in which the man who interviewed Mrs. Hasegawa searches in vain for her missing husband among the massive crowds after hearing from an acquaintance that Hasegawa had been spotted at the games. His wife finally gives up waiting for him after a year and a half has passed, and the narrative follows her throwing away his things that had remained in their home in the interim. The final scene includes a brief, but important, reference to another comet discovered by a Japanese astronomer: "'Even if you can't see it, if you think you can see it . . . then you become able to see it.' What sad words those are. And yet they seem to me to be like an astrological puzzle. Just as I calculated from the mystery of the Crommelin Comet that disappeared the moment it was discovered, searching for it, tracking it down, the way this single businessman's route got pinched between Leo and Corvus, it just couldn't be true. You can't retract a human heart that's grown distant with only the strength of Newton's universal gravitation."[72] This short statement is extremely dense. The creation of existence through belief in existence can be read as a broad comment on the nature of knowledge or as a more specific reference to the creation of stereo space by the radio announcer's speech act claiming himself to be a centered presence between the speakers. The Crommelin Comet is also of particular interest because it was discovered several times throughout the nineteenth century, never by Crommelin himself, and was first photographed by Yamazaki Masamitsu on October 26, 1928. Yamazaki was not credited for the discovery, however, because poor weather conditions prevented confirmation until after the comet moved out of visible range—it had literally "disappeared the moment it was discovered."[73] Had Yamazaki been able to communicate with Tokyo (and Tokyo with Copenhagen) as quickly as Ikeya could in 1963, there would have been a better chance of him being recognized for the discovery. Advances in the speed and range of international communication by the 1960s set up a structure in which this nineteen-year-old could be fully credited and his comet known to astronomers around the entire world as Comet Ikeya. The global recognition is marked in the domestic name for the comet (Ikeya Suisei, with Ikeya's name in the phonetic katakana), and further extended in the radio drama to its international name: Kometto Ikeya, or Comet Ikeya.

The blind narrator, a fairly obvious self-reflexive comment on the relationship between listeners and the medium of radio, is not the only case of a blind character showing up in Terayama's radio dramas. They are so common, in fact, that the Terayama scholar Moriyasu Toshihisa concludes, "The use of blind protagonists in this aural medium of the radio drama, where listeners are forced to experience the aural experiment together with the characters, might rightly be seen as no more than an orthodox device based on the particularities of the medium."[74] It is doubtful, however, that radio audiences ever felt "blind" before the popularization of television, so if this is a comment on the properties of radio, then it might be better understood as a statement about the way particular aspects of a medium do not reveal themselves until a new technology threatens to replace it. Because Terayama's radio dramas were all written during the period when television was first threatening, and then truly overtaking radio as the normative medium for broadcast news and entertainment, any reflexivity would naturally engage the historical nature of this situation—Terayama was writing blind protagonists into his radio dramas at the very moment radio was *becoming* a blind medium in the face of television's vision. Ikeya's discovery of the comet correlates, then, with the moment the transition from radio to television was effectively complete.

Looking carefully at the meaning of blindness in the text of *Kometto Ikeya*, it quickly becomes clear that sensory perception is closely linked to the production of truth value. Unlike the sighted characters, the blind narrator refuses to believe in the existence of things until she can physically touch an object. It may seem a pedantic point to make, but Terayama is suggesting some fairly sophisticated ideas. One is the rhetorical power of visual media, with this visual addition to broadcasting serving as a force against the perhaps natural tendency for the truth value of any particular medium of communication to fall (i.e., are new media ever less persuasive than the old?). NHK was particularly attuned to the truth value of this new "seeing-is-believing" medium. The opening question the section of their 1993 survey on television, which compared television to newspapers, was "Which one do you think conveys the truth?" Respondents favored television to newspapers 39 percent to 28 percent (but clearly distrusted both).[75]

The narrator's insistence that she would not believe in anything she could not touch invokes Diderot's *Letter on the Blind for the Use of Those Who See*. Diderot's piece is concerned with insights made possible by the restriction of perception in much the same way Terayama seems to have been interested in the possibility of radio in the age of television. Much of Diderot's text focuses on the blind Cambridge mathematician Nicolas Saunderson, including the following striking refusal delivered on his deathbed to a clergyman offering his last rites: "'Ah, sir,' replied the blind philosopher, 'don't talk to me of this magnificent spectacle, which it has never been my lot to enjoy. I have been condemned to spend my life in darkness, and you cite wonders quite out of my understanding, and which are only evidence for you and those who see as you do. If you want to make me believe in God you must make me touch Him.'"[76] The narrator of *Kometto Ikeya* has a similar exchange with Ikeya Kaoru:

GIRL: Mr. Ikeya! What's a star?
IKEYA: Stars are visible all the time, but only the people who realize that stars are shining up there can see them. Even if you're blind, as long as you realize that it's there you can see it.
GIRL: Have you ever touched one?

IKEYA: No, I've never touched one. Meteorites are a kind of star,
and I've touched one of those. Your hand can't reach them, not
even if you stand on tiptoe. They're really, really far away.
GIRL: Then no one really knows the nature of the stars![77]

Terayama would return to Diderot's text again in his play, which borrows its title (*Mōjin shokan*, quoted earlier), further exploring the problem of knowledge's relationship to perception, the production of truth value in that process, and the paradoxical advantages to perceptual restraint.

There is one final feature of *Kometto Ikeya* that is less apparent in the script than in the sound recording but that recurs enough to become conspicuous and provides further evidence that the interaction between audio and visual representation forms the core of this experiment with stereo. While stereo technology allows voices to be placed left or right along a line between the two speakers, the project seems far more interested in creating illusion of depth and verticality: layers of sound moving forward and back from the listener or up and down. Such a sound field is technically impossible without additional speakers and so must be approximated using distance from the recording microphone, muffling, amplification, and other techniques. These methods manipulate tone color and trigger our perception to categorize the sounds as nearer or farther away based on memory of similar sounds and their qualities relative to other sounds within the drama. (It is useful to remember that the daily experience of three-dimensional sound fields is always mediated by our two ears, meaning that sound recorded with two microphones and replayed through two speakers or headphones can accurately reproduce the biological apparatus.)

But why would Terayama focus energy on developing depth in a radio drama specifically designed to exploit the new possibilities of stereo? There are a few interesting possibilities. The first is that this parallels the longer history of stereo technologies, which were first (and for a much longer time) a visual, rather than audio, means to fool human perception. Using two slightly different photographs, one viewed with the left eye and the other with the right, stereoscopic images with the illusion of depth entered world culture in the mid-nineteenth century. Charles Wheatstone's reflecting stereoscope (1838) was popularized by its exhibition at the first World's Fair, the "Great Exhibition of All Nations," in London's Hyde Park in 1851. In 1862, the Holmes stereopticon was released and quickly became the world standard, again popularized through the World's Fairs. The mass-market View-Master, which has almost managed to keep stereo photography alive to the present day, was introduced in 1939 and sold well at the New York World's Fair that year.[78] Stereoscopic images add positionality forward and back from the viewer, and the *Kometto Ikeya* production crew may have been attempting to create a similar kind of sonic depth of field.

Another compelling possibility is that the *Kometto Ikeya* production staff wanted to emphasize the stimulation of imagination that occurs when expression is pushed beyond a medium's ability to faithfully represent it. If the medium itself offers the placement of sound on only one dimension (the line between the speakers), Terayama wants to push it to two dimensions (a plane stretching from the speakers to the listener) to demonstrate the presence of human imagination in the creation of the sensation of presence—a presence both artificial and under the subject's control. Sasaki Shōichiro, the production director for *Kometto Ikeya* and interviewer of Ikeya Kaoru, worked with the sound technicians at NHK to attempt to make an approximation of sound so that it sounded as though it was moving vertically upward toward the heavens, which would extend the flat, two-dimensional sound plane formed between the speakers and listener into a fully three-dimensional (*rittai*) space.[79] The constant tension between people on Earth and stars in the sky throughout the piece reflects this fundamental problem facing stereo sound—that is, the material difficulty in creating the illusion of vertical movement with right and left channels. The NHK radio director Okino Ryō, who worked with Terayama on the 1967 radio drama *Mandara* and the 1969 *Mokushiroku*, addresses the problem of hearing vertical motion through stationary speakers in a 1970 round table:

> Speaking of waterfalls, when I dove into stereo in probably 1961 or '62 an overwhelming majority of people thought the downward motion of a waterfall would come through in stereo. But stereo is just right and left, so that was absolutely impossible. And even today, a lot of people believe that with a flowing river the sound itself moves. But when a river is flowing, the sounds don't move at all. What's making the noise is water hitting rocks or pilings, so the noise itself doesn't ever move side to side. But if we visualize it we

see a moving river. We think the sound must be moving, too, but we're being fooled. Stereo seems to cause these sorts of illusions.[80]

Here we can return to the taped quotation from Ikeya that is repeated like a mantra throughout the piece: "You see it because you believe you can see it. Even if you can't see a comet, once you believe you can see it, then it becomes visible."[81] This line was not scripted by Terayama but came directly from Ikeya in interviews with Sasaki and thereby forms the most important part of the documentary side of this project. Had Ikeya said the same thing about sound, he would have been nicely in line with Okino's point, making a perfect summary of the technology of stereophonic radio and the conceptual prerequisite to "hearing" a voice as centered between two speakers. His comment is even more extraordinary, however, since it implies that vision, too, is not a pure sensation but one inflected, and possibly enhanced, in its interaction with imagination.

CHAPTER 3

Boxing—Stuttering—Graffiti

WHAT GENERATES THE SENSATION OF presence and immediacy in the sport of boxing? Is it the flirtation with death (and murder) that excites both boxer and boxing fan? If so, is the possibility of death in the ring required for that excitement? Does boxing need an occasional sacrifice to maintain its truth value? Joyce Carol Oates confesses (as do many others) that she is drawn to this descendent of gladiatorial battles with deep, conflicting emotions about her complicity in the injuries that result.[1] The allure of the sport may be as simple as a desire to see a human life end in spectacle—which may not be as ugly an impulse as it seems if it is ultimately a drive to rewrite knowledge of the more typical banality of death and the way it dovetails so seamlessly into the flow of everyday life.

Is this sport a sample of pure violence, held just within the limits of legality? It can look like sanctioned assault, brought to the edge of murder—or at least a simulation of murder in cases of a clean knockout, the unconscious boxer felled like a tree in the ring, rendering the score and all the judges irrelevant with the winner upright and the loser prone on the mat. Boxers may seem more alive because of this tangible risk of death, and the sport may be appealing because the audience can participate vicariously in that affirmation of life and will of the winner exchanged for the denial of life and will of the opponent. This may be a structure at work in generating the sport's appeal, and if so, it creates a zero-sum system that requires not only death but also occasional homicide in order to generate the perception of human life.

Boxing, however, may appeal less for its reality effect than for its fictionality. The sport is filled with simulation: shadowboxing against imaginary opponents, knockouts that in another context would be murders, punches driven by fear of failure rather than anger. It fascinates because it stands in the liminal space between the upper limit of civil society and the bottom limit of war culture. It may be this insight into human nature—the ability to will transitions between brute and compassionate behavior—that creates the fascination with the sport. The "reality" of boxing, then, may have something to do with this mixture of real and fictional elements, and it may appeal to fans and others because it parallels the mixture of direct and imagined events within our everyday experience.

Terayama spent much of the 1960s fascinated, along with much of the world, with boxing and the problems it forced viewers to face. The sport encapsulated a debate between self-determination (let 'em fight) and interventionism (call off the fight) that would resonate with Third World independence movements, civil rights, and the students behind the barricades. Terayama's spin on this discourse, however, would be to position boxing in a cluster of formations, including stuttering, graffiti, jazz, and gambling, which, in their ad-libbed style, enhance a sensation of presence and a feeling of being in the now.

Death in the Ring

The ethical dilemma of death in the ring—letting the boxers fight with the goal of a knockout versus the obligation of intervention by authorities (doctors or referees) to protect the prizefighters from themselves—would become the dominant boxing narrative of the 1960s. But Terayama's first boxing piece, a screenplay called *Jūkyūsai no burūsu* (The nineteen-year-old blues, 1959) also opens with this very problem:

> SCENE 1: In a boxing ring. A middle-aged boxer is continuously punched by a younger boxer, Shōji. Pushed against the ropes, he can no longer put up a fight. Next, faces of the crowd laughing hard, cramming hotdogs into their mouths, drinking Coca-Cola, hooting, and whistling. Suddenly the crowd quiets. The middle-aged man is dead.[2]

The scene that follows depicts another middle-aged man, accompanied by a young sidekick, running up to the top of a building with a chicken in his arms. They have apparently made a bet about whether chickens can fly, the older man claiming that the bird will manage to slow itself down enough in the panic of free fall to land safely on the pavement and the boy demanding cigarettes if his own prediction, that it will fall like a rock and die, turns out to be correct. The older man drops the bird, and it falls hard to the ground only to get run over by a truck—moot point.

Why this strange juxtaposition? Why open with the middle-aged man being battered to death in the ring followed by the killing of this bird? Did the older man exempt himself from blame for the bird's death with his good faith that it could fly (as gamblers at the fight might exempt themselves from blame by arguing that they had bet on the dead man)? Terayama may be opening with this pair of images to inaugurate a debate about the nature of responsibility for death in the ring—namely, by asking if the act of stepping into a boxing ring amounts to a relinquishment of a claim to murder, if the boxing ring functions as a tiny square of extraterritoriality inside of which the rule of law does not apply. Or Terayama may be asking whether this was a case of criminal recklessness—was the man on the roof responsible for the death of the bird despite believing it could fly? Did Shōji kill the older boxer, was it pressure from the crowd that kept the fight going too long, or was this criminal neglect on the part of the referee or the man's trainer? Alternatively, is the flurry to name a murderer or a set of complicit parties actually driven by our discomfort with this extralegal space—do we start pointing fingers because even one small square of lawlessness is too much for us to handle?

These are the questions of individual or combined culpability that Bob Dylan would later ask after a March 1963 ring death in his song "Who Killed Davey Moore?" Dylan interrogates the referee's judgment, the crowd's desire for blood, the manager's nonchalance, forces of the gambling economy, the boxing critic's dependence on the sport, and the challenger's need for a job and then follows each with a predictable excuse. Moore's death was particularly troubling because it was the third title-bout case of death in the ring in as many years during the early 1960s.[3] The first, Harry Campbell's routine loss of a ten-round decision to Al Medrano at Madison Square Garden, occurred in May 1961. After the fight, Campbell fell into a coma and died a few days later. This was reported in the newspaper *Asahi shinbun* with comments that the fragility of veins and arteries in the brain make it possible to burst them during a match, but aneurysms are difficult to diagnose and almost impossible to predict.[4] This first case was dismissed as a freak accident. The weekly magazine *Shūkan Asahi* ran an article that asked, "Is Boxing a Murder Contest?" after the similar ring death in 1962 of Benny Paret, which occurred not even one full year after Campbell's. The article runs through an interrogation of possible suspects (referee, manager, mob, and audience) similar to Dylan's list and settles on the likelihood of a multiple and tangled complicity that might call for outlawing the sport.[5]

The *Asahi jānaru*, in a telling break from the other Asahi weekly, responded just two days later with a counterargument, stating that boxing is actually one of the safer sports and citing the following statistics: in 1961, there were thirty-one student deaths recorded for American football and only nine deaths worldwide for boxing; between 1955 and 1958, there had been fifty sports-related deaths in the United Kingdom, among which one was a boxer and fourteen were cricket players—and yet there was no public outcry for the banning of football or cricket. According to the article, "In a rank-order of risk for personal injury insurance in the U.S., boxing ranked seventh, even lower than American football and pro-wrestling."[6] Norman Mailer makes an astute comment on Paret's death in an article he wrote for *Esquire* in February 1963 (one month before Davey Moore's death): "Children had seen the fight on television. There were editorials, gloomy forecasts that the Game was dead."[7] The strong reaction to death in the ring may have been due to its having been televised, although Mailer quickly deflects his analysis to blame the "establishment doctors" and "mass media." Still, Mailer defends the sport because "it showed a part of what man was like, it belonged to his ability to create art and artful movement on the edge of death or pain or danger or attack, and it had much to say about the subtleties of human style." Mailer seems even further drawn in by the sport after witnessing Paret's death in person: "No, I was not down on boxing, but I loved it with freedom no longer. It was more like somebody in your family was fighting now."[8] Terayama read Mailer's essay in its Japanese translation and praised it in a profile of him published in *Asahi jānaru* in December 1964.[9]

Mailer seems to support the notion that the appeal of boxing is in its flirtation with injury and that the spectacle's tingle rests in our knowledge (perhaps subconsciously) that we may witness a human death. It almost goes without saying that the pleasure of watching boxing is the guilty pleasure of witnessing sadistic behavior—that we enjoy the vicarious infliction of pain. Yet there are elements unique to the sport that remind us that it is primarily a clash between two masochists who have trained themselves ruthlessly, and particularly in the lighter weight divisions, who have been on painful, near-starvation diets in order to stay within a weight class before the bouts. Each of the three major ring deaths in the early 1960s occurred in the lighter weight divisions, and two of them were title bouts.

A champ who cannot make weight before a title contest sacrifices the belt without a fight, and it was likely the combination of these anorexic diets and the blows to the head caused the aneurysms that killed Campbell, Paret, and Moore.

Terayama became friends in the early 1960s with a boxer named Harada Masahiko, known at home and abroad as "Fighting" Harada, who would become a world champion amid the series of major ring deaths. Born in 1943, he joined a boxing gym and began training at age fourteen. Two years later, he went professional in the lightest weight class, the flyweight division with a limit of 51 kilograms (112 pounds). In February 1960, at age sixteen, he took the national flyweight belt from Ebihara Hiroyuki, who would go on to win a world championship himself. Harada's first chance at a world title came in October 1962, when he was given a fight with the champ, Pone Kingpetch of Thailand, who was looking to pad his record with a series of easy wins. Harada surprised him in front of the home crowd in Tokyo, knocking Kingpetch out in the eleventh round. At age nineteen, Harada was the youngest flyweight world champion on record. Three months later, he would lose the title back to Kingpetch in Bangkok and vow to leave the lightest division. In May 1965, Harada moved up a weight class to bantamweight and took the world title from the Brazilian Eder Jofre, whom many critics rated to be the strongest boxer at the time, pound for pound. Harada defended that title four times, including a rematch with Jofre in 1966, until he finally lost it to the Australian Lionel Rose in February 1968. All six of those bantamweight title matches remain to this day in the top twenty-five most-watched events in Japanese television history.[10] At the end of the 1960s, after losing his bantamweight belt, Harada moved up yet another weight class to try for what he called a "triple crown." He challenged Australian Johnny Famechon in the featherweight division in July 1969 but lost a controversial one-point decision. After being beaten decisively in a rematch back in Tokyo, Harada retired after the match (at age twenty-six) and has managed a boxing gym ever since.[11]

There are three important ways in which "Fighting" Harada should be historicized. First, his career overlaps perfectly with both the rise of a broad international interest in boxing (driven largely by the career of Muhammad Ali) and the period Terayama was writing on the sport. Second, his all-attacking style (running from his corner to meet his opponent each round, punching constantly with both arms) risked shifting the sport away from the gracefulness Mailer so appreciated, seemingly confirming the sport's reputation for simple aggression. Third, his dramatic weight loss before matches (several divisions worth) put him at risk for the same type of aneurysm that killed three lighter-weight boxers in the period of Harada's rise. These elements of Harada's career emphasize, and sometimes establish, the themes that dominated Terayama's writing about the sport throughout the decade. Terayama writes in 1965,

> What was an "angry sport" is now in the process of shifting toward being a "hungry sport." At the time of his title match the buzz wasn't "How much does Harada hate Jofre?" or "How angry is Jofre?"—it was only questions about dropped weight. If you eat you might go over the weight limit, so they fight after starving themselves. In the ring they end up swinging wildly just to try to knock away their visions of meat and fish. But weight is just a problem of external restrictions, the problem of passion is different. This problem of "dropped weight = empty stomach" links up to the genre of politics.[12]

The combination of Harada's all-attacking style with his brutal training regimen sets him up perfectly as an embodiment of the sport's contradictions. By linking this to politics, Terayama seems to be asking who is in power and by what structure that power might exchange hands.

Terayama is one of many boxing writers who focuses in on a particular image from the sport to answer this question. The image is of a boxer, usually late in the fight and being badly beaten, struggling to see because his eye has swollen shut from too many punches to the brow. He wants to continue, though, often to save his pride by finishing the bout even if the decision is already obvious. In those circumstances, a boxer might ask his "cut man," whose usual job it is to close wounds, to pierce the swelling around his eye with a razor. That drains the blood from the contusion, and the new cut can be quickly closed with clotting agents, allowing the boxer's swollen eye to open up enough to see. Terayama writes a tanka with this image that is included in a collection called *Den'en ni shisu* (Death in the Country, 1965):

> *miru tame ni ryō mabuta o fukaku sakan to su kamisori no ha ni chihei o*
> *   utsushi*
> About to cut both eyelids deep in order to see—
>   the horizon reflected on the razor's blade[13]

This poem juxtaposes the image of a boxer having his eyelids cut open with an homage to Luis Buñuel and Salvador Dalí's surrealist short film *Un Chien Andalou*, in which a woman's eye is famously depicted as being sliced with a straight razor. There should be little doubt of the nature of this act—the boxer is willing to be cut for a chance at winning the fight or at least salvaging his pride. If this were a suicidal moment, then he would have the razor turned on his neck; if it were murderous, then he would turn it on his opponent.

A similar image appears within a novel that Terayama claims was the model for the screenplay quoted at the start of this chapter: Nelson Algren's *Never Come Morning* (1941). Near the end of Algren's novel, the boxer-protagonist has the following exchange with his manager between late rounds of a match:

> "Cut the eye for me, Case," Bruno asked. "It's swellin' tight as a drum."
> He closed his eyes when he felt the knife: then the loose wetness of the blood down his cheek and the cool touch of collodion as it began to freeze over. He sat then, his eyes watering and his mouth dripping from the sponge, with the towel about his neck, looking like an oversize baby on a stool about to blubber for oatmeal.[14]

The same scene would appear again at the end of *Rocky*, with Rocky Balboa begging, "Cut me, Mick," but his manager imploring him to give up: "You don't wanna do it, kid!" In each of these cases, the interest is in this masochistic element in an otherwise apparently sadistic sport. The impulse among critics and theorists of boxing to search for a culprit in their analysis of death-in-the-ring cases may, then, have to do with a discomfort with not only the legal exceptionality of the ring but also the type of psychology that could, in such a moment of intensity, still direct the blade inward, onto oneself. The great irony here may be that we recognize this kind of self-sacrifice as emblematic of the sport but still resist the idea that boxers possess the autonomy to accept risk of injury in the ring.

The Reality Effect of Boxing

In a short piece introducing profiles of Japan's world-championship boxers (forty-one between 1952 and 2000), "Fighting" Harada concludes with the following lines on the appeal of boxing as a sport: "Thinking back, I really believe that boxing is a wonderful sport. After punching each other in the ring the two always naturally embrace the moment the bout ends and say, 'good fight.' That's not a scene you see very often in other sports. It's because you battle in earnest, it's not faked, it's real [*tsukurimono de wa nai honmono dakara*]."[15] The suggestion here is that the reality effect of boxing is established not by its relationship to death but by its relationship to "faked" action.[16] Boxing stands as real against the falseness of scripted entertainment.

If boxing has a pure opposite, then it may be professional wrestling. One is ad-libbed and real, the other choreographed and fake. And yet boxing and professional wrestling, historically, are not the distant cousins they may seem to be. Under the nineteenth-century London Prize Ring rules, boxers were allowed to grapple with each other, and the signature headlocks and throws of pro wrestling were integral to the sport. It might be accurate to think of pro wrestling as an offshoot of boxing, comprising the elements that were shed as boxing became the pure punching sport we know it as today. The London rules were abandoned only after a famous two-hour, bare-knuckled match between John Sullivan and Jake Kilrain in 1889, for which Sullivan had trained with champion wrestler William Muldoon.[17]

Kōrakuen Hall, next to the Tokyo Dome, to this day alternates between boxing and pro wrestling matches, as did the Kuramae Kokugikai stadium, just south of Asakusa, before it. Kuramae was primarily, at least in name, the home of Sumo from 1954 until 1984, before that sport moved to its exclusive location in Ryōgoku. But it was also at Kuramae that both the professional wrestler Rikidōzan and the boxer "Fighting" Harada came to fame, and the audience sat in the same seats as they would to watch the *yokozuna* on other nights. Kuramae, then, was used specifically for these particular one-on-one contests of strength and quickness, as well as various, and never fully determinable, levels of choreography. We would be wise to remember that the greatest amount of gambling money is made by fixing contests the public trusts to be left purely to chance and skill.

The reality effect of boxing in the 1960s, as well as the privileging of that element of the sport, may have been set up in contrast to the popularity of pro wrestling in the 1950s. At that time, Rikidōzan was challenging American wrestlers with his "Karate Chop" and almost single-handedly popularizing television in Japan, then still something people watched as huge crowds in the streets. It is fitting, too, that the transition from the peak of pro wrestling (roughly 1953 to 1963) into that of boxing (roughly 1964 to

1970) perfectly overlaps with an update in the reality effect of television, which moved from black-and-white to color broadcasts at approximately the same time. The color technology allowed boxing's clearest proof of its reality—red blood—to transfer directly from the ring to the living room.[18] Yet, there remains a great deal of reality within pro wrestling as well: Rikidōzan had been a real Sumo wrestler, he really weighed 250 pounds and had to do a lot of real training to maintain that physique, he really did lift other huge men up into the air and slam them down on the mat—all of which required a very real amount of strength and agility. The athleticism and spectacle of pro wrestling were both very real.

The fundamental difference between pro wrestling and boxing might be what we watch for and what we hope to see. In pro wrestling, we want to see rules broken, the excesses like throwing opponents out of the ring, or the cheap shot behind the referee's back. It is the treachery and the vigilante-style revenge that follows that appeals to the viewers and participants. In boxing (one would hope), we do not watch for the ear bitings, low blows, or cheap shots after the bell but rather for a clean, fair fight where the stronger boxer wins a deserving victory. We want the rules followed strictly. And if we accept Gilles Deleuze's delineation between sadism and masochism—the claim that these are fundamentally distinct and incompatible libidinal systems—then we ought to see pro wrestling as a sadistic sport, one in which the violation of a contract is eroticized, whereas boxing is a masochistic sport where the maintenance of the contractual agreement (amid great pressure to break it) is the basis of pleasure.[19]

It is important to note that within the broad history of boxing commentary, an emphasis on the reality of boxing is rare. We usually find contextualizations of matches within frameworks of struggle between races (Max Schmeling defeating Joe Louis for Hitler's Aryanism) or classes (the working-class boxers performing for a bourgeois audience), or as proxy battles between nations, or most recently as a comment on gender. But it may be a great disservice to the boxers themselves to reframe their sport as anything other than as one skilled and well-trained fighter against another. Terayama writes an interesting piece on this topic in December 1965, profiling a Zainichi Korean boxer named Kaneda Morio. One might expect reportage on a minority boxer to celebrate the channeling of discrimination-fueled anger into motivation in the ring: "There are many boxers from his home country who can only capture glory by 'knocking down the Japanese.'"[20] But Terayama points out that assumptions about the symbolic meaning of a bout can end up being just as discriminatory. In Kaneda's case, concern over the political implications of a North Korean competing for the Asian championship led to him being banned from international competition, despite having won the middleweight belt within Japan. The audience's desire to have boxers stand in as metaphors for hot-button political issues might fuel ticket sales and even motivate the boxers themselves, but it is also alienating. In this case, the boxing association's inability to handle a case of hybrid nationality resulted in a lower level of competition and a potentially false belt for whomever Kaneda would have faced.

This reality effect of boxing—its relationship to the sensation of presence, to an enhancement of perceived vitality—was precisely the theme that Terayama would focus on in his major boxing project of the mid-1960s. In March 1965, Terayama began serialization of a novel called *Aa, kōya* (Ah, wilderness). It was published in monthly installments in the magazine *Gendai no me* until September 1966, then edited somewhat and released as a book in November 1966. The narrative concerns the simultaneous development of two new boxers, Barikan (an introverted, shy stutterer) and Shinjuku Shinji (an optimistic, proud ex-con)—they train in the same gym, and the narrative leads up to a showdown between them in the ring.[21] The first direct mention of enhanced reality through boxing comes midway through the third chapter (of fifteen): "Once their first opponents were decided, boxing suddenly began to have a sense of reality [*genjitsukan*] for Barikan and Shinji. But it was completely unlike the blurred photos of loudmouthed Clay or Liston the Bear. The reality that *someone's muscles in this city of Tokyo were being trained in order to break their jaws* was reality enough."[22] The reality effect (literally "reality-sensation" in Japanese) originates with the imagination of physical pain in the ring, a pain coupled with the humiliation of defeat, and that pair is sufficient motivation for Shinji, who revels in the opportunity for glory. But Barikan cannot fight driven only by fear—the avoidance of a negative result is not enough for him—he needs something positive driving his punches. What he needs is genuine anger toward his opponent, which Shinji can generate at will (by creating a fictional version of his opponent in his mind, then transferring the anger from that fiction into reality in the ring), but Barikan lacks that capacity. He seeks out his first opponent before their match, hoping that something in their interaction will frustrate him enough to cultivate the anger needed to fight: "Barikan was puzzled about why he should punch out this man without having any sort of individual reason to do so. Wouldn't he have to meet him at least once before the event?"[23] So he finds the address of his opponent and visits him at home, but has nothing to say once he arrives. The other boxer brushes him off, suggesting that if he has something to communicate, he should do it through their managers. Barikan ends up feeling jealous that his opponent had already developed a loathing for him and concludes that generating anger must be part of his training.

Barikan is quintessentially passive, as his personality is purely reactive. His emotions and actions are completely determined by those around him, and he never has an assertive moment in the entire novel—never an imaginative moment, never an original thought, never a spontaneous idea. In the ring he is a counterpuncher: "He always fought in a crouching style, never using his long reach, and fought only by countering."[24] He is a pathetic protagonist, but it is extremely difficult to sympathize with him, which may be why the novel itself was not a great success in Japan (it was, however, translated into both German and French).[25] The narrative becomes far more interesting when reconceived as a socially critical parody of counterpuncher politics, however, especially when Terayama juxtaposes this portrayal with a collage of contrasts: a series of extemporaneous forms, chance operations, and ad-libbed culture.

The first, and most important, of these spontaneous forms is modern jazz, the improvisational mode that flourished in Japan and around the world in the 1950s and 1960s. Terayama's afterword to the novel opens with the following:

> *Aa, kōya* is the first full-length novel I have ever written. I tried to write this novel using the method of modern jazz. The way I did it was to treat the characters like instruments in a combo, decide on the basic story as a chord name, and then fill it in with completely improvised depiction. It is, therefore, very haphazard and far away from any sort of composition or design. But this form of manipulation, deciding by ad-lib as I wrote where the characters would go (and myself with them), was a fresh experience for me. Typically novelists give themselves over to a particular pre-determined idea, then take the position of confirming it throughout the writing process, but in this novel there was not a single thing set at the start.[26]

This combination of structure (in the chord name, or the selection of a scale) with improvisation within that structure is a perfect cognate for boxing itself—the boxer enters the ring with a set of punches (jabs, hooks, uppercuts) and combinations (two- or three-punch sets like riffs) but must improvise the arrangement of those elements on the fly and in relationship with the movements of the other boxer, just as the musicians in a jazz combo will play off of each other. Structure and improvisation coexist here. Terayama speaks explicitly on this issue in an interview with the composer Takemitsu Tōru: "Jazz taught me that 'fixed forms and freedom are not an antinomy.' When I was young I thought that the opposites of form and structure were freedom and liberation. But jazz showed me that form and structure are synonymous with freedom and liberation. To put it another way, there is a superimposition in jazz of images of bondage and confinement with images of liberation and freedom."[27] Jazz and boxing are emblematic of improvisation here—Terayama calls boxing "a physical ad-lib"[28]—as they constitute a tangible example of a dialogic process that creates something beyond the initial imagination of the participants.

Terayama had been interested in jazz since the 1950s, and it is likely that he first encountered it while living in Misawa during his middle-school years in the late 1940s, during the Allied occupation. Misawa was a major military base for Japanese forces during the war and was quickly overtaken by American forces once the war ended—a major U.S. military installation remains there today. Two of the tanka from Terayama's public debut mention "black men's blues songs" (kokujin hika), the first of which was mentioned in chapter 1, and the second of which makes specific reference to a military base:

barakku no rajio no kokujin hika no basu hirogaru kagiri mugi aomi yuku
Just as far as the bass of the black man's blues song carries
   from the radio in the barracks—there the wheat greens[29]

These songs could have been anything from gospel to blues to jazz, but it is likely that his first experience of black music occurred there in Misawa. Terayama's interest in jazz gained momentum once he was in Tokyo, resulting in a book called *Jazu o tanoshimu hon* (Enjoying jazz, 1961), which he coedited with the music critic Yukawa Reiko. Terayama writes of being a "Yellow Negro" in those days, playing off of Mailer's essay, "The White Negro: Superficial Reflections on the Hipster" (1956).[30] In 1962,

Terayama mused on the possibility of "action poetry" that would operate like a modern jazz performance—not the re-presentation of a score or
enaction of a theory, but an instigation, a new "action" generated spontaneously. In the first section, he writes of his interest in jazz as it developed
by spending time in a jazz club called Kiiyo in Shinjuku's seedy Kabukichō
district: "A friend of mine asked me, 'Why do you listen to modern jazz?'
I'm interested in modern jazz because it's action. When someone mentions a piece by Wynton Kelly, they're not talking about the chord name
of a song he played or the score he arranged. They mean the action that
took place in some club near dawn with rotten apple cores and cigarette
butts and whiskey bottles strewn all over—people are able to powerfully
connect their consciousness with his by taking his work to be that action
alone."[31] Terayama is interested in reconnecting poetry to action in a way
that would have particular poems remembered as embedded in space and
time, rather than severed from life and dehistoricized in the form of books,
mediated by the mechanical, antihuman, timeless, and placeless medium
of movable type.

Returning to *Aa, kōya*, we find the text documenting an *act* of writing
from a particular place and time—it is more analogous to a live recording of a concert than an engineered studio production. Terayama moves
in this direction by overwriting the specificity of location and historical
moment, and his references to establishments in Shinjuku's Kabukichō
district are so obscure that nearly every page has two or three footnotes
(necessary even for the primary target audience of fellow Tokyoites).
The text is peppered with references to pop songs that had just been
released, news items, and television commercials, all probably timed with
the monthly installments during its serialization. This method may have
been more than just a way to document the era—it was a creative process
(maybe the only one) that allowed the artist to continue living in the present tense during the creation of the work. Rather than imagining the final
product and then spending the time creating it, waiting to arrive at that
future moment, or reliving memories of the past in order to recreate a situation that is already over, Terayama wrote within the moment of his life
as it was being lived. He was certainly not the only artist using an improvisational style during the 1960s—it may have been the dominant mode
within popular, and certainly within countercultural, forms. The graphic
designer Uno Akira, for example, who designed several posters for Terayama's theater troupe and collaborated with him on many projects, describes

his method as one in which he begins a drawing with a single human figure somewhere on the page, then adds other elements that the figure he has drawn reminds him of—if the shape of a girl's leg calls to mind a horse's head, he draws a horse's head near the girl's leg; then when part of the horse reminds him of something else, he adds that to the piece. Uno, like Terayama, seeded his projects with form, then allowed it to develop, as if on its own, through a kind of iterating dialectic between the artist and the artistic product itself.[32]

Terayama's position in relationship to the problem of boxing and death begins with a redefinition of "life" that limits its meaning to life led in an ad-libbed fashion. By reconceptualizing life to be the perception of physical, and especially mental, presence in the here and now—something enhanced by improvisation and the witnessing of improvisation but suppressed by resigning to a reactive stance—Terayama also redefines "death" to be stasis, stability, and predictable routines. The salaryman, then, is willfully already dead, whereas the boxer—despite risking injury (not because he risks injury)—is alive, particularly in the ring. Death in the ring, in Terayama's framework, is more a return to society's norm of stasis than an extraordinary event. This deconstruction of the simple opposition (and codetermination) of life and death parallels a relationship between rationality and insanity in regard to jazz that Terayama comments on further along in the interview with Takemitsu cited previously: "Rationality and insanity are not simply opposites—the actual opposites are rational insanity versus insane insanity, or else insane rationality versus rational rationality. In the 1960s, Marcuse led us to expect an anti-linguistic trend that takes insanity created by rationality to be fake, and only deranged insanity to be truly insane, but I still feel like that's ineffective. I do think, though, that there is a great suggestion in his 'distancing from language,' and 'suspicion of rational decisions.'"[33] Similarly, it seems that Terayama (along with much of 1960s counterculture) had reconceived of the relationship between life and death to be primarily between dead life and live life. This position distances Terayama from aligning boxing's allure with death. Both the pitying of boxers for facing such danger as well as the use of ring death to enhance the potency of fiction tighten the link between death and boxing in public discourse, which then leads to increased fetishization of the death spectacle and demands to ban the murderous sport (removing another avenue of social mobility). But Terayama seems to be claiming that this sport can be about life without simultaneously being about bodily death. In fact, he makes a clean distinction between the life-force of boxers and the death drive of university students and salarymen within *Aa, kōya*.

Only one group of characters in the novel has no substantive relationship to Barikan, Shinji, and their boxing gym: the members of the Waseda University Suicide Research Society. This parody of Terayama's alma mater stands in contradistinction to the virility of Shinji in particular. Their first appearance in the novel occurs in the third chapter—they are sitting next to Shinji in a cafe debating plans for the group:

> A student with a face just like the movie actor Kawasaki Keizō is explaining the construction of a suicide machine. "It's a device that lets you die while you're sleeping," says Kawasaki Keizō. "I thought of it while I was looking at a drawing of François, and the principle is the same as a bucket in a well. On one side you hang an ax, and I'd be sleeping under that. On the other side you hang a bucket filled with water and the weight balances them both out. But the bucket has a hole in it so the water leaks out and makes it lighter. I'm sleeping, so I won't be able to know how light the bucket that's holding up the ax is getting. Suddenly the ax will fall and I'll die. Well, that's the general idea."[34]

One of Kawasaki's friends argues that the machine (clearly a twist on Edgar Allan Poe's "The Pit and the Pendulum") would fall too slowly to kill him—the design was flawed. Kawasaki brushes off the comment and says to the group, "I've spent twenty-one years preparing to die, every day since I was born." At this point, Shinji, who had been listening in from the next table, says to him, "So, how much time have you guys spent preparing to live?" Kawasaki then turns to his girlfriend: "There are some optimists in this world . . . but the optimistic people die, too."[35]

There may be more to this than just associating higher education with preparation for a deathlike existence and juxtaposing Shinji's life-force with the pessimism of these students. They are flippant and cool in their rejection of the possibility of successful opposition to fate, but they eventually reject the potential for any sort of self-determination whatsoever. Terayama might have been playing with an association between self-determination and suicide, two meanings embodied in the single Japanese word *jiketsu* ("to decide for oneself").[36] The students, fundamentally, want to take possession of their own lives by being the agents determining their own deaths, perhaps as an expression of free will, but one that eliminates that same human will in the process of its demonstration. Their vicious circle has just enough internal logic to maintain itself. Shinji argues with them for a bit longer but then closes his eyes and starts to daydream about his girlfriend.

The Suicide Research Society reappears occasionally through the novel, almost for tragicomic relief. Realizing that they are all too timid to test their own suicide machines, the group places a want ad for a suicide volunteer. It is at this transitional moment, when the suicide club decides to go out looking for someone to murder (in the name of euthanasia), that "a sense of reality [*genjitsukan*] began to grow in the suicide machine blueprint sitting on the table."[37] The same word is used here for the suicide club students as had been used for the boxers. This suicide discussion draws us back to the second chapter of the book, where Barikan is reading a *manga* in the gym while Shinji trains. It is called *Gasu jisatsu* (Suicide with gas), and the protagonist wants to kill himself but frets over the best method. Finally, he decides to buy a sweet potato snack for his sister and he kneels down behind her as she eats it, his hands clasped together in prayer until she farts on him. Standard scatological *manga* slapstick, but Barikan does not laugh. Suicide is something you ought to do on your own, he thinks. He contemplates the disillusionment in the protagonist—"Reminds me of someone," Barikan thinks.[38] It is reminding Barikan of himself, of course, and Terayama suggests through his ironic tone that what Barikan needs to get out of his humorless rut is a willingness to immerse himself in illusion.

Barikan's reason for taking up boxing is made clear in the first section of the novel. He has a stutter, and the self-help book he bought—*How to Cure a Stutter*—recommends that he try nonlinguistic methods of self-expression, such as athletics: "Languages have national boundaries but sports do not."[39] After seeing an advertisement for a boxing gym in the newspaper ("Come on in, Weaklings!") and concluding that his stutter is due to physical weakness, he joins the gym. Boxing does not help, though, so he tries visiting a treatment center for "stuttering, embarrassment, and fear of people," but cannot afford the costs of therapy. Terayama satirizes Barikan here for assuming his stutter to be a sign of weakness, when in fact he is using it to rationalize his own reactive and overly cautious personality. In other works, Terayama revisits the theme with scenes that praise stuttering—it is the one form of language that carries proof of its improvisational nature. This issue will come up again in Terayama's 1971 film *Sho o suteyo machi e deyō* (*Throw Out Your Books, Let's Hit the Streets*):

> To keep from stuttering I pick words I definitely won't stutter on, but then I end up saying things I didn't really want to say ... They told me singing could cure my stutter, so I sang "The Woman from Hakodate" a hundred times. But isn't stuttering a kind of philosophy? The rising sun stutters its way between the buildings. Beethoven's Fifth stutters "da, da, da, daaaan." Peace stutters over the scorched earth in Vietnam. Clouds are stuttering vagabonds. The Straits of Korea are a stuttering borderline, have you seen it! Order and subordination are smooth, but the sun has a stutter, the human heart has a stutter, every kind of resistance stutters, it stutters and stutters and stutters as it shouts.[40]

This is an homage to a short 1960 essay by the composer Takemitsu Tōru called "Kitsuon sengen: Domori no manifesuto" (Stammering declaration: A manifesto on stuttering):

> We should stutter when we're looking for a method to communicate our ideas clearly to another person. The most moving part of Beethoven's Fifth is the theme of Fate knocking on the door, it stutters so wonderfully:
> Da, da, da, daaaan.
>   Da, da, da, daaaan.
> Stuttering lets you digest your words once more inside your heart.[41]

This juxtaposition of fate and stuttering is made even clearer in Terayama's script, where Beethoven's Fifth is referred to as his *unmei kōkyōkyoku* (symphony of fate). Takemitsu continues, "Stuttering is not regressive. It is progressive. It may be medically categorized as a type of functional problem but within my metaphysics stuttering is a song of revolution."[42] This praise of stuttering is a recognition that polished language is scripted, evidence of a time in the past lived for the future (coupled with a time in the present lived as repetition of the past), whereas the stutter itself confirms the extemporaneousness of the stuttered speech—and its challenge to fate. Fate knocks on the door in a stutter as though to gain entry to a serendipitous space from which it has been excluded.

Yet Barikan never embraces his own stutter—he seeks only to hide it, to escape it, and to tidy it up. As the novel progresses, he comes to embody all that is not spontaneous. He loses his first match by knockout after entering the ring and virtually forgetting to fight. After a few punches glance his face, he throws a few in return, but the reality effect and heightened sensation of presence associated with boxing are completely lost on him; in fact, he becomes even more distant inside the ring: "He wanted to escape the loneliness of being in the ring as soon as possible. He felt like he was in a ridiculously 'distant place.' Expanding completely beyond the edge of his psyche, the audience on the other side of the ropes was suddenly millions of light-years away."[43] Barikan loses focus again later in the match and is caught by a straight shot to the brow, which knocks him down and, briefly, unconscious. Shinji, however, in the following match, makes quick work of his opponent, pounding him until even his own manager has to shout for him to stop.

There are hints in the text that this core difference between Barikan and Shinji's personalities in the ring is linked to each boxer's relationship with his father. As Shinji slams his opponent in the ring, he replays in his mind a memory of his father being beaten up by a bartender: "'It's over?' Shinji asked as he returned to his normal self. Who is this guy sprawled out next to my new shoes?"[44] Shinji's vigor, then, is the product of a smooth transfer of vengeful anger toward the bartender who abused his father to his opponent in the ring. Barikan's father, however, left home when Barikan was young, leaving him with an unfulfilled longing for that relationship. Locked in a hold in the middle of his match, Barikan thinks to himself, "I want to stay just like this"—a proxy embrace with his missing father.[45] Barikan constantly fantasizes about father–son communication. Looking out over the "neon wilderness" of Shinjuku one night, he focuses in on the Suntory whiskey sign: "Why does the Y in the 'Suntory' sign on Nishi-guchi Hall always take longer to light up? (He was dull-witted enough to think that it might be some kind of key to understanding his life.) Is the Y some kind of secret code to me from my missing father? Or is that Y a lonely stammer among the other neon lights? It's probably a stutterer like me."[46] Barikan's frustration with stuttering throughout the narrative is paired with Terayama's inconsistent, episodic, lurching style—he stutters his way through the composition, jumping from one narrational mode to another, from first- to third-person narration, and he inserts poems, song lyrics, and bold-faced lines sporadically throughout the text. While Bari-kan retreats in shame, Terayama pushes forward, embracing the sensation of presence delivered by the roughness of that linguistic texture.

The sensation of presence is mentioned again immediately after Bari-kan and Shinji's debut fights. Shinji is at the horse-racing track with their trainer, One-Eye (Katame), who has taken him out to celebrate his win. Terayama opens the chapter with the following description: "The horse-track was packed with people. Thousands of vagrants were enjoying the mood of 'the lost home' up in grandstands in the clouds. Everything pro-gresses in the present tense [genzaikei] here, once something has passed it's instantly worthless. Bets from the previous race, old newspapers, empty beer cans. Property-less men and forgotten women. 'The Present' [genzai] throws all that away and continues bounding forward."[47] An ear-lier reference to horse racing appears when Barikan and Shinji first visit One-Eye's boxing gym, where they find horse-racing newspapers scattered all around. Immediately following that description, and in conspicuous juxtaposition, is a scene where One-Eye has both of them strip down and show him their bodies, poking at their legs so he can size them up "just as though he were sizing up horses at a stable."[48] Here again we find box-ers in a liminal space—human, and yet functioning precisely the same way as animals do in the gambling economy (One-Eye mentions his sup-port of the two boxers as an investment of his capital in a gamble on their careers).[49] And yet the existence of gambling in both of these arenas speaks to the unpredictable nature of the events and their tangible demonstration of an unknowable future. Losing at the track, then, might be even more exhilarating than winning, in that it concretely confirms the ad-libbed nature of an unscripted future. At the track, One-Eye explains to Shinji that one horse, one of a family of horses that consistently wins, is far faster than the rest. Shinji asks him if there is anyone foolish enough to bet on other horses. "'Oh, there sure are,' One-Eye said, cracking a smile. 'Every-body wants to beat their own fate. We always try to believe in the power of human intervention. Don't you think a life led without challenging the star you were born under would be flavorless and cold?'"[50] One-Eye goes on to pick an underdog and wins big. Gambling stands with stuttering here as a challenge to determinism itself, as wins at the track become a tangible means of exploiting other people's belief in inevitability.

There is a moment about halfway through the novel when it seems that Barikan has willed himself into independence and broken from his cycle of introversion, shame, and reactive thinking. After finally winning a tough match, he quits One-Eye's gym, moves out of his apartment, and joins the Sasazaki Gym in Meguro (where "Fighting" Harada trained in the 1960s). In a letter he writes to Shinji, however, it becomes clear that the sudden severing of connections is actually driven by a desire to link back up again:

> Depending on my record, we might have a chance to cross gloves (as equals) in the ring. Actually, that was the goal I had in mind when I decided to change my registration. (We couldn't fight each other while we were in the same gym).
>
> Until now I was like your sidekick [otōtobun], and I used to think that being near someone who's got good luck would some-how rub off on me and I'd become lucky, too. But when I thought about it, I realized that there are some lives that just don't involve chance. That's when I gave up on "chance" and decided to try mess-ing things up on my own. Goodbye, and thanks.[51]

It is Shinji who suffers more from Barikan's departure, getting more and more depressed and longing for his old friend. Barikan, however, seems to be strengthened by his new independence. He starts frequenting a bar near his new apartment, makes some friends, and even seems to finally begin curing his stutter: "As he spoke to them he felt an inexpressible sensation of liberation [kaihōkan]; it was because he was unexpectedly speaking without stuttering."[52]

At this point in the novel, Barikan's program for curing his stutter is finally starting to work. He has found a way to communicate through sports, which has given him the confidence to liberate himself from power-less relationships and stand on his own. Paralleling this development in the text is commentary about the relationship between violence and commu-nication. Terayama channels this topic into the narrative through the diary of Miyagi, the owner of a discount store in Kabukichō and the brother-in-law of One-Eye: "Lately, I've become more interested in 'violence' than in 'language' or 'sex.' Violence as communicative action. Violence as a method of solidarity . . . at any rate, there is no room for alienation within 'violent' action. That's how I've gotten interested in boxing recent-ly. This lonely violent action where you understand your opponent by punching him, it's a society of two without a third party intervening . . . You can't love someone without hurting them. And you can't hurt someone without loving them, either."[53] Violence here is direct, unmediated communication—a form of language not deflected through the slipperiness of signification.

Terayama would take up the opposite relationship as the theme of a series of essays called *Bōryoku toshite no gengo* (Language as violence), which was serialized in the monthly *Gendai no me* (the same monthly that *Aa, kōya* was published in) starting in 1968. With subsections on topics such as "Poetry Read on the Run," "Group Poetry," "Unaccounted-for Poems," "Linguistic Engineering," and "Graffitology," Terayama works to generate a metaphysics of violence as it relates to language and poetry. It is important to recognize from the start that the definition of violence that Terayama uses throughout this inquiry is specific and limited: "Sorel, in his *Reflexions sur la violence*, divides violence [*bōryoku*] into two categories: that which is directed from the low toward the high is called 'violence,' and that which is directed from the high toward the low is called 'force,' or what we might call 'authority' [*kenryoku*]. Adapted to language, I feel that the printed word is authoritative, and that spoken language is violent."[54] Terayama is reworking and extending an argument he made first in the 1962 essay on action poems and then again in a book of literary criticism from 1965 called *Sengoshi: Yurishiizu no fuzai* (Postwar Poetry: The Absence of Ulysses): that the formality and universalism of standardized language and its monopolization of publishing stifle the soul of living language, with its regional accents, awkward phrasing, and unpolished texture. The piece on graffiti in *Bōryoku toshite no gengo*, however, is new. Graffiti appears briefly in *Aa, kōya*, but without much evidence of the level of theorization Terayama had devoted to stuttering and boxing. There is penciled graffiti of boxers' names on the walls of a training gym and later a reference to the walls of Barikan's apartment, which he has punched until they are blackened and dented, as a "diary written with his fists."[55] There is also a quotation from a Vladimir Mayakovsky poem—"Some people's hearts are in their chests, but mine fills my entire body"—that appears twice in the text, first without explanation and later as a line Shinji liked enough to copy into his journal.[56] The poem would appear again in the film *Sho o suteyo, machi e deyō*, this time written as graffiti on a wall. Terayama's graffiti comprises literary quotation, chalked statements on rugby fields, and absurdities on walls in the city or written on the pavement itself—these are suggestions for new directions graffiti might expand.

The directness of graffiti is similar to that of boxing in that there is no mediation by the printed word, editing, market-driven apparatuses of distribution, or state censorship. Comments on the wall of a bathroom seem to speak directly and yet with an anonymity perhaps unique to the form:

> Whether or not it's true for poetry, graffiti is doubtlessly a sacrifice made through language. Writers of graffiti become "Invisible Men" in the process of writing on the bathroom walls. Contrary to the way the Negro has been painted into the dusk of history through social discrimination like Ralph Ellison's protagonist, graffiti writers erase themselves as they write—"the generation of erasure"—a single wall, with language as its medium, provides the appeal to erase the self. We might say that this is the sacrifice of graffiti's poetics, one which corresponds to the way in which poets of the past sought to erase nature by writing.[57]

The practice of graffiti is linked to an effacing of the individual's place in the process of communication, an erasure of the narrator in parallel to the fictionalization of the poetic voice discussed in chapter 1. But in poetic graffiti, left unsigned on the walls of a bathroom, Terayama finds new hope in a form of communication devoid of self-promotion: "When I was younger I thought that the fantasy of becoming invisible and the desire to become a poet stood in an antinomy. But now I can positively say that these two dreams are not contradictory at all."[58] Here again he returns to this consistent theme of apparent opposites revealed as noncontradictory—rationality and insanity, structure and freedom, and here the Invisible Man and the poet.

The final showdown between Barikan and Shinji is described from all sides as a communicative act. At the initial handshake, Barikan says to Shinji, "It's been a long time," but he receives no reply. As the first round begins, Barikan follows Shinji around the ring "as though he wanted to talk to him," but Shinji continues to deny him communication.[59] In the second round, Barikan starts longing to have a "meaningful conversation with Shinji, but Shinji's words only transmitted pain to his body, they never sank in with any meaning."[60] By the third round, Barikan is slower still, feeling light-years away (again), and Shinji is gaining momentum. The bout becomes so imbalanced that Miyagi begins to wonder to himself if Barikan is actually suicidal—whether he stepped in the ring and dropped his guard, hoping to die. Here some of the novel's themes, which had each taken solos as chapters during the course of Terayama's text, begin interweaving into a final ensemble. It is beginning to look like there might be a death in the ring, and the audience has started to search for a culprit. Shinji had begun preparing for this process well in advance, thinking to himself, "He is probably hoping that I'll knock him down. That by being beaten to a pulp and completely bloodied up we'd have some kind of inevitable relationship. That's his trap. But even knowing that, I'll train hard to fulfill his desire—this is going to be a brutal match."[61] He is correct in a way: what Barikan wants is a confirmation of the role of fate that he senses binds him to Shinji—and Shinji, although inclined to challenge what he perceives as his fate, also feels bound as a sort of guardian figure for Barikan to provide him with what he desires. Shinji is rewriting his role from proactive sadist into that of the masochist's partner, following the instructions of someone who desires pain—this is the moment in which responsibility for any possible damage to Barikan is transferred onto Barikan himself.

In the fourth round, Barikan's mind has begun wandering as Shinji continues to punch him—there are shouts from the crowd to throw in the towel and the referee tries to stop Shinji but he, too, is no longer mentally present in the ring. The punches continue, numbered for us up to eighty-nine, well beyond the point when the match was decided, and in a strange parallel to Mailer's description of the twenty-five unanswered blows to Benny Paret's head in 1962 and to "Fighting" Harada's style of wailing away until he got the total knockout. The last page of the novel is a copy of a death certificate confirming that an aneurysm sustained during the match killed the twenty-year-old boxer; and so Terayama did end his novel with a ring death, after seeming to spend the majority of the text working to break down the codeterminative relationship between the reality effect of boxing and the risk of death in the ring. It reads like an easy out, a simple way to tie things up, and even when read symbolically—completing the walking-dead counterpuncher's drift from one kind of death to another—it still leaves one hollow. Why finish with such simplicity, with no effort to frustrate the coupling of boxing with death? There is one strange part of the death certificate, however, that may be suggestive: Barikan's real name (Futaki Kenji) has been replaced with that of his missing father (Futaki Takeo). It is possible that this was a simple mistake, but it would not be unlike Terayama to slip a strange puzzle into a place like this. Takeo has a shadowy existence in the text—Barikan searches for him unsuccessfully, he is the one recruited by the suicide club as a potential guinea pig for their machine, and he wanders Kabukichō alone—but he never interacts directly with the main characters. Barikan looks to Shinji as a replacement for his runaway father, but here the missing (but living) father replaces his present (but now dead) son. Maybe this is the best Terayama could do to frustrate the process of naturalizing the boxing-equals-death equation, a wrench in the works at the very moment of ring death. It is accomplished with sufficient irony to throw the awkward twists in logic used to justify the beating—he must have been suicidal—into relief. Barikan was the least suicidal character in the novel—certainly less so than the Waseda students, lonely Miyagi, and his ethereal father. He may have been the one most interested in cultivating a meaningful, real-time interaction with others, even more so than Shinji. Yet it was his efforts in the direction of sociality that made him a social outcast. Terayama's critique may ultimately have been directed at the paradox of a society that alienates those working against alienation.

The Funeral of Rikiishi Tōru

Terayama would be involved with a third death-in-the-ring narrative at the end of the 1960s. It came midway through the wildly popular manga *Ashita no Jō* (lit. Tomorrow's Jō, but with the sense of an underdog that fans hope will "beat 'em next time"). This series by Takamori Asao and Chiba Tetsuya ran in the weekly *Shōnen magajin* from January 1968 until the protagonist, Yabuki Jō, dies in the ring in the final episode, five years later. Around the halfway point in its run, however, there is a showdown between Jō, the underdog working-class hero, and his rival (almost more of a coprotagonist than an antagonist), the handsome and talented Rikiishi Tōru. They are also friends, congratulating each other on particularly good punches and politely shaking hands after their bouts. The two are a good match, as well. Rikiishi has a longer reach, but he drops so much weight before the bout that his stamina is low. Jō has a smaller frame, but fights with the heart readers expect from a boxer from the slums. Midway through the fight, Jō is clearly losing the long-awaited showdown—he is completely exhausted, falling to the mat from the momentum of his own missed punches—but then manages to land a lucky temple shot on

Rikiishi. This turns out to have been the killer left hook, which bursts a vein in Rikiishi's brain. But close inspection reveals that Rikiishi may have been set up for the deathblow by comments from the crowd. The fans, seeing the pathetic state Jō was in, were first screaming for the referee to stop the fight, or for Jō's trainer to throw in the towel. But Jō's trainer (another "one-eye") thinks he sees enough "fight" in him to keep Jō in the match. Rikiishi is distracted by the heckling, however, and loses his focus. The frames immediately preceding the temple punch show Rikiishi glancing toward the crowd, taking his eye off of Jō for a split second—precisely the moment Jō lands his punch. What could have distracted him?

One fan shouted for Rikiishi to "finish him off" [*todome o sashite yare yo*], and another yells out that leaving him half-dead [*namagoroshi*] would be a sin. The direct reference to death, although probably metaphorical, draws Rikiishi's attention enough that he glances conspicuously to the side. The announcers comment that he looks exhausted, too, and that he may have dropped too much weight before the match. It is in this state of contemplation that Rikiishi receives the fatal punch, cleverly tipping the scales on the common conception of death in the ring. It is the fear of killing Jō that paradoxically kills Rikiishi—had he just remained focused on the fight, he probably would have blocked the punch and lived. The irony, in this case, is that Rikiishi actually wins the fight, by an uppercut knockout in the eighth round. Jō regains his senses after the ten count only to witness Rikiishi collapse as he reaches forward for their postbout handshake. Recovering in his locker room after the match, Jō learns that Rikiishi died and screams out in grief.

Terayama writes an analysis of Rikiishi's death for a newspaper about one week after the episode was published in *Shōnen magajin*. The title of his article, "Dare ga Rikiishi o koroshita ka" (Who killed Rikiishi?), invokes the press following the ring deaths of the early 1960s as well as Dylan's song. His critique and conclusions, however, deviate considerably from previous iterations on this theme. Terayama opens by claiming that "there were two deaths depicted in the most recent episode of *Ashita no Jō*. One was the death of 'tomorrow' as Yabuki Jō lost by a knockout."[62] Jō's potential to become a star boxer was stopped short by this loss, but what Terayama focuses on is the shattering of his dream to use boxing prize money to clean up the slums, adding parks to the riversides, a hospital, eldercare, apartments, and a supermarket—that was the future [*ashita*] that died in the ring. Terayama's sympathies are not with Rikiishi, who he sees as reflective of authority within the social establishment: "He dominates with his American Superman-like face, his backing by capitalists, his rationalist decision-making, and advanced technology." Rikiishi is the technocracy personified here. Acknowledging that the meaning of the text is a collaborative production by the writers and the readers, Terayama asks whether the meaning of Rikiishi's death was effectively "a lynching by the eyes of the readers of the authority that toppled Jō?" Terayama answers his own question in the negative, adding that "to boxers, death outside the ring isn't 'death'—it's nothing more than a rest from life." But in Rikiishi's case, Terayama argues, this was not even an honorable ring death because "Rikiishi was dead from the start." Unlike Jō, he never had a reason to fight and only played a reactive role in the text (another counterpunching figure like Barikan): "Rikiishi was born as an illusion in the heart of Jō, and he disappeared along with Jō's bankruptcy in the ring." For Terayama, Rikiishi proxied for the illusion of establishment authority, an authority that disappears once relinquished. He concludes the piece with the following: "Rikiishi did not die, we just lost sight of him—an almost maliciously accurate reflection of the sentiment of 1970. There might be a bit of the chalked graffiti saying 'Shatter Illusions' still left inside Yasuda Hall at Tokyo U., and you can strain your ears all you want but what you hear isn't demo chanting or broadcasts from the clock tower. It's not even the 'shu, shu' of Jō's breath as he shadowboxes. All you hear are the empty, February winds."[63] Rikiishi died with the fading of the antiestablishment movement. The public response to Rikiishi's death, however, was anything but illusory.

Kōdansha's editorial division was flooded with consolation letters, funeral flowers, and even gifts of money following the death of Rikiishi on the pages of *Shōnen magajin*.[64] The idea to hold an actual funeral for Rikiishi came first from Higashi Yutaka, the original stage director for Terayama's troupe, who had recently left to form his own company. Higashi's troupe, the Tokyo Kid Brothers, had integrated *Ashita no Jō* into their third production, called *Ōgon batto* (The Golden Bat), which ran from late 1969 into 1970. One scene of the play was a reenactment of the latest episode of the boxing *manga*, changing each week to stay current with the narrative. That play was already doing live-action reproductions from the *manga*, including Rikiishi's death and the funeral scene from the print version itself. Higashi suggested to Terayama that he organize a formal, public funeral for Rikiishi, and Terayama's proposal to Kōdansha was approved enthusiastically.[65] The date was set for March 24, 1970, and the event would take place on the sixth floor of Kōdansha headquarters (Figure 3.1). The event was advertised in *Shonen magajin* itself, alongside the continuing serialization of *Ashita no Jō*. The organizers had planned for five hundred, but over seven hundred people attended to watch an actual Buddhist priest perform the death rite and to see the Tokyo Kid Brothers reenact the fateful bout. Judging from photographs, the audience was a mix of elementary-school students and college-aged men, and they did line up at an altar complete with flowers, candles, incense, and a large image of Rikiishi to pay their respects.[66] The newspapers reacted with headlines like "Predictably Manga, an Expression of Discontent with the Times" (*Asahi shinbun*), "They Know It's a Joke—Is This the Mood of the Era?" (*Tōkyō shinbun*), and "An Unprecedented Manga Funeral!" (*Sankei shinbun*) (See Figure 3.2.). Terayama's support for a project like this is consistent with his efforts to demonstrate that the path between imagination and reality is not

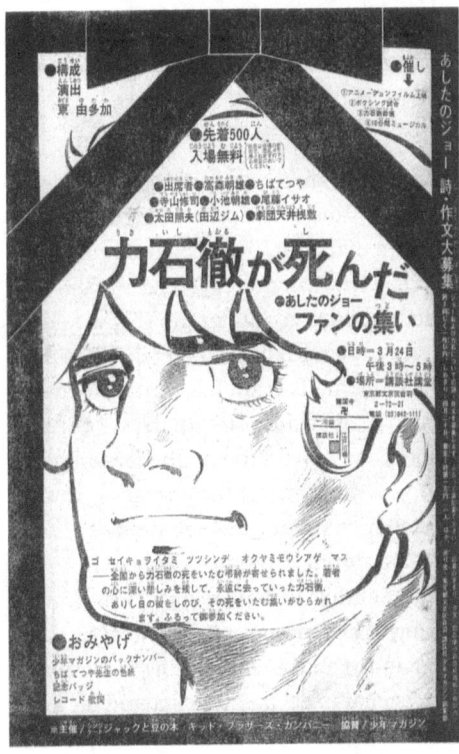

Figure 3.1. A full-page ad in the weekly Shōnen magajin for a funeral service to be held at Kōdansha headquarters for Rikiishi Tōru, the rival boxer in the manga series Ashita no Jō *(*Tomorrow's Jō*, 1968–73)*

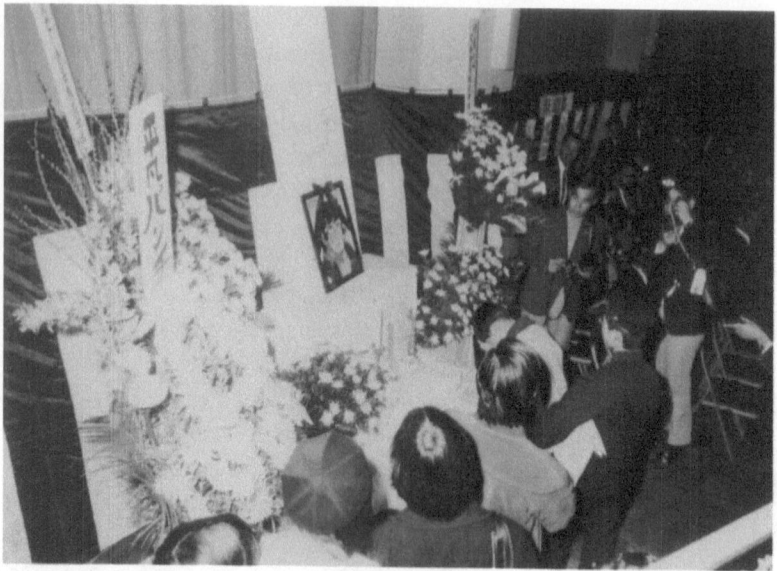

Figure 3.2. A mix of teenagers and college students line up to pay their last respects to Rikiishi Tōru at the funeral service at Kōdansha headquarters. Terayama helped organize the event. Courtesy of Kujō Kyōko and Terayama World.

a unidirectional flow in which real events are filtered through consciousness and reworked into fictional texts. This is fiction moving concretely into the real and life integrating, more than imitating, art. Terayama again reminds us that real events are conceived of and executed within consciousnesses flowing with a mixture of fiction and truth. This would be further exemplified exactly one week after Rikiishi's funeral, when nine radical college students from the Red Army Faction hijacked a Japan Airlines domestic flight and then forced it, at swordpoint, to deliver them to Pyongyang, which it did, and where they remain today. The leader of this so-called Yodo-gō incident (Yodo was the name of the airplane), Tamiya Takamaro, concluded his public statement about this underdog's victory during the hijacking by famously proclaiming, "We are *Ashita no Jō*."[67]

Paralleling this process of documenting instances of fiction moving into reality was Terayama's clustering of extemporaneous cultural forms—jazz, boxing, gambling, stuttering, and graffiti—and linking them to the enhanced sensation of presence. His characters are not centered on a diachronic timeline; they gain no self-awareness from knowing their position within a historical lineage. It is the crosscut in time—the experience of synchronicity—that grounds them and provides a base for their experience of being. The broader project may be to fictionalize and shrink both the future and the past so that the present becomes bigger and more real, an inhabitable space.

The commonsense understanding of the present moment as an infinitely brief, one-dimensional point crushed between the monoliths of past and future is flipped on its head here. The structure is inverted so that the present expands to become the only experienced (and therefore real) form of time, overwhelming both past and future. By severing the present from the web of diachronic causalities—all the deterministic causes and effects that generate the notion of fate—Terayama can zoom in on moments that demonstrate the unpredictability of experience by highlighting ad-libbed forms. It is there, in the three-dimensional present, that we find potential for a true sensation of presence—one produced not in contrast to death as biological death but in alignment and solidarity with life conceived as mobility, as visceral consciousness of being in the now.

CHAPTER 4

Deinstitutionalizing Theater and Film

THE CONSPICUOUS AMOUNT OF ATTENTION paid to the relationship between sex and violence in the late 1960s might best be understood as an attempt to expose the erotics of war as a first step toward deconstructing that relationship. Too much emphasis, however, has been placed on simply repeating the link between Eros and Thanatos. Social realism as a tactic is always vulnerable to being misinterpreted as a statement on the immutables of human nature, whereas satire or nonrealist forms of representation are often clearer in their critique of aberrant psychology or society gone wrong. The focus within cultural production on sadism, something we might paraphrase as eroticized violation, may have resonated in the 1960s with the presence of American troops in Vietnam and the Soviets in Czechoslovakia, but we must admit that sadistic narratives failed in the greater project of decoupling sex from violence and, in fact, may have served to further concretize and naturalize that association.

While Shibusawa Tatsuhiko was fighting an obscenity charge on his translations of the Marquis de Sade's writings, while Ōe Kenzaburō and Mishima Yukio were writing sex-and-violence fiction, and while Wakamatsu Kōji and other "pink film" directors were shooting sex-equals-violence films, Terayama Shūji began an inquiry into the dialectical libidinal economy of Leopold von Sacher-Masoch. Where de Sade eroticized the breaking of social and personal contracts, Masoch eroticized the production and strict maintenance of a contract between two free subjects. The masochism of *Venus im Pelz* (*Venus in Furs*) is not so much a masochism of whips and chains as it is a testing of the limits of contractual agreement. Masochism, argues Gilles Deleuze, is a libidinal system fundamentally incompatible with sadism—there can be no mixing of the two into a coherent system of sadomasochism because the sadist severs contracts and establishes a new set of laws while the masochist deinstitutionalizes and sets loose calcified social relations by moving from a model based on the inherited laws to one based on individual contracts negotiated only between the parties impacted by them.[1] Sadism appears revolutionary in its destructiveness but it reinstitutionalizes a new order even more brutal than the old. Masochism, on the other hand, might be seen to represent a postrevolutionary rebuilding of the social contract on a synchronic rather than diachronic model. Terayama produced two texts that read well against these ideas of masochism and deinstitutionalism: a 1967 play called *Kegawa no Marii* (Marie in furs) and the 1971 film *Sho o suteyo machi e deyō* (*Throw Out Your Books, Let's Hit the Streets*). This chapter will explore these two projects in depth in order to root out the particular set of institutions Terayama targeted for intervention as well as the counterproposals he suggests to replace them.

Masoch's *Venus im Pelz* was translated into Japanese (from an English version) by the novelist Satō Haruo in 1957 as *Kegawa o kita Viinasu* (lit. "The Venus who wore fur"). Terayama's title for Tenjō Sajiki's third play, *Kegawa no Marii*, certainly his most famous makes direct reference in its title to the locus classicus of masochism itself. The play was in fact translated into German for performance in Frankfurt as *Marie im Pelz*.[2] Terayama's play does not follow Masoch's narrative at all, however, and the reference may have been mainly a joke. The protagonist is a transvestite named Marie, played by the transgendered lounge singer Maruyama Akihiro (now Miwa Akihiro), who opens the play by having his legs shaved by a servant while he sits in a bathtub in the center of the stage. Never in the play is there a fur coat like the one Wanda taunted Severin with in Masoch's text, so we are left to conclude that the "fur" here is that on the human animal himself and that the removal of the fur from Marie's legs is what creates a woman from the man.

The main narrative is the story of an eighteen-year-old boy named Kinya, who is locked up in the apartment he shares with Marie, who insists on being called "mother." Marie treats Kinya as though he were half his age, claiming to be sheltering him from the ugliness of the outside world. Kinya is fully indoctrinated and nonresistant, dallying his time away in fantasies, occasionally chasing butterflies (indoors) that his mother has painted to resemble exotic species, and pressing them in books to expand his already large collection. Marie, for her part, flirts with a sailor. Conflict begins when the neighbor girl stops by while Marie is away and she tries to explain all the things he is missing by staying inside. As she moves to kiss him, he attacks her, strangling her to death with the same ruthlessness as he dealt to his butterflies. He escapes the apartment briefly, but returns dutifully to Marie in the final scene.

The narrative is a spin on a play that Terayama admired, Arthur Kopit's *Oh Dad, Poor Dad, Mamma's Hung You in the Closet and I'm Feelin' So Sad* (written in 1959, performed in London in 1961 and Off Broadway in New York in 1962).[3] It was Kopit's debut, and in his case, the boy's mother, Rosepettle, was genetically female and kept her son Jonathan locked up in their hotel room in Havana—he has collections of stamps, coins, and books, but there are no butterflies; what becomes a carp in Terayama's play was a piranha in Kopit's, and Terayama omits reference to the dead, stuffed father in the closet and the monstrous, constantly growing Venus flytraps on the veranda featured in the original play. The central problem of both narratives is the logic driving the boy's acceptance of his imprisonment and his full assimilation into the disciplinary regime—a nearly perfect example of Gramsci's understanding of hegemony. The following is Jonathan's defense of his house arrest to the girl next door in Kopit's play: "No! You-you don't understand. It's not what you think. She doesn't lock the door to kaka-keep me in, which would be malicious. She . . . locks the door so I can't get out, which is for my own good and therefore . . . beneficent."[4] Jonathan's degree of indoctrination reflects his mother's level of faith in the righteousness of her decision, and it does have its own internal logic. Jonathan's mother begins dating "The Commodore," a wealthy man with a huge yacht, who empathizes with her overprotected son, to which she replies:

And I feel sorrier for you! For you are *nothing*! While my son
is mine. His skin is the color of fresh snow, his voice is like the
music of angels, and his mind is pure. For he is safe, Mr. Roseabove, and it is *I* who have saved him. Saved him from the world
beyond that door. The world of you. The world of his father. A
world waiting to devour those who trust in it; those who love. A
world vicious under the hypocrisy of kindness, ruthless under the
falseness of a smile. Well, go on, Mr. Roseabove. Leave my room
and enter your world again—your sex-driven, dirt-washed waste of
cannibals eating each other up while they pretend they're kissing.
Go, Mr. Roseabove, enter your blind world of darkness. My son
shall have only light![5]

The narrative is a spoof of security overdone and concludes with an interesting twist. The neighbor girl who seems to be encouraging Jonathan to break away from the bonds of his mother and escape into the world turns out to be motivated by just as monopolistic an attachment: "Forget about your mother. She's gone . . . Come and let me keep you mine. Mine to love when I want, mine to kiss when I want, mine to have when I want. Mine. All mine."[6] Her focus is so intent that she carries on even as the stuffed corpse of his father falls twice out of the closet right onto her lap. The strangulation may not have been overly pathological, then, with Jonathan trapped on both sides by women demanding absolute control of him (something both of the women conceived of as "love").

Terayama writes about Kopit's play in the early 1960s, well before the founding of the Tenjō Sajiki, as part of what would become one of his most representative books. The text, a suggestion to run away from metaphorical "homes" of all types, is now known as *Iede no susume* (In praise of running away from home), a play off of Fukuzawa Yukichi's famous *Gakumon no susume* (In praise of learning) from the mid-1870s. Terayama's project started as a half-year serialized column (July through December 1962) in a high school and university student–targeted bilingual newspaper called the *Student Times* (published by the *Japan Times*), which was repackaged and lengthened into a 1963 book called *Gendai no seishunron* (On contemporary youth) before being rereleased under the title *Iede no susume* in 1972. The very first installment in the newspaper series describes the basic plot of Kopit's play: "This drama begins with an only son and his mother on a world tour staying in a hotel room in Cuba, but because she's afraid to let her beautiful boy see the 'ugly world filled with vulgarity,' she keeps him locked up in the room of their hotel."[7] Terayama's text, both in the newspaper and as a book, is agitation for relinquishing (rather than attacking) comfortable but tightly controlled conditions over the lure of security found in the status quo—this is a liberation politics based on exodus. As such, it is primarily interested in institutions and in the competing forces of institutionalization and deinstitutionalization—particularly in how the institution of the family is replicated in municipal, regional, and national structures to fully integrate a citizenry. Terayama seems interested in unwinding institutionalized society (the *kokka*, or "nation family") not from the top, by dismantling the structure of nations, but from below, by dissolving the family with its internal class structure and set of prescribed responsibilities. The family or, rather, the family system (*ie seido*) is the focus of his attention—but it is important to remember that this is primarily metaphorical, speaking to all family structured institutions ("home" [*ie*] appears in quotation marks throughout the text). The basic proposition is for disinterested abandonment rather than violent destruction, since any attack carries with it a strong trace of attachment—the object of attack must be destroyed for fear that its existence might lure the rebel back. Abandonment implies the opposite: runaways demonstrate their independence from that which they relinquish by walking away. Yet Terayama recognizes that the unwinding of one institution is no guarantee against the rise of another in its place: "It is, of course, an error to examine the 'home' only from the perspective of the vertical axis between parents and children. The reason being that the thing which begins disintegrating is a 'home' created by the two parents. Even as humans are being liberated from an institution (whether matriarchal or patriarchal) they begin assigning roles to other people and transitioning into another institution—which is a flawed form of thought, and the deformation that results from that mistake is extending outward into every part of the world."[8] Deinstutionalization initially done in the name of classlessness is too often betrayed by the reestablishment of new class-based structures in the place of the old. It is here, then, that Terayama's inquiry into the nature of institutionalism and the invocation of Masoch in *Kegawa no Marii* cross paths. Gilles Deleuze makes a useful distinction between masochism and sadism in his analysis of *Venus in Furs*, phrased in terms of institutions and contracts:

> We are no longer in the presence of a torturer seizing upon a victim and enjoying her all the more because she is unconsenting and unpersuaded. We are dealing instead with a victim in search of a torturer and who needs to educate, persuade, and conclude an alliance with the torturer to realize the strangest of schemes. This is why advertisements are part of the language of masochism while they have no place in true sadism, and why the masochist draws up contracts while the sadist abominates and destroys them. The sadist is in need of institutions, the masochist of contractual relations.[9]

Deleuze further delineates the masochist's contract from the sadist's institution: "The contract presupposes in principle the free consent of the contracting parties and determines between them a system of reciprocal rights and duties; it cannot affect a third party and is valid for a limited period. Institutions, by contrast, determine a long-term state of affairs which is both involuntary and inalienable; it establishes a power or an authority which takes effect against a third party."[10] A transition between institutionalism and contract-based relationships, then, is also a shift from a diachronic system of rights and duties to a synchronic one in which social relationships are renegotiated by the members of that society itself rather than by their forebears. This is a shift seen before in Terayama's work, and it may be the most critical to understanding the thrust of his greater project. At every opportunity he urged an adjustment in perspective from chronological flows toward cross-sections of the present.

The central problem of both Kopit's and Terayama's plays concerns the way in which the mother creates an authoritative institution out of the imprisonment of her son while keeping him convinced that he is there under his own will. This means that these are plays about the disguising of institutions as contract-based systems. This is further complicated by Marie's transvestism, a conspicuous assertion of the persuasive and performative (and therefore contractual) nature of gender.[11] Marie operates within a masochistic mode in terms of her identity and in relations with those outside of the family, but in a sadistic mode within it. She is a sadist who has manipulated her victim into conceiving of himself as a masochist, which may seem a stable system. But the moment he fully accepts the situation is also the moment that the erotic crumbles, for it needs resistance to uphold it (violation equals pleasure). Kinya and Jonathan are both trapped in the apartment but not in the way that they seem—we might expect them to resist, but resistance is precisely what their sadistic mothers desire (to confirm the violation), and so their strongest form of effectual opposition to that desire appears to be complete sublimation. They fight back by not fighting back at all—perpetuating the stasis and demonstrating nicely how a sadistic power system maintains both its own power and the logic of sadism as a structure for maintaining order. The better option, which neither boy seriously considers, is to simply sneak away alone without a fight—to become a runaway. A sustainable relationship between mother and son within this structure requires a cycle of resistance, counterresistance, and restabilization of self-discipline.

In Terayama's play, Marie disciplines Kinya with a tape-recorded message that entertains, instructs, and gives orders while she is out of the apartment. Her voice lectures him first on educational institutions:

There are lots of different kinds of schools, my boy! It's not just those buildings with blackboards that you ride your bicycle to carrying all those textbooks. Reformatories can be schools, and bars can be classrooms.

Your mother's school was a prison. A school of old, nasty concrete, and my classmates were murderers, pickpockets, and thieves! But I didn't go there looking for glory or adventure, it was for serious education.

At a normal school they teach you to be good. That amounts to saying, "All you do is lie, so force yourself to be truthful." But what I learned in prison was the opposite. "All you do is tell the truth, so force yourself to lie."[12]

This link between educational and correctional facilities resonates with Erving Goffman's description of "total institutions," where the social spheres typically separated into spaces for work, play, and sleep—with different authorities in each realm—are conflated here into a single system under a single authority.[13] Marie's control over Kinya is totalitarian, but the situation does not fit the second part of Goffman's description, that "each phase of the member's daily activity is carried on in the immediate company of a large batch of others, all of whom are treated alike and required to do the same thing together."[14] And yet the crux of this second requirement may not be the mass nature of daily activity so much as the lack of any counterexamples to the disciplinary regime. Without contrast, the totality maintains its logic whether the institutionalized number one or one hundred. Goffman goes on to make the strange claim that "the formation of households provides a structural guarantee that total institutions will not be without resistance."[15] He is profamily but antiasylum. But in the case of Marie and Kinya, or Rosepettle and Jonathan, the household *is* the total institution. Terayama may be effectively challenging Goffman's solution to the problem of total institutions by asking if the proposed structure of resistance is not just as totalitarian as the institution it seeks to displace. Is a strong household just as imprisoning as an asylum? Is reinstitutionalization, rather than deinstitutionalization, a true solution or only a superficial changing of the guard?

A text that may resonate more closely with *Kegawa no Marii* is Wilhelm Reich's *The Sexual Revolution*, which Terayama would make repeated and specific reference to starting in the late 1960s.[16] Reich's theory was that mass sexual repression enforced through a socially compulsory system of heterosexual monogamy and the denial of sexual self-determination to minors creates a widespread neurosis as well as a mysticism that maintains and regenerates that repressive system. He credits this repression with everything from pedophilia, prostitution, and rape, to fascism and Stalinism. The only escape, Reich claims, is a fundamental revolution in sexual ethics and a rewriting of the sexual economy itself. Committed relationships would demonstrate their commitment not through institution-based certificates issued by state authorities but by loyalty within a mutually agreed-upon contractual arrangement including the possibility of sexual freedom beyond that relationship. Reich argues that the existence of sexual enforcement is evidence against its claim to the naturalness of that being enforced—that "natural" sexuality would never require a system of restrictions.[17]

Goffman and Reich's ideas can open up Terayama's play in two ways. First, there is a parody of the "structural guarantee" against total institutions that Goffman finds in the household: Marie's apartment is a prison. Second, and this is where Terayama's play parts with Kopit, we find an inversion of the typical compulsory heterosexual upbringing of children by heterosexual parents. Marie forestalls the gendering of Kinya until the final scene of the play once Kinya has returned after escaping into the streets. The scene could have been staged in a lighthearted and parodic way, but Miwa Akihiro's performance, overplaying the adoring voice of a mother dolling up her genetically male child in dresses and bows, came off as chillingly sinister:

> Look, you've come back. (*To the servant*) Just as I told you he would. (*Happily*) You've been a bad boy, making a mess in your room and not cleaning it up. You must do as you're told or there'll be no more butterflies. (*Puts her arm around him and sits him down on the bathtub*) Kinya, I bought you a wonderful present in town today. (*Takes out a wig*) From now on you're going to be a very beautiful little girl. (*Places the wig on Kinya's head*) Look! It suits you perfectly, just as I thought! (*Prepares lipstick, the theme song begins playing quietly*) Look up at me now, that's it. (*Begins making up his face, the boy gradually changes into a girl*). Kinya, you're going to be the most beautiful girl in the whole world! (*Curtain closes slowly as Marie laughs while the doll's features come into relief*).[18]

The power of this scene is in the implications of its social inverse: the forcible gendering and heterosexualization of children within the institution of the family. This is simultaneously a defense of transvestism on libertarian grounds and an indictment of the top-down social institution of gender formulation that we are accustomed to as the status quo.

This call for social reflection on gendering is paired with theatrical reflexivity in *Kegawa no Marii*. While Kinya is listening to Marie's lecture on the tape, there is a clatter at the window of the apartment that Marie seems, impossibly, to hear, saying, "Someone's here. Stop the tape!" Kinya does as he is told and the neighbor girl pops in through the window to convince Kinya to run away with her. The moment is jarring, though, calling attention to the scripted nature of the play in a way that might not be possible without the use of prerecorded lines delivered via a recorded-sound apparatus. Our suspension of disbelief is forcibly shattered in quasi-Brechtian fashion through this moment of reflexivity, but then, just as quickly, illusionism reincarnates itself in its previous framework. "Someone's here. Stop the tape!" is particularly important because it acts to disassemble the institution of realism into which the play's audience will always drift without these reminders. And yet even with these moments of reflexivity, the reinstitutionalization process begins immediately following realism's breakdown, recalling Terayama's comment on the error of reformulating institutions immediately after our liberation from them. Suspension of disbelief returns, again and again.

Once the girl has asked Kinya to leave the apartment, Marie's tape starts up again on its own: "Get out, whore! Harlot! Make a pass at my little boy and you'll never know the end of it!" Marie's spirit returns to break again the illusion and to make the play simultaneously more real and more fictional. The things happening on stage cannot occur in everyday life; they contradict the material properties of the technology of recorded sound—and yet the play is being performed by very real people using conspicuously materially bound technologies. We, as an audience, are of a split consciousness at this point, aware that we are watching a fabrication but suddenly entering a more truly fictional text, one in which the fundamental nature is becoming unclear. What had been an exaggerated but still plausible narrative shifts here toward the fantastic. Kinya turns off the tape recorder and begs the girl to leave, but she wants to stay and take a stand against Marie: "Let's wait here, together, and watch that old bag lose her composure. Life is about calling the bully's bluff—without lies, the truth goes away; without masks, you can never see someone's real face."[19] The dual presence of truth and fiction, and their codeterminative relationship, is right here on the surface of the play at the very moment that the dual nature (plausible and fantastic) of the play is being reconstituted and enhanced with these tape tricks. Marie does return, but as a ghost with her angered voice booming from all corners of the apartment—her disembodied voice is at once impossible and yet still integrated into the narrative as it interacts with Kinya and the girl.

This libidinal drive to draw fiction into reality or reality into fiction whenever either is getting too close to dominance is something Terayama wrote on in other places around this time, including his analysis of the motives driving nineteen-year-old Nagayama Norio to go on a shooting spree between October and November 1968, killing two security guards and two taxi drivers in Tokyo, Hakodate, and Nagoya: "There are no means of investigating his motives other than pursuing the reason he sought 'theater' within reality, just as we seek reality within theater. However, finding reality within theater is a design for happiness, whereas we can say that 'seeking theater within reality' signals a loss of imagination."[20] This is not a process simply of drawing elements of reality into a fictional realm but of seeking a clearer view of reality from the standpoint of fiction—of exiting the real in order to get a clean look at it from a viable vantage point. This recognition of fiction's codeterminative relationship with truth, and therefore of theater's codeterminative relationship with everyday life, constituted Terayama's theory of performance, that is, his dramaturgy. The art critic Hariu Ichirō puts it in the following terms: "The core of Terayama's ideas is the effort to find a point of departure for emotion to flow once we realize that there is no hometown we need to return to, that there is no home at all. At that point reality can be seen as a type of fiction, or alternatively, we try to find a way to recapture reality from the side of fiction—that was Terayama's unique methodology."[21] There is an urgency here to recognize that the effort to purge fiction from reality or reality from fiction is not only an impossible task but also a volatile and potentially dangerous one.

Terayama's metaphorical project of deinstitutionalizing lived reality occurred at several important real institutions in Tokyo. The first of the Tenjō Sajiki plays, *Aomori-ken no semushi otoko* (The hunchback of Aomori prefecture) was performed at the Sōgetsu Art Center, the nominal home to the Teshigahara family of ikebana (flower arranging) artists and instructors but that also functioned as an important site for contemporary fine art and performance through the 1960s. Teshigahara Hiroshi's interest in filmmaking led to the use of the hall for a number of film festivals and screenings, and it served as a gathering place and performance venue for artists such as composer Takemitsu Tōru, novelist and playwright Abe Kōbō (both of whom collaborated with Teshigahara on film projects), poet Tanikawa Shuntarō, Fluxus artist Yoko Ono, critic and filmmaker Donald Richie, poet and composer John Cage, and others. Terayama was a fringe member of the clique and performed several poetry readings at the Sōgetsu Art Center during the early 1960s. When Terayama's troupe formed in 1967, with Yokoo Tadanori designing posters and stage sets and a group of amateur actors and a stage director (Higashi Yutaka) fresh from Waseda University, the Tenjō Sajiki debuted at Sōgetsu, likely the most important institution in Japan at the time supporting the contemporary arts.

The troupe's second play, *Ōyama debuko no hanzai* (The fat girl of Ōyama's crime), was performed at another landmark institution—one of the last remaining vaudeville houses in Tokyo, the Suehiro-tei in Shinjuku. This time the theme of the play was matched to the venue—it starred a fat lady and a circus-like cast and played to packed houses for its run of four days. Seats in the upper balcony (*tenjō sajiki* in Japanese) were discounted. The troupe's producer, Kujō Kyōko (a former actress and, at that time, Terayama's wife), reports calling the Suehiro-tei daily for weeks to persuade them to rent out their theater for a play, a practice without precedent and one that has never been repeated, particularly after the rowdy mobs broke the ticket-booth window as they jostled in line for seats.[22]

Kegawa no Marii was the third of the Tenjō Sajiki plays, and it was performed not on a typical stage but on the narrow strip of space in front of the screen at the Shinjuku Bunka Art Theater, the flagship for films distributed by the Art Theatre Guild (ATG) and a central institution for Tokyo counterculture. The ATG, a subsidiary of Tōhō, was run by a group of film critics granted relative autonomy in selecting, promoting, and distributing art films to seven ATG cinemas in Japan. They formally began coproducing domestic films in 1968—the first three of Terayama's feature films were granted half of their budget from ATG funds and they were screened at ATG cinemas. Shinjuku Bunka was emblematic, then, of the new, quasi-independent art institutions supportive of (or at least catering to) young, baby-boomer era countercultural trends during the late 1960s. This is where students went to see Godard's and Ōshima's films. It was half a block away from Hanazono Shrine where Kara Jūrō pitched his red tent for the first plays of the Japanese underground theater movement, around the corner from the gay quarter, and down the street from Beheiren's "folk guerillas" who were singing songs against the Vietnam War in Japan's busiest train station.

The slippage between fiction and reality at work in *Kegawa no Marii*, then, was enhanced by the institution in which it was performed. To the audience, most of whom would have been used to watching films in Shinjuku Bunka, this play was a truer kind of live action and a challenge to the perceived reality of cinema.[23] This may have been conceived as a film performed in the home of filmed plays. Such a theatrical affront to the reality effect of cinema might first seem to claim relative realism for theater over the illusionism of celluloid. But the juxtaposition, paradoxically, also cannot help calling attention to the extreme fictionality of theater itself. These are real people on stage, after all, pretending to be something they are not, saying words divorced from their true character, and moving in ways willed but not fully free. How could things be any more purely fictional? Film's mediation between the profilmic moment (actors in front of the camera) and the audience's reception adds a layer of documentation—we watch a truthful capture of the purely fictional act of theater. Terayama's mantra, and his fascination with the potential of theater, was that this description of the nonreality of actors on the stage is an almost perfect description of everyday life. This type of fiction *is* reality for most people; we are alienated from our own characters, from our words, and from our actions—reciting lines and performing acts according to the script of our various institutions (e.g., jobs, family, etc.).

The interaction between film and theater in the Tenjō Sajiki project can be traced back further than *Kegawa no Marii*, however. Terayama named the troupe after the Japanese title for Marcel Carné's *Les enfants du paradis* (*Children of Paradise*, 1945), which was released in Japan as *Tenjō sajiki no hitobito* (The people in the upper balcony). Carné's film is itself a film about theater—specifically the bohemian theater of the Boulevard of Crime outside Paris in the decades preceding the revolts of 1848. The free exchange between actors and audience, near anarchy on the streets, and the prerevolutionary spirit of the masses in the upper cheap seats with whom the actors most closely identify and for whom they perform: these elements form a nexus of culture that Terayama likely sought to evoke and recultivate by naming the troupe after this film. It is possible to trace a set of possible direct influences—the protagonist Baptiste alternates between masculine and feminine personae much like Marie—but those specific links are less useful for understanding Terayama's project than broader ones regarding medium crossover and its relationship to reflexivity. Much of *Les enfants du paradis* has to do with Baptiste's mime acts on stage within an otherwise talkative play, and he inevitably steals the show with his masterfully expressive gestures. Presented in the medium of film, this might be read as some sort of comment on the exaggerated expressivity of silent films once contextualized by the talkies, or it could be a warning against letting the silent form go extinct. But it also shows the fascination with restricted perception to be something that predates the cinema— mime acts started well before the silents. The will toward silent film may date back to the mimes, or even farther back to Diderot and his effort to access gestured communication by covering his ears at the theater. Carné's film tells us something about our assumptions about film and theater in the course of this interaction—Terayama's film-referencing theater and theater-linked films will likely do the same.

As a play performed in a cinema, *Kegawa no Marii* functionally removed the mediation of camera and projector, offering audiences true "live-action." The performativity of gender that forms the core theme of the play—particularly the satire of sadistic gendering of children by parents within a totalitarian family structure, and the call for gender to be recognized as a contract-based prerogative of the individual—also comments on the institutionalization of our assumptions about theater and film. These themes and problems would be carried over to Terayama's first feature film, *Sho o suteyo machi e deyō,* a film that when read against the Tenjō Sajiki's theater projects of the same period should reveal more about the process of deinstitutionalization.

Throw Out Your Books, Let's Hit the Streets

In April 1971, around four years after the *Kegawa no Marii* performances in Shinjuku Bunka, Terayama's first major feature-length film was screened in that same cinema. Titled *Sho o suteyo machi e deyō,* it was one of the "ten million yen" ATG coproductions (around US$28,000 in 1971), each of which received half of that already rock-bottom budget and were expected to pull together the other five million independently. The film is a collage-like rock musical that traces the coming of age of its young male protagonist, Kitagawa Eimei (played by Sasaki Eimei), within the bohemian counterculture of Shinjuku circa 1970. Eimei's family is already somewhat bohemian: he is being raised by his petty-thief grandmother and his delinquent father (who owes him money). Eimei in turn looks after his sister, Setsuko, who the family worries has developed a romantic attachment to her pet rabbit. Eimei tries to join a soccer team but never gets promoted above janitorial duties, and his sexual initiation with the team's patron prostitute is a disaster. Eimei's grandmother arranges to have Setsuko's rabbit killed in order to force her to socialize, which sends her wandering distraught into the soccer team's locker room where she is gang-raped by the entire team while Eimei tries in vain at the door to stop them. All of this is intercut with footage of street theater and "happenings" from Shinjuku: video versions of homosexual wanted ads, hippies smoking marijuana on the streets, fantasies of human-powered airplanes, a manifesto on stuttering, graffiti everywhere, and other seemingly random excerpts from Tokyo's counterculture. By the end, Eimei has become confrontational and assertive, his sister has fallen in love with her rapist and moved in with him and his girlfriend, and Eimei's plot to liberate himself from his family is foiled when the ramen cart he bought to put his father back to work turns out to have been stolen.

Sho o suteyo machi e deyō compares well with *Kegawa no Marii* in several ways. The core narrative concerns the emancipation of a young man, particularly the process of recognizing the manner of his entrapment and the following effort to escape. In both cases, they ultimately fail: Kinya returns to Marie obediently, and Eimei is dragged away in the final scene by police officers. Both narratives are driven by audience curiosity regarding the sexual or gender ambiguity of these young, male protagonists. To these thematic parallels we must add a direct quotation of the play within the film: Miwa Akihiro is again in the bathtub demanding to be shaven (this time his underarms rather than his legs)—in this case, when Eimei visits a queer brothel in an apparent fantasy near the end (Figure 4.1). But *Kegawa no Marii* was ultimately about a masochistic alternative to sadistic power structures—which is to say, about a deinstitutionalization rather than a reinstitutionalization of power. Does the continuity between *Kegawa no Marii* and *Sho o suteyo machi e deyō* stretch beyond these links—the parallel narratives, the crossovers from theater to film, and the direct quotation of the play within the film—all the way to this larger discourse on the problem of institutionalism? If Terayama's engagement with the problem of institutionalism continues here—particularly the problem of diffusing a calcified structure of laws into a new set of negotiable contracts—there is an exciting possibility that this film could speak to issues of power and stability within an antiestablishment institution such as the ATG itself.

Rather than simply charging the ATG with hypocrisy, Terayama's work seems to ask whether film could still exist in a deinstitutionalized form or if its material dependencies will always require change to be a reinstitutionalization of some kind. The ATG was an institution established in opposition to the larger institution of commercial narrative film, which was already in serious decline in Japan by the time the ATG began officially coproducing domestic films in 1968 with Ōshima's *Kōshikei* (Death by hanging). But as a subsidiary of one of the surviving major studios, Tōhō, it had little potential for completely overthrowing the system of film production and distribution, since any substantive resistance would have gotten the entire project cancelled. The available options appeared to be hedging bets and hoping for reform of the studios by reinstitutionalizing

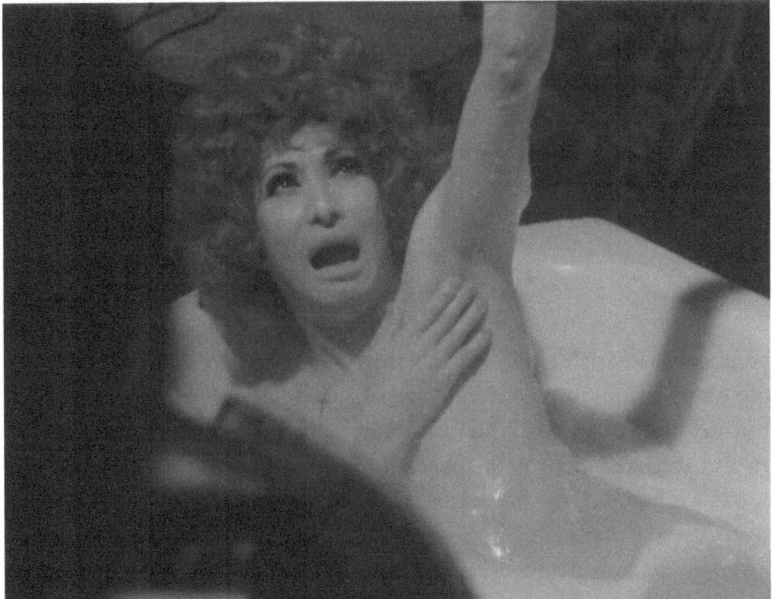

Figure 4.1. Miwa Akihiro is a prostitute named Jigoku (Hell) in the film Sho o suteyo machi e deyō *(Throw Out Your Books, Let's Hit the Streets, 1971), a twisted reprise of his role in the play* Kegawa no Marii *(Marie in furs, 1967).*

them on ATG's art-house model (conscious of dependence on the support of the profit-seeking majors and their investors) or abandoning the existing system of production and distribution altogether and starting anew with full independence from both those existing systems. These alternatives sparked a lively discourse among filmmakers, and one way to read *Sho o suteyo machi e deyō* is as a contribution to this debate.[24]

The film version of *Sho o suteyo machi e deyō* was the final installment of a larger project that had first been a book done as a collaboration between Terayama and the graphic designer Yokoo Tadanori and later became a Tenjō Sajiki play. The book version of *Sho o suteyo machi e deyō* was published first in February 1967, and another printing was timed with the release of the film in 1971. Its physical appearance is striking: the dust jacket is printed on both sides with Yokoo's trademarked rising sun and disembodied mouth on the front, a blond woman topless and lactating on the back, women's underwear as if on an invisible person on the front flap, an image of Terayama encased within layers of decorative frames on the back flap, and the Beatles on all four panels of the opposite side. The cover itself has yet another design with a jockey sitting on a horse skeleton straddling train tracks, on the back is a photograph from behind of a nude, blond woman standing in water.[25] The table of contents is modeled on monthly magazines but does not begin until page twenty-two, following two vignettes. Cheap newsprint is used throughout, with sections near the beginning and end printed in red ink, probably to simulate the look and feel of *manga* weeklies like *Shōnen magajin*. Drawings, newspaper clippings, photographs, and mock advertisements decorate most pages. There is a flipbook cartoon in the upper left margin that shows a countdown from the number seventy down to zero followed by a finger poking a woman's nipple, which then triggers an explosion that shatters the entire planet to bits. A half-sized, glossy blue insert appears midway through the book with a brief autobiography of Terayama. Text is in one, two, or three columns on the page, suddenly shifting its orientation in one section to force readers to rotate the book ninety degrees, but then back to normal ten pages later. The content of the pieces ranges from "introductory" instruction manuals on delinquency, jazz, and running away from home (selections from the *Iede no susume* essays), to sex, sports, profiles of entertainers, and neomythology. Which is to say that it is not "about" anything at all, and that any attempts to read this text looking for a core theme would face not only a realization that there is none but also (and more importantly) a realization that we have been conditioned to unify texts no matter how fragmentary they appear. The entire project could be described as a foregrounding of bookmaking style itself as well as an exposure of the rigid uniformity within most printed matter. When rereleased in paperback, Yokoo's embellishments and the range of printing styles were removed, leaving only Terayama's collection of essays in a tidy and uniform format—and more than missing the point in a gross distortion of the original. At its core the original publication was a conspicuous treatment of the materiality rather than transparency of words as distributed through the printing industry, and a showcase for the eclectic style both Terayama and Yokoo were using at the time.

The theatrical version of *Sho o suteyo machi e deyō* was a loosely scripted play that featured teenage poets reading their poems on stage—it was conceived as an experiment in *stage verité*. Sasaki Eimei, the lead in the film, was one of the young poets recruited to perform in the play, which was performed in Tokyo during August and September 1968 and then again in March 1969 before moving to Nagoya in October 1969, Sapporo in January 1970, and Ashiya in April 1970. The play shifted as new poets were constantly integrated, and it drew material freely from Terayama's *Iede no susume* essays.[26] The script found in Terayama's collected plays, then, must be considered just one manifestation of the performance, which was willfully designed to change with time, exaggerating theater's assurance that each performance be slightly different. By launching these high schoolers onto the stage and into the public eye, Terayama was fast-tracking them into the entertainment industry, bypassing the universities altogether. This position is consistent with his argument against the university system as discussed with the young poet Kishigami Daisaku (see chapter 1) and with Marie's lecture to Kinya in *Kegawa no Marii* when she lists off prisons and bars as alternatives to the classroom. At a moment when much of the student movement was sparked by tuition hikes and overenrollment, Terayama was promoting the abandonment of university education (including the personal and family debts incurred and the expectation of mainstream employment after graduation) in exchange for immediate participation in an independent, bohemian movement in the arts. The one fully scripted scene in the stage version of *Sho o suteyo machi e deyō*'s narrative speaks directly to this problem and merits close attention.

In this scene, the two characters that appear amid the poems in the theatrical version of *Sho o suteyo machi e deyō* are a high school student

preparing for the university entrance examinations and his Japanese teacher. We first encounter them as they sit in adjacent stalls in the bathroom,
talking about reading on the toilet:

> TEACHER: All I want is to read to my heart's content someplace
> where I'm not interrupted by life . . . There is nothing more
> pleasant that "reading in the toilet" in our modern rushed soci-
> ety, even from the standpoint of time efficiency.
> STUDENT: They should just go ahead and put bookshelves in the
> stalls.
> TEACHER: Exactly, I agree. It's the Ministry of Education's duty to
> fill all public restrooms with books! (*laughs*)
> STUDENT: It is an education issue, isn't it. But with that plan the
> more constipated you are the better your chance for joining the
> intelligentsia![27]

Satire of the joys of social atomization misconceived as independence
appears throughout Terayama's work. Reading here stands in broadly for
antisocial introversion. In a later scene, the teacher is literally walling himself into a room of books, using them like bricks. The student approaches
him and asks if he has read anything interesting lately and then uses the
typical word for "book" (*hon*), which is quickly corrected by the teacher
to the snootier "volume" (*shomotsu*)—used in an abbreviated form in
the play's title. The title of the work was likely taken from the afterword
to André Gide's *Les nourritures terrestres* (*The Fruits of the Earth*, 1897) in
which the narrator repeatedly demands that his imagined reader, Nathan-
iel, "jette mon livre" (throw out my book). Gide's paradoxical recognition
and rejection of his own didactic impulse (still in the didactic mode:
"Don't obey me!") is something found in Terayama's project as well. The
title used for the French release of *Sho o suteyo machi e deyō*, in fact, was
Jetons les livres et sortons dans les rues, collectivizing in Terayama's case the
film audience and suggesting that all books must go.[28] The title draws this
line from Gide together with a more explicitly revolutionary one—a 1911
work by the philosopher Tanaka Ōdō called *Shosai yori gaitō ni* (Out from
the studies and into the streets), which was a slogan used by proletarian
writers to protest the anticommunist Peace Preservation Law (*Chian
iji-hō*) of 1925. But rather than a return to the pastoral countryside as in
Gide's narrative (or a dispatching of college students to farms as in Mao's

Cultural Revolution), Terayama's title suggests that his audience abandon the false comforts of their isolation and begin to interact with real people within the streets of the cities—he promoted urban immigration similar to his own. At the time of the play version, this walling up behind books would have particularly resonated with the barricades strategy the students were using in their opposition to tuition hikes, embezzlement, the Vietnam War, the 1970 renewal of the U.S.–Japan Security Treaty, and other grievances. Often misunderstood as opposition to the student movement, Terayama may again (as he did in 1960) have been calling for a broader insurrection, one that did not do its opposition the favor of containing itself within the campuses.

With *Sho o suteyo machi e deyō* existing in these three forms—book, play, and film—but with tenuous, if any, narrative links between them, the project as a whole refuses both the typical link between genre and medium as well as the unity of a single work of art. The project has a rhizomatic structure, appearing here and there in different forms, and hinting at something much greater lurking beneath the surface and out of sight. But it would be a mistake to conceive of even this greater *Sho o suteyo machi e deyō* project as complete unto itself because elements within the text link not only to other manifestations of *Sho o suteyo machi e deyō* but also to Terayama's other projects. The quotation within the film of Miwa's performance as Marie in *Kegawa no Marii* draws a tangible and undeniable link to that play, breaking apart the possibility that the greater *Sho o suteyo machi e deyō* project could be a closed text. Miwa's appearance in the film rewards Terayama's fans who knew his work well, but it also jars those trying to make sense of the film—we have shifted so many times by that point (the scene occurs about two-thirds of the way through the film) between fictional and documentary modes that most viewers had probably given up attempting to understand it through a customary framework.

The film's attack on audience comfort begins with the opening sequence. It starts with a full minute of blank screen, in which we hear shuffling sounds, some muttering, then Terayama's directorial voice over a megaphone calling out blocking, and finally the sound of film running through the camera. Then a jump cut to Eimei (it is left unclear whether this is the actor Sasaki Eimei or the character Kitagawa Eimei) in monochrome facing us directly with his accusatory challenge: "What the hell are you doing? (*Nani shiten da yo*) All of you sitting there waiting around in a dark cinema. Nothing's gonna start." In these ten seconds of film, Terayama has already severed the typical bundling of film viewership to pure image consumption—our passivity and vulnerability are being attacked (Figure 4.2).[29] Eimei continues:

> It's empty back here behind the screen. All the people back here are getting sick of waiting just like you. "Isn't there anything cool going on?" (*Lights a cigarette*) The difference between out there and back here is that it's no-smoking for you, but back here we're free. (*Takes a long drag*)[30]

Behind the gag about smoking is a more serious reference to two important critiques of the medium of film and the way it is typically received. The first is to the willful passivity of the audience mentioned previously. If cinema operates sociologically to mass produce an agency effect within the everyday lives of audience members in contrast to their sedated consumption of films—that is, passivity inside the cinema making us feel subjective outside of it—then Terayama may have been attempting an

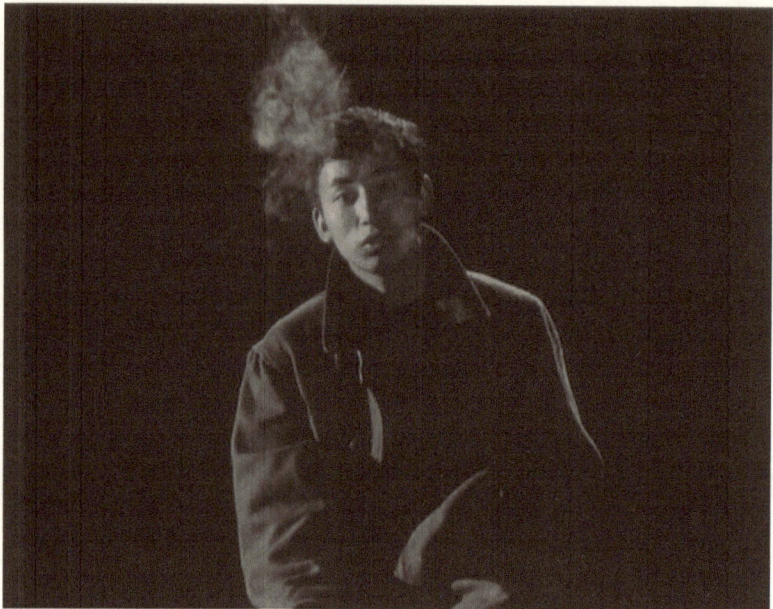

Figure 4.2. Eimei addresses the audience directly at the beginning of Sho o suteyo machi e deyō (Throw Out Your Books, Let's Hit the Streets, *1971*), *distinguishing the smoke-free cinema from the freedom actors have behind the silver screen.*

inversion of that structure here. By attacking that passivity and demanding active participation in the creation of the film, the cinema becomes the locus of agency for the audience, throwing the passivity of the everyday into relief.[31] Cinema more real than reality itself risks sparking despair in its attempt to motivate action—this cinema could agitate for a requestioning of agency in everyday life and the social system of illusions that produce false sensations of agency.

The other critique of the film medium present in these first lines has to do with the temporal disconnect that separates the moment of filming from the moment of projection. Film mechanically severs the human link between actors and audience that participatory theater sought to reconnect. Here, as Eimei speaks directly to us about this screen behind which, or, to follow Eimei's lines literally, *within* which (*sukuriinu no naka de*), the actors wait for some kind of beginning along with the audience, we are made conscious of the material impossibility of synchronicity between the human actors behind the celluloid images and audience in the seats of a cinema. We are also made conscious of how strange the moment of filming must have been for Eimei—speaking directly to the camera but imaging it to be the audience separated from him by a not-yet-present screen that would collapse his three-dimensional body into a two-dimensional image. It was certainly as strange for him to make as it is for us to watch. Suddenly we are thinking about production rather than immersing ourselves in consumption, recognizing the properties of the distribution apparatus of images, and becoming conscious of the severing of the people who produce from the people who consume.

Engaging the material and imagined properties of the screen in this first shot was the first of several screen-related "expanded cinema" experiments Terayama did through the 1970s. The most famous of those was a nine-minute 16mm film called *Rōra* (Laura) from 1974, in which three prostitutes on-screen face the audience directly and begin taunting an accomplice in the audience for expecting to see nudity in an avant-garde film, eventually challenging him to join them inside the screen.[32] The accomplice (always Morisaki Henriku) stands, and they continue to beckon him on until he physically pushes himself through the screen and, somewhat predictably by this point, then appears on the screen as part of the film—the trick screen uses Ace bandages stretched vertically over the front of a wooden frame. The three women proceed to strip him naked, forcing him to actively show something that he had hoped passively to watch, and then shove him back out of the film and into the audience, where he exits the cinema nude, clutching his clothes. The point is a simple one: the seemingly material constraints of the filmic medium are not actually capable of restricting expression in the ways they first appear. In fact, the opposite may in fact be true: by establishing an assumption like the screen's impenetrability, the materiality of cinema creates fictional potential using those expectations. *Shinpan* (The trial, 1975) used the screen in the opposite way, ending with accomplices and audience members physically pounding nails into the white, plywood screen used for the film. *Nitōjo: Kage no eiga* (The two-headed woman: A shadow film, 1977) uses shadows both existing on the film image and others added to the screen from two sources: the projection booth and by backlighting people walking behind the screen. The shadows they cast on the back of the image are visible to the audience due to the semitransparency of the silver screen. Terayama often mentioned his high school days spent living behind the screen of his uncle's cinema in Aomori as the root of his interest in the back surface of the screen, which may be the source of the idea, but the effect of these projects is to destabilize and exploit audience assumptions about the material properties of the apparatus of cinema and to open new possibilities for fictionality in the process.[33]

The use of camera noise in the moments before Eimei appears on-screen in *Sho o suteyo machi e deyō* contributes to another instance of cinematic reflexivity, but it does so with an interesting ambiguity. Because we can only hear the sound of film running through a machine and are unable to see the apparatus itself, we cannot be certain whether this sound is coming from a camera or a projector. It could be either, and as such we should read it as being both, which puts the audience in a strange place. The running film sound is loud relative to the other background voices and even loud enough relative to Eimei that it seems that we, the audience, are being positioned adjacent to whatever it is that is making the noise. We could be in the position of the cinematographer holding the camera at the moment of shooting, of that of the director sitting next to a projector in a small screening room preparing for editing, or of the projectionist in the booth during the film's exhibition. The ambiguity opens the possibility of these three important moments in the creation of a film being collapsed into a single productive instant—of impossible synchronicity made possible—and this impossible subject position is offered to the audience of the film. These are three moments of production exposed, conflated, and repositioned onto the viewer.

Eimei continues his monologue, suggesting that the rebellious ones in the cinema could use the darkness and their own anonymity as an alibi: "If you were thinking of pulling off something devious there in the dark, it won't do to just sit there all proper like that. Try stretching your hand over toward the next seat. Stroke the knee a little, see what happens. Don't worry about botching it up . . . no one even knows your name. No one knows my name either."[34] Again the gag veils a more serious critique, this time of the notion that watching a certain type of film (political, counter-cultural) in a certain type of cinema (ATG, other art houses) is in itself a "devious," political act—Terayama denies the claim to substantive politics within one's selection of products in the marketplace. But this line is also about the hidden power of anonymity. Too often we assume that power comes only with prestige or social status and that our ability to impact social structures is dependent on being close to the top of those structures. Here the opposite is true—anonymity provides cover. Most important, however, is Eimei's identification with the audience in terms of their equally anonymous status. Despite this Brechtian breaking of the fourth wall in facing and addressing us, Eimei manages to link himself to us in a direct way. Rather than imagining ourselves in his position, we identify both ourselves and Eimei as members of the same collectivity.

This countercultural collectivity contrasts with the newspaper head-line Eimei mentions near the end of his monologue about a young man, ethnically Korean but living in Japan, who has crashed a hang glider he was trying to use to fly back to his homeland:

"Fixed-Wing Glider Crashes into Tsushima Channel: Adolescent Korean Male, Ji Hōgen, Dead on Arrival"

I was stunned and looked up into the sky. Cloudy, then clearing; occasional showers. On wings of cheap steel, an unarmed Korean trying to fly back to his homeland. As envious as I am of those few meters of sky you flew through, that air gives me a bitter chill. Like a steel-press operator groaning under the weight, I'm a human-powered airplane [jinriki hikōki], only make 28,000 yen a month.[35]

Images of this human-powered airplane appear throughout the film, and considering that the production company Terayama set up to coproduce the film with ATG was called Jinriki Hikōki Sha (The human-powered air-plane company), it would be difficult to overestimate the importance of this image to it. The human-powered airplane never flies in the film; the attempts are always futile. In the newspaper headline the glider's flight is an attempt to return to an ethnic homeland this Korean probably never knew. Later, when Eimei runs away from his father down the railroad tracks, the film cuts to a fantasy with Eimei's first attempt to fly the glider, but his father is easily able to keep up with him on foot (Figure 4.3). The glider appears twice after Eimei's encounters with the soccer team captain girlfriend, who he is clearly attracted to. The second fantasy depicts Eimei trying to persuade her to fly away with him, but she is unconvinced that it would work. After this series of escape fantasies, the final appearance of the human-powered airplane shows it engulfed in flames, with the impli-cation that Eimei had lit it on fire. This image of the destruction of a failed means of escape is critical to the film, and more complex than simply an image of despair preceding a reassimilation to the status quo. This incin-eration image follows important lines by the member of the soccer team who "went political" and is now being pursued by the police: "Once in middle school I picked up a baby lizard in a park. Put it in a Coke bottle and raised it there. It got bigger and bigger until it couldn't escape. Liz-ard in a Coke bottle! Lizard in a Coke bottle! Do you think you have the strength to break free? It's the same for you, Japan! Isn't it the same? Japan! Shame blows across the Korean Straits again, could you be worth me throwing away my life for, oh Homeland? My Homeland, are you worth it?"[36] There are at least four major narratives being pulled together in these lines. The lizard grown too large to escape its home is from Ibuse Masuji's "Sanshōuo" (The salamader, 1923), in which a salamander grows too large to fit through the opening of the cave it lives in. The Coke bottle update to that narrative, which probably represents capitalist expansion to the Left and American corruption to the Right, could have been a reference to the huge Coke bottle on the poster for Satō Makoto's play *Isumene chikatetsu* (Ismene subway, 1966), which was probably the first Japanese play to pro-claim itself "underground theater." The third reference is to the hang-glider death in the waters between Japan and the Korean peninsula, linking back to the start of the film, but it is cast through a fourth reference to Teraya-ma's famous tanka on patriotism: *misutsuru hodo no sokoku wa ari ya* (is there any homeland worth forsaking?), as discussed in chapter 1. So added to the critique of willful atomization mistaken for freedom that we saw in the

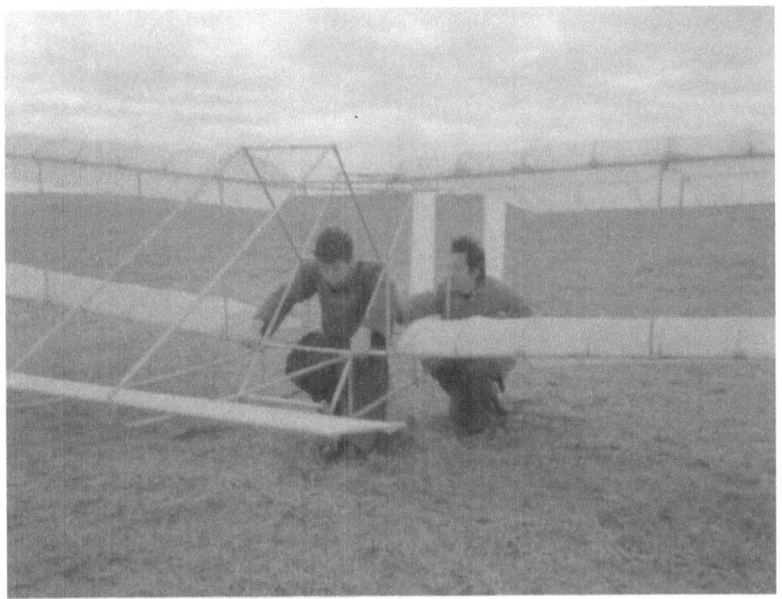

Figure 4.3. Eimei escapes from his father in a human-powered airplane (jinriki-hikōki) during a fantasy sequence near the beginning of the film Sho o suteyo machi e deyō *(Throw Out Your Books, Let's Hit the Streets, 1971).*

play version of *Sho o suteyo machi e deyō,* here we find what first appears to be an attack on the will to freedom when that has become impossible. Is the nation even worth attempting to rescue—are we not trapped inside it? And yet it may be possible to read this burning glider as perfectly consistent with Terayama's critique of liberation misconstrued as freedom from social ties. The juxtaposition of these lines raging against entrapment with the image of Eimei burning his own glider makes a powerful suggestion about the proper target for abandonment. What would Eimei have been free from in his human-powered airplane other than a web of connections to other people? Realizing that is what he sought to escape, Eimei burns the airplane to relinquish that false hope, in the spirit of recommitting to sociality (Figure 4.4).

This burning human-powered airplane also forms the ending of a Tenjō Sajiki play called *Jinriki hikōki Soromon* (Solomon: The human-powered airplane, 1970). It was first performed in November 1970 as a street theater project in Shinjuku, part of which took place just outside the

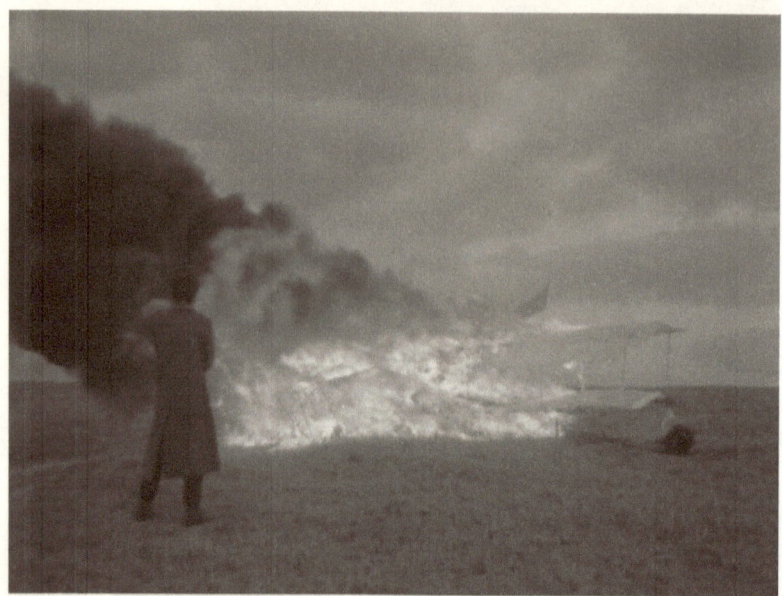

Figure 4.4. Eimei watches his airplane burn in a sequence near the end of the film Sho o suteyo machi e deyō *(Throw Out Your Books, Let's Hit the Streets, 1971), which was borrowed from the end of the Tenjō Sajiki street theater performance called* Jinriki-hikōki Soromon *(Solomon: The human-powered airplane, 1970).*

Shinjuku Bunka where *Sho o suteyo machi e deyō* would be screened about five months later. The audience for the three performances was partially recruited by offering free tickets to bystanders willing to participate in preperformance events. The homage anthem to *yakuza* film star Takakura Ken in *Sho o suteyo machi e deyō*, for example, is a reworking of one of these recruitment techniques in which a Tenjō Sajiki actor posed as a street musician outside the Shinjuku Tōei cinema (just around the corner from ATG's Shinjuku Bunka), singing an ode to Takakura and his line "*shinde moraimahyō*" ("I need you to die" in the working-class Tokyo dialect). Takakura Ken's films were screened in nonstop succession at that cinema, between about eight and thirteen per year throughout the 1960s, with this particular installment, *Shōwa zankyōden: Shinde moraimasu* (Shōwa tales of brutality and chivalry: You will die for me, 1970), opening in September, just two months before the Tenjō Sajiki's street theater performance. Terayama's song is filled with homoerotic innuendo toward Takakura's fanbase, but it also suggests that the all-night screenings may also have served as a homeless shelter for Tokyo's working poor. Airline-style tickets for the street theater play were given out free to anyone who spontaneously joined in with the Tenjō Sajiki actor's anthem (Figure 4.5). Recruitment for the play also took place at a busy intersection on the opposite side of Shinjuku station, where actors rewarded those willing to answer a survey with questions such as "Are you satisfied with monogamy?" and "What type of crimes have you enjoyed lately?" There were three meeting points for the 4:00 P.M. start of the play: at Shinjuku station's east exit, the west exit, and on the second floor of the Kinokuniya bookstore between the station and the cinema district. At the heart of the project was a flirtation with quasi-spontaneous revolution in the streets. This loose coordination of action across several parts of Shinjuku was paired with the alibi of theater's fictionality—"It's just a play, officer, don't worry"—energizing the dynamic between the actors, the audience, and the urban space itself. Shinjuku was reconceived as the sky through which this "human-powered airplane" of the coordinated groups would fly, as is made clear by the clouds on the maps that all participants were given (Figure 4.6). There are a few more possibilities that suggest other meanings for this project, some of which hinge on how we handle the name of this airplane: "Solomon." This may refer to King Solomon, the monarch who reigned over Israel's empire at its greatest size before seeing it crumble. After two major film versions of *King Solomon's Mines*, the name "Solomon" may have been more associated with adventures through uncharted parts of Africa than with Israel, but reference, in 1970, to Israel's historical empire must have invoked the Six-Day War of 1967 when contemporary Israel expanded its borders

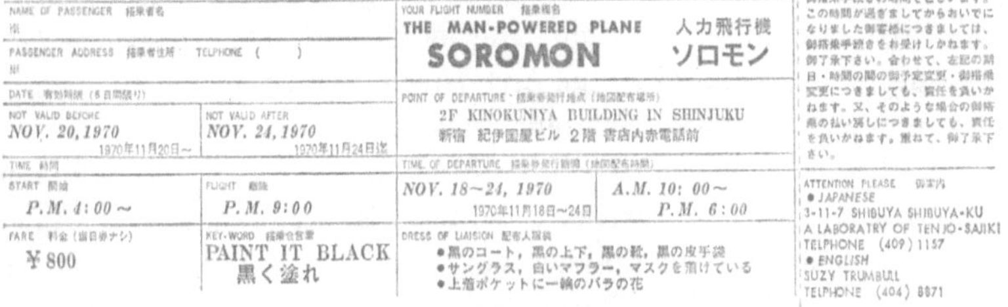

Figure 4.5. The airline-style ticket for participating in the 1970 street theater performance Jinriki-hikōki Soromon *(Solomon: The human-powered airplane). Courtesy of Kujō Kyōko and Terayama World.*

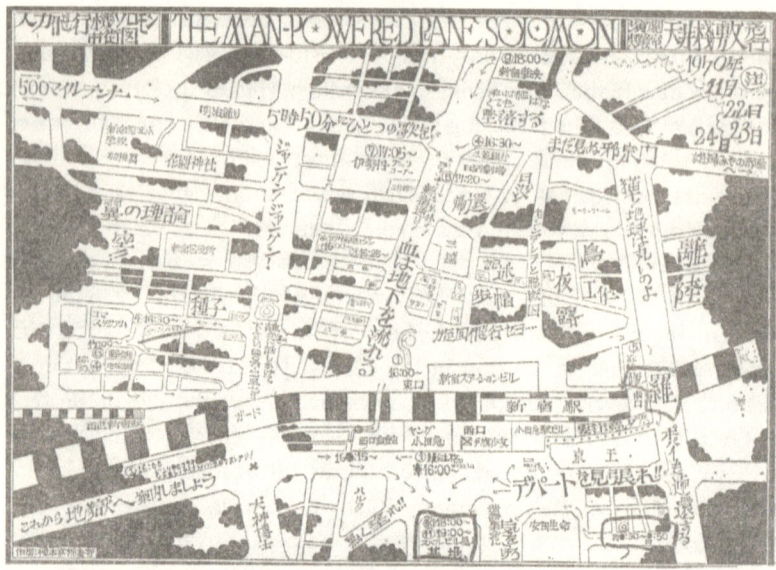

Figure 4.6. The map envisioning the streets of Shinjuku as a clouded sky through which would fly the street theater performance Jinriki-hikōki Soromon (Solomon: The human-powered airplane). *Courtesy of Kujō Kyōko and Terayama World.*

significantly. When this play was performed, Terayama would have just returned from a 1969 trip to Israel on an Israeli government grant, so these issues would have been fresh in his mind.[37] Juxtaposing Solomon with the Six-Day War is politically clever in that it simultaneously reminds Israel of its own expansionist precedent and the failure that followed, just as it also undermines the logic of opposition to Israel's right to exist on historical grounds—that this is "Arab soil"—since the Israelis could also restake a claim to the Solomonic kingdom if previous historical borders justify war. The suggestion, then, is that the Arab-Israeli negotiation will need to be done on synchronic, not diachronic, terms.

Another possible source for *Jinriki-hikōki Soromon* is the Solomon Islands, which hosted the fierce Guadalcanal Campaign between the Allies and Japanese forces, made famous as the location of Kennedy's shipwreck and rescue. Supply routes to Australia were at stake, so the area around the Solomon Islands was a critical space in the Pacific war. Recall, too, Minami Yōichiro's 1941 adventure novel for boys, *Soromon-tō tanken* (Expedition to the Solomon Islands). That novel includes a scene in which a shipwrecked boat is burnt by the heroes to help them keep their cover in the jungle, but results in them being rescued by a seaplane.[38] Terayama may have been deliberately invoking these historic battles or Minami's book, something he may have read as a boy during the war. The broader implication may be that the performance was partly a military operation conducted in the Shinjuku "theater" of war.

An important hint for understanding the function of this street theater performance comes in Terayama's introductory notes to the project: "For *Jinriki-hikōki Soromon* to fly, it will require 'resistance' more than anything else. When George Cayley invented humankind's first airplane he clarified a structure in which flight did not depend on the wings creating upward thrust, but rather, where liftoff was achieved using air resistance and directionality. The basis of aeronautics is that 'when a bird flies its wings have power sufficient to uphold a set weight using the resistance of air.'"[39] By moving the project into the streets, Terayama may have been attempting to give conceptual flight to the group involved in this play by provoking resistance from either other bystanders or the police. The goal, as he describes it, was to begin by creating a "one-square-meter, one-hour-long nation" through the theatrical interaction on the street between one actor and one viewer. That limited, temporary polity would then extend to become a "two-square-meter, two-hour-long nation," then become a "four-square-meter, four-hour-long nation," and eventually conquer and fictionalize the entirety of Shinjuku.[40] *Jinriki hikōki Soromon* performed the theatrification and transformation of urban space. This notion, not of performing a theater of revolution (*kakumei no engeki*, a slogan of Satō Makoto's Theatre Center, or Black Tent, troupe), but rather of making the revolution theatrical (*kakumei no engeki-ka*) and of theatricalizing the revolution already in progress, is critical to making sense of the Tenjō Sajiki's position at this time.[41] This is effectively an assertation of the radical possibility of theatricalized revolution—precisely opposite of the points of Robert Brustein, who bemoaned this trend in his 1971 *Revolution as Theatre*.[42]

Reconsidered in terms of urban space, it is interesting that the Tenjō Sajiki, which had in 1969 set up a base of operations in Shibuya with the establishment of the Tenjō Sajiki-kan (the troupe's headquarters, which consisted of a performance space in the basement, a café on the first floor, and office space on the second), would have returned to Shinjuku for this performance. As Yoshimi Shun'ya outlines in his history of the geographical movement of Tokyo's primary entertainment district, the center of

Tokyo's energy had historically moved from Asakusa to Ginza in the 1920s, from Ginza to Shinjuku around 1960, and then from Shinjuku to Shibuya in the 1970s, by which time the Parco department store anchored the rising consumer culture:

> Parco provided an environment of fashion on Shibuya's Park Avenue [Kōen-dōri]in which the leading role would be performed by us [watashi]—the keyword here was "staging." The key toward understanding Parco's spatial strategy, then, is to look at the way they made the entire town into one giant theater, which required the creation of individual elements in the town that would establish the situation of seeing and being seen, after which the value system of the participants had to be expanded. As Parco's founder, Masuda Tsūji, has said regarding the cluster of theaters on Park Avenue, "We sought to pull the stage out into the audience, we wanted to make small theaters that let customers feel that they were in the leading role," but the same could be said of the entire district.[43]

The opening of Shibuya's Parco department store in 1973 contributed to the shift, as did the demise of Shinjuku Station–based "folk guerilla" protests of the Vietnam War, but Terayama's establishment of a countercultural icon in Shibuya even before the 1970s began should not be overlooked. Masuda was a close friend of underground theater leader Kara Jūrō, who did a performance on the Parco grounds as they were being prepared for construction, and the theater on the top floor of the main Parco department store in Shibuya has supported (or has been supported by) Miwa Akihiro's solo performances and Tenjō Sajiki plays since its opening.[44] The reinvasion of Shinjuku with *Jinriki hikōki Soromon* was therefore motion against the nascent flow of youth culture out of Shinjuku and toward Shibuya around 1970, and might most effectively be understood as an effort to spread countercultural urban theatricalization across the whole of western Tokyo. The reference to the Solomonic empire, rather than the former expansionist Davidic one, may have hinted at the need to maintain countercultural territory already won by previous exploits. This flow links well to the possible readings of *Jinriki hikōki Soromon*'s role within the film version of *Sho o suteyo machi e deyō*: we could either take the presence of street theater in a film to be an extension of the outdoor street theater project to the indoor theater, or the image of the play could be seen as a conceptual portal from the enclosed cinema back out into the streets. Critical here is the revisioning of urban space as itself performative, its nature shifts depending on how it is used, and once reconceptualized as one big theater or cinema, the underground can burst out of its "little theaters" (shōgekijō) and tents to reclaim entire urban areas.

Another notable aspect of the human-powered airplane scenes in *Sho o suteyo machi e deyō* is the conspicuous use of color. The first of these scenes is tinted magenta and occurs when Eimei is running away from his father near the opening of the main narrative of the film. This magenta tint contrasts with the monochromatic green-tinted scenes in which Eimei introduces his family—this green tint will be used to mark the family scenes throughout the film. Magenta is also the font color used for the title of the film, printed against a green tinted image of an empty boxing ring (boxing being the future Eimei dreamed of before he joined a gym and realized how much it hurt—as with Barikan from *Aa, kōya*). Green is coded to the family, then, and magenta typically to this fantasy of escaping it. It is not until thirteen minutes into the film that full color is used—a first for an ATG coproduction—saved here for the soccer team that Eimei joins. Life in the Shinjuku streets, in restaurants, on the soccer field, and in the brothels and locker rooms: all of this is polychromatic and vivid in parallel to the heteroglossia of the streets. Monochrome returns after Eimei's visit to the brothel in which he remembers playing doctor as a child. Here the tint is red in the office and blue as the woman chases him outside. The magenta tint appears again with the series of visual want ads, probably based on those in the back of magazines, and again in a brief shot of the empty soccer field. The second image of the human-powered airplane is tinted magenta but over what appears to be color stock—there are blues and reds clearly visible. Black and white monochrome is used again as Eimei's sister Setsuko walks in despair down the train tracks, ignoring the surrealistic image of Jennifer Merin (an American who had joined the Tenjō Sajiki) running toward her flying a kite. The magenta tint is used again during the homage to Takakura Ken in stills intercut into the song. Black-and-white monochrome is used for the "fountain of youth" sequence of tales and the family portrait, but the magenta tint returns for the final images of the human-powered airplane and the brothel images with Miwa—in both cases again a magenta tint over color film. The "lizard in a Coke bottle" lines are delivered within black-and-white monochrome with a magenta tint, which cuts directly to the magenta tinted image of Eimei's airplane burning to the ground.

In order to sort out the codification of tint colors in *Sho o suteyo machi e deyō*, it will be useful to consider another experimental short film from 1974 that used tinting conspicuously. The multiprojection 16mm film, *Seishōnen no tame no eiga nyūmon* (The young people's guide to film) is only three minutes long but comprises some of Terayama's most striking cinematic images.[45] Three films are projected simultaneously, each tinted one of the three primary colors for light. The image on the left is tinted green and consists of a series of surrealist images—unlikely and provocative juxtapositions of random objects. The center image is tinted blue and features an image of a naked young man (Morisaki Henriku again) urinating directly onto the camera lens. The image on the right is tinted magenta and consists of a series of personal, autobiographical images from Terayama's life. Terayama's choice of color implies that these three mininarratives could combine into one full color production, which when understood against the title—that is, an introduction to film—might suggest that the process of filmmaking could be thought of as a combination of attacks against the cinematic apparatus, autobiography, and unexpected juxtapositions.

If this use of tinted images was codified to the color wheel in this "introductory" short film, then a similar semiotic may operate in *Sho o suteyo machi e deyō*. The magenta tint is always used to represent Eimei's interior fantasies (whether good or bad), in contrast to the brief concrete memories marked red or blue. Magenta is a mix of red and blue (in both light and pigment color mixing), and the suggestion here may be that Eimei's fantasies (magenta) result from a combination of past memories (red and blue). Even the personal ads could represent Eimei's interiority, since these are likely visualizations of text-based ads from magazines processed through his imagination of faces to match the text. The centrality of this exploration of Eimei's interiority is signified by the magenta font used for the title, posing the possibility of addressing Eimei's interiority on film as a central problem. This problem is particularly clear in the screenplay itself, where Eimei's lines are all attributed to the first-person pronoun *watashi*. Eimei, then, was playing "me," as he had in the *stage verité* style of the play version *Sho o suteyo machi e deyō*, but this time with a script. Rather than bringing himself further and further into the on-screen character, he may have been expected to bring the on-screen character closer to himself. This refashioning of Eimei using the film is addressed in the final scene of the film in which Eimei addresses the audience directly again, as in the opening sequence:

> When I hear the sound of the clapperboard, I start to talk. Lines someone else wrote, someone else's words. Once the camera's rolling I have to call Mr. Saitō "father," and as I repeat it over and over it starts feeling real. Just when I start wondering if Mr. Saitō is my real father I hear, "Cut!" Then, "Good, next is scene 103. Eimei, hurry up, here we go." Then on to the next scene, the next lie . . . it starts again. A lie within a lie. But in the tiny gap between cuts I get reflected into the cold, cold February sky, trapped inside an illusion.[46]

The creation of a new family in the course of the film is reinforced here by the use of a green tint over this sequence, reserved until this point exclusively for Eimei's biological family in the film. Here it is the entire assembled cast (including Eimei's on-screen "family") tinted the familial green. Rather than the audience suspending their disbelief and allowing the fictional characters on-screen to become real, Eimei emphasizes the way that process operates on the production side of a film as well—that is, of actors beginning to lose track of themselves as they transform into the characters they perform.

One important subtheme in the film remains—that of rape and prostitution—and we need to look closely at it in order to understand the film's engagement with institutionalism. Rape, in the abstract, can stand in for sadism in its simplest form—eroticized violation, the conflation of sex and violence, and the severance of a social contract and the one-sided establishment of an authority structure. This symbolic form of rape is one we see again and again in Wakamatsu Kōji's films, for example, and is typically put into a binary relationship with unforced nudity (e.g., on the roof of a building) representing liberation. Prostitution, in contrast, could be seen as similar to Deleuze's description of masochism—pleasure based on the negotiation of a mutual contract between both parties. In neither case is sex itself the primary locus of eroticism: the erotic of rape is in the entanglement of violation with sex, and the erotic of prostitution is in the dynamic between sex and contract. *Sho o suteyo machi e deyō*, however, does not present rape and prostitution in such simple terms. There are four scenes on the topic in the film: Eimei's trip to the soccer team's prostitute, the gang rape of Setsuko, the brief scene with Setsuko and her classmates stripping off the tops of their school uniforms while singing about becoming prostitutes, and Eimei's daydream about the transvestite brothel with Miwa. The first brothel trip fails partially because Eimei is there to impress the team captain, who is also paying for the trip—had he negotiated the arrangement himself, it may have turned out differently. Ōmi assumes that Eimei desires what he himself and the other team members desired: that after being broken in by this woman, he would start to enjoy it. But Eimei's desire is clearly to escape, even to the desolate fields of the countryside if necessary.

The same logic drove the gang rape of Eimei's sister Setsuko. The soccer players seem to have thought that she was getting what she wanted—why else would she have wandered into the men's locker room and then all the way into the shower? She may, in fact, have been flirting with a player in the locker room at the time. It seemed, for an instant at least, that she wanted the same thing as the men who would attack her in the shower, something they would use to justify the action as ethical. Rape here, and perhaps more generally, may expose a glitch in an ethical system institutionalized under the principle of reciprocity. A man forcing a woman to have sex is likely treating her exactly as he would want her to treat him. The problem with reciprocity is its solipsism—it does not require a contract with the other party impacted but only the identification of the rights and desires of others with oneself. Such an ethical system would work perfectly if all parties were perfectly homogeneous, and in fact, it requires the homogenization of needs and desires in order to become ethical. Socially heterogeneous desire—whether based on gender difference or, more conspicuously, with homosexuality—may be threatening foremost because it threatens the universalist logic of reciprocity ethics. A truly social, rather than solipsistic, ethical system would require the negotiation of relationships on a case-by-case basis, the tedium of which may be the greatest force operating against it. The irony in the film is that Ōmi—who talks constantly of new social relationships, Kommune 1 (the famous urban commune in West Berlin that signaled a split from the German SDS), and free love—is the least likely to negotiate relationships at all. He is a classic hypocrite, possibly representative of a broad sexual hypocrisy on the fringes of 1960s counterculture.

In contrast to the sadistic scenes, suddenly we find Setsuko and her classmates gleefully stripping off their tops and singing about becoming prostitutes:

If I end up to be a call girl
Gonna get me a big bar of soap
And wash up all the men I like!
If I end up to be a call girl
Gonna leave my door open all the time
And let in the swallows from the sea[47]

The song is visually linked to the previous scene in which Setsuko's father tries to reendear himself to her by offering her a new pet rabbit, but she refuses, saying, "I'm not a child anymore," as she is making up her face and demanding privacy—clear signs of coming of age. It is at that moment that he spots an old photograph of her in her school uniform, an image that immediately precedes Setsuko and her friends stripping off that same uniform. The juxtaposition of the father's glimpse of his pubescent daughter in the photo and her sexual awareness in the house reveals the stripping song to be a representation of the father's fear of his daughter gleefully skipping into sexuality—ironically idealistic compared to how her initiation actually occurred. What becomes evident at this point is that all of the sexual experiences in the film are plagued by slippages between the dominant party's perception of the other's experience and the actual experience of that person. This is never more painfully clear than when Ōmi nonchalantly invites himself to join Eimei and his sister at their table in an expensive restaurant that Eimei had splurged on specifically to console Setsuko after the rape Ōmi had just supervised and participated in. These juxtapositions foreground the disconnect between the fiction in the minds of these dominant men and the realities of those they dominate—and open the possibility for a realization among viewers that the problem at its core has to do with the absence of any form of genuine negotiation or even an awareness of its need.

To push this further, by recognizing the dangers of representational sex itself—including rape as sadism and prostitution as masochism—the film's critique might come full circle, unwinding its own representational mode. As Setsuko's rape seems to parallel the violation her grandmother committed in killing the rabbit she saw as blocking Setsuko's social development, or as Eimei's failure in the brothel looks like another representation of his inadequacy on the soccer team, the rawness of those scenes and true discomfort on the faces of these novice actors pulls that representational layer away and leaves us looking at what seems (relative to the rest of the film) to be something very real. But our cognizance of the profilmic moment, when these were real people actually naked in front of a camera rather than images on the screen, must then ultimately conflict with the reality effect it produces. We are convinced by the potency of the depiction within the film's narrative and yet simultaneously aware of its necessarily fictional and scripted nature. But even so, the nudity of the actors and the clarity of their physical sensations pushes us all the way back to the moment of filming, making them human again. The juxtaposition of Setsuko and Eimei immediately after the rape with a man carrying half a butchered pig down the street is a powerful metaphor for the soccer team's treatment of Setsuko, but it is also a conspicuous reminder that this is a fiction film. This reverse dialectic proceeding from the film image back to the moment of production—from shades of light reflected off the screen back to human actors—is an unwinding of the representational apparatus of cinema with an important politics. If the same logic could be applied to the use of rape as metaphor, then we might make the important step of deinstitutionalizing the use of rape for symbolic purposes, a distancing of the act from its immediate meaning that replicates the semiotic slippage necessary to justify rape itself. Terayama may have come away from *Sho o suteyo machi e deyō* with the realization that there may be no responsible way to critique the logic of rape within a realist mode—even one that makes the scene extremely uncomfortable for the viewers and forces us to recognize and confront our own desire to simultaneously block out that image and to see it more completely. Setsuko in the shower was the first and last scene in a Terayama film of a man violating a woman. In the case of Eimei at the brothel, and in many of his later films, however, we find woman sexually dominating and violating men, an inverted form of critique far more effective in de-eroticizing rape.

The reverse dialectic, moving back from cinema's illusion through the production process and to the human actors behind the image, is a maneuver that challenges the notion that the medium of film itself possesses any sort of political potential. Eimei, in his final musings at the end of the film, ponders the ethereality of the medium:

Please turn on the lights. The film ends here, now it's just my turn to talk. If you think about it, a film can only exist within the darkness of a cinema. The world of the film ends the moment the lights come on—it just disappears.

... Even the worlds of Polanski and Ōshima Nagisa and Anto-
nioni, all of them disappear when you turn on the lights. Think you
could show a film on the side of a building during daylight?[48]

This is partially a corrective to the notion that certain filming techniques
or content constitute a "political" film. Here we are reminded that politics is a set of power relations between people and that the film can only
mediate information and images about human power relations or the link
between the producers of the film and its audience. The film itself is not
a political object. But this is also likely a reference to a specific event that
occurred in 1969 at the Sōgetsu Art Center where the Tenjō Sajiki had
debuted two years previously.

Sōgetsu hosted an experimental film festival planned for October 14
through 30, 1969, that would have featured new noncommercial art films
from around the world under the title "Film Art Festival 1969."[49] However,
around thirty members of a student movement faction opposed to the
1970 World's Fair in Osaka, a group called Banpaku Hakai Kyōtō-ha (The
Expo destruction joint-struggle faction), disrupted the festival on opening day. They charged the selection committee with collaboration with
the expo (Teshigahara Hiroshi and Matsumoto Toshio did shoot films for
pavilions, but Teshigahara's was anticapitalist and Matsumoto's was quasi-
pornographic) and accused the inherited leadership system (*iemoto seido*)
of the Sōgetsu school with feudalistic patriarchy. Sōgetsu decided to can-
cel the entire festival rather than risk involving the riot police. Matsumoto
wrote an angry response to the intervention arguing that the nature of film
requires a space (*ba*) for it to be shown, and that until a better space was
formed, there was little use in destroying one of the few locations willing
to do experimental film screenings in Tokyo.[50] Art and *manga* critic Ishiko
Junzō countered Matsumoto's argument, claiming that the social standing
of a cinema impacts the film itself.[51] Several years later, Kawanaka Nobuhiro, one of the members of the group that raided Sōgetsu, wrote of the
event and described the alternative venue that they tried to set up—a tent
in a nearby park that clearly would have struggled with the darkness problems Eimei mentions.[52] In 1977, Kawanaka and Tomiyama Katsue would
launch the Image Forum in Yotsuya (roughly halfway between Sōgetsu
and the ATG's Shinjuku Bunka). The Image Forum got its start, however,
as a monthly screening called the "Underground Cinematheque," which
screened films at a number of sites around Shinjuku before eventually

settling into the basement of Terayama's Tenjō Sajiki-kan for a period of over four years.[53] Terayama's name is now on one of the classrooms in the new Image Forum building in Shibuya as a tribute to that origin.

The reference to this 1969 Sōgetsu event within *Sho o suteyo machi e deyō*, then, was probably directed toward the difficulties Kawanaka's group faced in screening films before they had a stable cinema space. But the reference to Roman Polanski invokes the famous disturbance at the Cannes Film Festival the previous year (1968) when Polanski joined François Truffaut, Jean-Luc Godard, and others to shut down the entire event. Terayama's reference to this moment links it to a global interrogation of the institutionalization of cinema—a nexus of distribution, festivals, criticism, production, form, content, style, and modes of viewership—literally bringing the discourse out of the cinema, out of the books, and back into the streets. This film is ultimately a film against film itself; against the way it historically replaced theater as a social entertainment and severed the human relation between actor and audience; against the way it fits so comfortably in a consumer society; and against the way it relies on a huge apparatus of cinema ownership, distribution networks, and upfront investment to begin production, a nexus that so often overruns the people involved. And yet what better medium in which to make this point than film itself? How fitting, then, that the film image itself derails at the end, splitting the image in half as though the projector has broken down (Figure 4.7). Eimei closes with an expression of his gratitude to the director, cinematographer, and other actors in the film, but then proclaims his hatred of

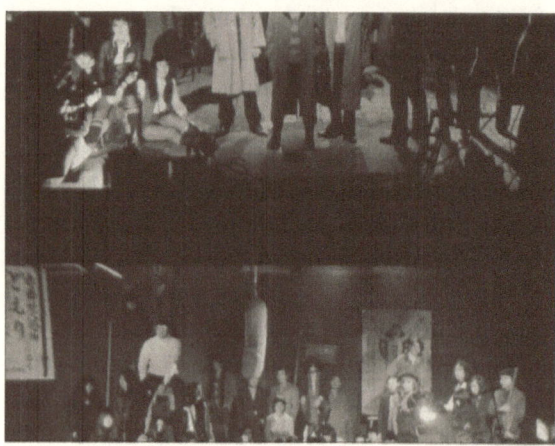

Figure 4.7. Eimei and the cast of Sho o suteyo machi e deyō *(Throw Out Your Books, Let's Hit the Streets, 1971) as the image derails during the lines of his final monologue.*

film itself—*sayonara eiga!* This film was ultimately not an effort to replace the institutions of cinema with something else—a reinstitutionalization—but to untangle all of cinema's mystification and get it back to people with their embodiments and entanglements of fiction and reality—a deinstitutionalization—and to move from there to renegotiate the contracts between actors and audience; between producers, distributors, and consumers of cinema; and between people and their conceptualizations of what cinema is and what it could be.

CHAPTER 5

The Impossibility of History

PAIRED WITH TERAYAMA'S WORK TO eroticize the present were texts that abject the past. Perhaps he realized that the logical impossibility of history—of a return to a now absent past—was itself insufficient to cause a shift toward a geographical orientation. Logic is often overwhelmed by the greater pressures of desire. So if the present and the past compete for our affections, then Terayama may have attempted to tip the scales not just by adding to synchrony's appeal but also by intervening to make diachrony uglier. Terayama treats the abject past most directly in a set of projects all titled *Den'en ni shisu* (Death in the country), and this chapter will be a careful analysis of these texts.

The *Den'en ni shisu* tanka collection from 1965 and the 1974 feature-length ATG film are widely seen as two of Terayama's most important works, but he used the same title for two smaller projects done earlier. One was the November 9, 1962, installment of the *Iede no susume* (In praise of running away from home) essays in *The Student Times*, titled "Rikyō no susume: Den'en ni shisu" (In praise of leaving your hometown: Death in the country). This concerns the pessimistic nostalgia for rural hometowns contrasted with the energy of a letter from a runaway. The title seems, then, to refer to the fear of dying in such a dismal place as one's own hometown, making abject the diachronically tinged space expected to embody one's familial history.

A few weeks earlier than this newspaper publication, on October 22, 1962, Terayama's thirty-minute television drama version of *Den'en ni shisu* aired on Nihon Television. It opens with lines that hint at the broader theme at play across all of these *Den'en ni shisu* projects: "The red flower blooms, hush-a-by, hush-a-by, let me be twenty once more."[1] The lullaby here is clearly designed for the caretaker more than the child, but what is striking here is this desire not for escape but for a return to a better past, perhaps a time of greater vitality, but likely a time of freedom. Terayama brings us to these moments again and again as if to ask why a desire essentially for freedom of movement—a geographical impulse—gets processed through this historical metaphor. A shift from diachronic to synchronic orientation might explode this sort of longing, so we are left to ask whether encapsulating desire within a diachronic framework functions to justify maintenance of the status quo—that what we have been taught to want is stasis, and we naturalize that desire by cutting off the possibility of geographical and synchronic motion.

These projects are important not only for their handling of issues of time, space, and abjection but also for the relationship between the texts sharing the same name. Whereas in Terayama's debut and the match-strike poem we found him incorporating and reworking material from other poets, pop culture, and film, the *Den'en ni shisu* series is a relatively closed and self-referential system in which Terayama repeatedly uses a set of signifiers that become closely associated with an attempt to (impossibly) revisit his own past growing up in rural Aomori. The system cannot be fully closed off from new information and historical change, however, so not only is the narrating subject a different person than he was as a child but Aomori has changed as well and has become mythologized both in his mind and in the popular imagination, inevitably inflecting this attempt at exposing the impossibility of "history."

An Impossible Japanese Avant-Garde

In an attack on the Centre Pompidou's exhibition of avant-garde Japanese art during the early 1980s, art historian Inaga Shigemi argues that the term "avant-garde" cannot be applied to any work of art identified as Japanese. Any such designation, he claims, would violate either the spirit of the avant-garde (to challenge dominant scales of value) or the nature of its content (historically something foreign to the artist's culture):

> It is logically impossible to find an authentically avant-gardist position within Third World culture. What causes this ambiguity? The notion of the avant-garde itself is based on a Eurocentric point of view. Not by accident did the avant-garde come into its own during the colonial period. The appropriation of the Other by a Western Europe hoping thereby to regenerate its own traditions attains at this point its ultimate manifestation, and brings with it an inevitable identity crisis within Western Europe itself.

That which is considered traditional in a non-Western context becomes avant-garde as it is integrated into a Western context. But this transplantation is a one-way dispossession. For a non-Western culture, this represents a double alienation: non-Western culture provides the Western avant-garde with an alibi but, in so doing, the non-Western avant-garde is uprooted, and is capable of basing itself upon its own culture only through reference to the Western avant-garde. From this indirect means, moreover, can only result an Eastern arrière-garde.[2]

While exposing the power dynamics behind European gallery and museum exhibitions of modern Japanese art may require this deconstruction of the term "avant-garde," Inaga may be relying on a dangerous loosening of notions of universal and particular to make his point—a move that could end up disenfranchising some legitimate forms of experimentalism in Japan. We may be tempted to imagine a temporally and geographically specific avant-garde consisting of disgruntled European art academy dropouts who "borrowed" African and Asian aesthetics in an Oedipal attack upon the values preached by their former teachers. The inversion of a scale of values as technique, however, certainly has not been limited by either time or geography. Any attempt to link a specific set of artists or artifacts with the "spirit" of rebellious creativity would be tautological. To cede aesthetic inversion and injections of foreign culture to a small group of French men is to efface similar antiestablishment projects going on around the world at the same time. The most important feature of the historical interwar avant-garde was its diffuse and decentered structure, in which some ideas may have transferred faster between Zurich and Tokyo than others did between Paris and New York. The necessary reconceptualization here is to abandon treatment of the avant-garde as specific to one time and one place—it is more accurate historically to keep the term a generic descriptor from the start. This decentralized avant-garde would materialize in different ways around the world depending on the nature of institutional art in its locality, confronting dominant aesthetic scales within each of its particular cultural settings. As long as we maintain the possibility of cultural difference, the avant-garde would necessarily texture itself differently within different cultural groups, which may be decreasingly consonant with national or ethnic boundaries.

What space, then, is left for experimentalism in Japan? Inaga's descriptive analysis skips one possible manifestation of avant-gardism within

Japanese art, namely, the inflection of premodern foreign and native content within traditional forms in which the standardized scale of values has been inverted. The resulting product could serve to challenge standard domestic aesthetics as well as the logic of the Eurocentrist version of the avant-garde Inaga posits as inherent in the concept. We must keep in mind that by the postwar period the cultural and aesthetic traditions often taken to represent Japan (noh, kabuki, etc.) were *at least* as exotic to young Japanese as to non-Japanese—making such traditions functionally foreign even to those most geographically proximate to them. John Cage's engagement with Zen Buddhism and Terayama's use of kabuki-style makeup on stage are actually structurally identical: both hinge on tension between a culturally distant form and an awareness of a very different present. While we might be tempted to argue that any adoption or importation of European methodology would necessarily reinforce off-balance power relations, such a claim is underwritten by an assumption that the techniques of experimentalism provisionally termed "avant-gardism" are somehow an essentially European property, a myth that Japanese experimental art, as well as this study, should serve to debunk.

This method of inversion is precisely what Terayama Shūji seems to have used in his third poetry collection, *Den'en ni shisu* (Death in the country, 1965). This set of tanka was preceded by the television drama and newspaper essay of the same title from 1962, all three of which would be followed by Terayama's second ATG feature-length film, also called *Den'en ni shisu* (1974).[3] The source material for the poetry ranges from Tōhoku regional customs to generalized Japanese myths to non-Japanese folklore and traditions. This material is then presented not just in the 31-syllable form of tanka but also in longer free-verse pieces labeled classical genres of *chōka* (long poem) and *sōshi* (storybook), gradually moving away from short-form poetry toward longer pieces in prose.[4] By the end of this so-called tanka collection, we find things such as a warped King Midas tale in which everything a certain man touches grows long body hair. This is flippant pastiche, but when such a narrative is written in classical Japanese despite its clearly postwar setting—the man lives in an *apāto* (apartment)—we are reminded of the link between the *genbun-itchi* movement to vernacularize fiction and the ideological politics of identifying modernization with Westernization.[5] Terayama could be reverting to premodern language for little other than playful style, but it might be hasty to overlook other possibilities. The presence of these short vignettes within a collection labeled "tanka" is an overt challenge to genre boundaries. By then reworking his own text into a film, Terayama has taken on notions of influence and expanded the attack on content and genre to include medium as well. The sum total of his *Den'en ni shisu* project, then, becomes a location for a rigorous reexamination of the physical and discursive structures that constitute notions of media, genre, and content of poetry and film. The following will be an attempt to trace out Terayama's engagement with these structures through several recurrent motifs and then to speculate about why he may have chosen to experiment in the way he did. Where Inaga questions the possibility of a Japanese avant-gardism, Terayama seems to use the techniques Inaga describes to question the nature of genre and medium and ultimately the limits of history and fiction in this *Den'en ni shisu* cross-media, cross-genre project.

Horror Poetry

Inaga was particularly frustrated with the way that traditional Japanese forms are categorized as "avant-garde" once they leave Japan: "One the one hand, one cannot automatically consider *haikai* avant-garde simply because *haikai* poets inspired Western imagists. On the other, one would obviously be overly selective to see Japanese avant-garde poets as coming exclusively from among dadaists and Japanese surrealists. Rather than attempting to draw a line of demarcation between the avant-garde and the non-avant-garde, our interest lies in questioning the very possibility of doing so."[6] *Den'en ni shisu* may be one of these strange cases that fits both the traditional model and the avant-gardist criteria, but simply debunking the term because of this conflict would deprive us of a useful framework for examining Terayama's method. In fact, we ought to expect avant-garde aesthetics to overlap in some way with canonized practice in order to first establish a connection before moving into critique. Consider Terayama's systematic attack on the traditional content of Chinese lyric poetry as passed on to Japan: the flowers, birds, wind, and moon (*ka-chō-fū-getsu*) are never the poignant lyrical reminders of natural beauty or our ephemeral human existence but are, for Terayama, rather the subjects and objects of horror. We find him decapitating flowers, for example:

> *noko no atsuki ha o mote waga hikishi yo no himawari tsui ni kubi nashi*
> That night I severed it with feverish saw teeth—
>   a sunflower suddenly headless[7]

The birds in the collection are shrikes, sparrows, and crows—portenders of death. But what ends up conspicuous about this inverted use of canonical poetic imagery is how *few* of the poems bother to attack the traditional lexicon. In exchange for classic content, Terayama begins building a parallel set of powerful signifiers. In this set we find things like wall clocks, *butsudan* (Buddhist altars for the home), the knifelike horizon, hell, hometowns, artificial eyes and limbs, murky water, and images of mothers. This new set of signifiers frees Terayama to develop associations from scratch and to manipulate them separately from the traditional signification of loaded words from the canon. It is important to recognize that in terms of the power of the image, however, he is choosing to relinquish the potential of long-standing associations. The aesthetic of increasingly refined and delicate allusion is exchanged for the perhaps more risky game of confrontation and fissure.

At the core of the aesthetics Terayama creates with this new lexicon is the abject pleasure of recognizing horror in everyday life. Again and again we encounter retrofitted explanations of brutality behind something that would have normally seemed completely peaceful:

> *mabikareshi yue ni isshō kesseki suru gakkō jigoku no otōto no isu*
> A nipped bud, he will be absent for life—
>   my little brother's empty chair in school hell[8]

Conceiving of an empty chair as being reserved for a brother lost to infanticide leaves us with several options for interpretation: an adult discovers his or her brother had been "nipped" and overwrites the image onto memories of childhood, a schoolchild makes the realization in real-time, or something uncanny about the chair itself suggests such a history. This technique of making horror out of a stationary object is seen again in the next section of the collection:

> *imada kubi tsurazarishi nawa tabanerare haigo no kabe ni furubitsutsu ari*
> Rope that has yet to strangle anyone hangs in a bundle
>   aging on the wall behind him[9]

Shifting horror from kinetic to potential sources of power may be at the root of Terayama's project here, and as such, it seems to be a valid case of his application of the inversion aesthetic of avant-gardism. That is, by identifying the aesthetic of horror as one that imagines active cruelty for cruelty's sake and then reversing that scale into a still and silent form of brutality waiting to happen, he has managed to double the horror effect: we are horrified by both the image itself and by the notion that our theory of horror had been incomplete (and is thereby incapable of protecting us with its predictions).

The problem with identifying this manipulation of the lexicon as an avant-garde technique is that major figures from the tradition (from Fujiwara no Teika to Masaoka Shiki) have repeatedly called for exactly that practice. So the energy avant-gardism stands to gain by confronting tradition is in danger of being deflated by falling within the requisites of the tradition itself. This problem with poetic tradition and rebellion is echoed by the literary critic Isoda Kōichi's take on Terayama's relationship with his hometown: "The feeling that 'there is no one in my hometown who will reject me certainly becomes, to the youth who wants to establish a notion of selfhood by using the restrictions of his hometown as a springboard, a paradoxical inconvenience."[10] It may be a stretch to claim that "hometown" operates as a metaphor for the poetic tradition throughout *Den'en ni shisu*, but it is interesting to note that they seem to be structured in the same way. A potentially more direct reference to the gravitational pull of tradition may be the repeated reference to family lineage:

> *kurayami no ware ni kakei o tōnakare tsukemono taru no naka no bōrei*
> Don't ask me about my lineage here in the dark—
>   spirits of the dead inside a pickle jar[11]

> *rōfu hitori oyogi-owarishi aki no umi ni ware no kakei no abura ukishiya*
> My aged father finished his swim alone in the autumn sea—
>   up floats the grease of our lineage[12]

Both family and poetic lineage are in the realm of horror and abjection here—it is almost as though Terayama shifts his poetic diction away from the standard allusions for fear of the ghosts that it might stir up. But it must be noted that the horror of these images is very clearly not only based in the past or on family but also specifically on the horror of diachrony as represented by "lineage." This is the familial past conceived as a set of birthrights, obligations, and genetic predispositions to disease.

The tanka tradition has encouraged—even demanded—periodic updates of the linguistic content of poetry. But if we look more closely at the expansion in terms of parts of speech, we find that the growth is almost always in new nouns. So we find Masaoka Shiki campaigning for the use of foreign words in tanka in order to revitalize the form that he claimed had nearly run through all available permutations of the traditional poetic vocabulary: "Any word which can express beauty is a proper word for tanka; there are no other tanka words. Whether Chinese or Western, all words that can be used literarily may be considered to belong to the vocabulary of the tanka."[13] If Terayama had recognized this pattern, then he may have chosen to confront the modern tanka institution by adding verbs instead of nouns. This tendency may not be quite as striking in his work as horror images, but considered in context, it could be the closest to a purely avant-garde move in the realm of content. Many of these poems use verbs of buying and selling. The first poem of the collection begins this pattern:

> daiku-machi tera-machi kome-machi hotoke-machi rōbo kau machi
>   arazuya tsubame yo
> Carpenter Town, Temple Town, Rice Town, Buddha Town, The Town
>   for Buying Old Mothers—
> Dear sparrow, are there not such places?[14]

This "Town for Buying Old Mothers" is likely a play on Obasuteyama, a real mountain in northern Nagano prefecture, the subject of Fukazawa Shichirō's 1956 novella *Narayama bushikō* (The ballad of Narayama), and originally a reference to the practice of killing the elderly to save food for the young. We should not be surprised to see Terayama tapping into the cruel tragedy, but it is the commercializing predicate that holds the true power of this line—if there is a town for buying used mothers then someone is also selling them. Like the doubling function of inert horror, here the commercial reference serves both to point toward the economic origin of the brutality and to debase the genre of expression, which despite all its transitions has never made economics its theme (other than the grief of poverty, perhaps, with Ishikawa Takuboku's work, but Terayama pushes this further). He maintains this doubled power throughout by limiting that which is bought and sold to putatively nonmaterial symbols of family, lineage, and identity:

hito ni uru jiden o motanu otokora ni odenya jigoku no onibi ga moyuru
The mirage of an *oden* noodle shop hell smolders
   for the men without autobiographies to sell[15]

hito no furusato kaisokonetaru otoko kite furugiya no mae tōrisugitari
A man came by who bought out another's hometown
   and passed right by the secondhand clothes shop[16]

It may be necessary to acknowledge here that Terayama could be referring to the very real problem of real estate developers exploiting rural areas, but he is also tapping into a more general discomfort with the perceived shift from the marketing of material goods to the service of purchasable identity. This could be read as either regret at the expansion of markets to this level of intrusiveness or relief over our collective disillusionment with the notion that trade was ever anything more pure. More important than speculating about which side Terayama stood on is the recognition that he has framed a timely dilemma in its most extreme form for us to ponder: either pay the market price for the material representations of "hometown" (land) and "lineage" (housed in the household shrine) or abandon those commercialized concepts and start fresh (run away from mother and home).

Linked Verse and Narrative

Challenges to the intuitive border between poetry and fiction generally seem to occur on two fronts: one side attacks the notion that literary form separates prose from poetry and another deconstructs the presence of narrative as central to the difference. The work on the first front is most obviously carried out by free verse and prose poetry; but the issue of narrative tends to be more slippery. It may not be difficult to produce examples of prose fiction with convoluted or disjointed narratives, but examples of tanka collections that develop narrative would yield a shorter list. Tanka collections are typically organized into sets of poems on particular topics, but there is a good chance that Terayama may have borrowed concepts from the separate tradition of linked verse (*renga*), a cultural formation that includes stricter rules against the production of linear narrative flow between poems.[17]

Looking at *Den'en ni shisu* as a whole, however, it is quickly evident that this tanka collection is not all tanka—it progresses from the thirty-one-syllable poems at the beginning to narrative-based imaginative prose at the end. Roughly the first half of the collection is tanka (with the two *chōka* used to divide the tanka into three parts), and the second half consists of short prose narratives in the *sōshi* form (the genre of Sei Shōnagon's *Pillow Book*). The shift appears abrupt at first, but the insertion of tanka into most of the first set of *sōshi* marks that section as transitional—the full purge of short-form verse does not occur until the last section of the text. This shift occurs in parallel to a progression in the section headings from references to childhood toward images of leaving home, again associating emancipation from poetic traditions with abandonment of hometown and mother. It is important to note, however, that although the *sōshi* at the end of *Den'en ni shisu* are written in prose and are labeled as a genre widely considered part of prose fiction, taken collectively the parts do not form a coherent whole. Rather, they operate as individual units surrounding a common theme and as such function more like lines of linked verse than as chapters in a unified fictional narrative. The implication, then, may be either that poetics can function within narrative prose or that such attempts at prose by a "poet" will never fully be free of the rhythms and structures of verse. Isoda's claim that antimony is central to Terayama's project becomes evident again here: "Although we might consider the antimony surrounding an adolescent conception of 'hometown' to be a universal phenomenon among the Japanese, Terayama's true originality is in pushing this universal sensation to its absolute limit and in defining with new language the fantastic self-reproduction of 'hometown' which occurs at the moment of abandonment."[18] If a parallel relationship to the poetic tradition holds, then we could similarly claim that Terayama's abandonment of tanka within *Den'en ni shisu* brought about a proliferation of notions of what that abandoned tradition actually was. In effect, he would have defined the object of opposition only after the separation from that object took place.

There are moments within the earlier tanka sections where Terayama has developed narrative continuity on a more subtle level. The first two tanka of the third section, "Komoriuta" (Lullabies), mark a shift from purely associative linkage toward syntactic flow between the poems:

> *yobu tabi ni hirogaru kumo o osoreiki jinsei izen no hi no yaneura ni*
> Each time I called out I was frightened of the spreading clouds—
>   the day before my life began there behind the roof

kakurenbo no oni tokarezaru mama oite dare o sagashi ni kuru mura
  matsuri
The seeker in a game of hide-and-seek is never freed, left to grow old—
  who will he come looking for at the village festival?[19]

The link between the two poems is generated by a *kakekotoba* (pivot word), of sorts, at the end of the first poem: *"yaneura ni"* acts as the direction the clouds move in the first poem, but also as the location of the seeker in the second. By shifting the location of the pivot from the standard middle to the end of the poem, Terayama has exploited the function of the traditional device to create narrative continuity *between* two poems—a clear violation of *renga* rules. Only when this pair is read as a single semantic unit does the beginning of the first poem make sense— *"yobu,"* in this context, refers to the seeker's call to the hiders, *"mō ii kai?"* (Ready yet?), as used in the game of hide-and-seek in the second poem.

A third technique Terayama has used to develop narrative is to gradually piece together plots with periodic reference to the same overdetermined objects. Isoda points out the *butsudan* and the wall clock images as examples of this "new language" Terayama used to represent a shift in notions of "hometown": "Although *butsudan* and wall-clocks have now become little more than objects with nostalgic flavor, to previous generations they were internal to the familial community and were objects possessing a deep-seated reality."[20] Isoda's connection of these objects to this shift in the meaning of "hometown" may have been generated by individual references to them in separate poems—in almost each case the object is being bought or sold, which may be enough to signify the shift from meaningful object to replaceable commodity. But it is more likely that Isoda based his reading on an understanding pieced together from the collective whole of these references. If that collective understanding were cumulative rather than just repetitive, then his interpretive stance would be one piecing together a narrative instead of one observing atomized images. In other words, if our reading strategy assumes that each occurrence of "wall clock" refers to the same object, then we have *already* been reading for narrative, violating the rules of *renga* ourselves via the logic of our reading strategy. Consider the following three references to wall clocks:

uri ni yuku hashiradokei ga fui ni naru yokodaki ni shite kareno yuku toki
Setting off to sell the wall clock, it suddenly strikes the hour—

I carry it under my arm and go into a desolate field

uragawa ni hissori to ke no haete imu hashiradokei no sopurano no hato
Hair will be growing silently on its back—
    the wall clock's soprano pigeon

shi no hi yori sakasa ni toki o kizami tsutsu tsui ni ima ni wa itaranu tokei
Measuring off time backward from the day of one's death—
    the clock which has stopped before reaching this very moment[21]

Distilling the poems, we find a few consistent facts: the clock is going to be sold, it is somehow organic by its link to a human life, and it marks time backward. The organic association developed in the second tanka fits well with Isoda's notion that the object may have been conceived of as much more tightly bound to the family by older generations. The clock, then, might be connected to family cohesion, a notion genuine to some and illusory to others. This association of the clock to life—either literally connected to mother's life or figuratively linked to the illusory life of a naturally cohesive family unit—is further established by the third poem in which the clock has just finished counting down that lifetime. We may be tempted to see the narrative developing chronologically: someone tries to sell the clock, it chimes again in the field, then grows hair and chimes once more in the voice of a pigeon, and then finally stops.

But it may be more plausible, actually, that the narrative is developing in a reverse chronology parallel to the reversed time-orientation of the clock itself. Under that framework we learn the most basic information about the clock in the last poem: that it works opposite to the conventional arrow of time and that it is uncannily connected to someone's life. Then the organic link is furthered in the second poem with this strange image of hair growing on the back of the clock. A partial explanation for that growth is that the poem sits at the end of the Midas-like tale mentioned previously, but it might be more satisfying to note the possibility that the hair growth occurs postmortem—precisely the type of biological trivia Terayama seems to have reveled in. In this context, the chronology of the clock continuing to grow hair in the second poem after its death in the third begins to make sense, especially given the use of the future progressive tense to describe the hair growth ("will [still] be growing" rather than "will grow"). But this interpretive schema stumbles on the ringing of the clock, both in the second and in the first poem. If the reverse chronology is to hold, the last rings of the clock ought to come before it stops working in the third poem. That is, unless this clock image is intended to resonate with the practice of *obasute* (disposing of old women), a practice marked by the gap between a socially scheduled and natural lifespan. During such a gap, the clock could ring even after it had stopped keeping time just as grandmother might speak even after her time is up (seventy years) and she is being carried up a mountain to be left for dead. We might then consider Terayama's inversion of the direction of narrative in *Den'en ni shisu* to be consistent with the inversion of standards associated with avant-gardist technique. But the result presents a paradox: in the process of this attack on the poetic traditions, the poetics have expanded to engulf "fiction" in terms of both form and narrative.

Translating Tanka into Celluloid

The film version of *Den'en ni shisu* was released in December 1974, nine years after the publication of the poetry collection. Using the same title for this narrative feature film poses several questions: How has the content of the poems been represented on-screen? Has Terayama exploited the features of the medium of film with techniques similar to those used in his poetry? Has he attempted to transfer aesthetic principles across media? Viewing the film, it is quickly apparent that much of the poetry collection has been abandoned, many new elements have been added, and the images and poems that are carried over have been significantly rearranged. Such dramatic departure begs questions regarding the elements or principles consistent across both works. In an essay on the film version of *Den'en ni shisu*, art critic Hariu Ichirō attempts to describe the aesthetic operative across many of Terayama's projects:

> Typically, images and photographs serve as the base for a commanding view of several objects as well as the space that surrounds them, which is to say that they occupy a comprehensive position. Words, in contrast, constitute only a partial essence of an individual object and, as Saussure has claimed, communicate according to a linear sequence. As such they are not able to form a complete narrative unless several narratives are woven together. However, in Terayama's works these two elements are continually confused in a characteristic

form. In his tanka, an image swollen with intense emotion is suddenly interrupted and collides with yet another intense image that has transcended time or space. Alternatively, two images are freely displaced. In his theater, stereotypical images doused in folk psychology along with words soaked with emotion, such as delirious nonsense or magical spells, are pulled together into an assemblage. As the established meanings are eviscerated the audience is assaulted with violence like bullets. In his films, and particularly in this film, after differentiating the links between images from the flow of the dialogue into a strict duality, the dialogue hints at desires hidden behind the discourse (the statements) and the images unfold psychoanalytically toward the root of desire. Furthermore, when both are linked up in order to construct a plot the scene changes, an uncanny image emerges, and the flow breaks off completely.[22]

By this account, it would seem that the entire project seeks to undermine not only genre and communication but also the very nature of the most basic units of those concepts: images and words. In this way, the film itself could trace out a process in which at each moment that it recognizes itself coalescing into a familiar form, a comprehensible narrative, or even anything realistic it abandons its course and starts again on a new tack.[23] This sort of take on the film works on a microlevel to explain the texture of the disjointed progression between scenes, but when viewed as a whole, a narrative still makes its way through to the audience: a boy attempts to escape his domineering mother by eloping with his neighbor's wife, she jilts him, and he proceeds onward alone. This narrative is then revealed to be a film in a film by a director struggling to retell his past; this director eventually encounters the former version of himself directly, and finally the two of them conspire, but ultimately fail, to murder their mother. We could claim, then, that the film ultimately failed to be nonnarrative, or that our hardwired drive to find (or produce) a narrative overrode Terayama's plan.

Alternatively, we could recognize that what appears to be a straightforward attack on narrative and genre might be a misinterpretation of the technique being used. If this film is an experiment in transferring poetry to celluloid, then many of the tactics of tanka may be controlling the shape of the film. Such an experimental technique may, in fact, have been used here in order to critique notions of genre, narrative, and medium, but to overlook the method behind that critique oversimplifies Terayama's application of tanka aesthetics to the medium of film. The following analysis will examine direct representation of tanka in the film, elements of the film likely influenced by tanka aesthetics, and parallels in the way narrative is developed in both media.

The film uses 13 out of the 102 tanka found in the poetry collection. Most of them are quoted verbatim, but some have been reworked slightly. They generally appear in pairs, first displayed on-screen, and then read aloud by Terayama himself. The first two poems from the collection are the first pair on-screen, but after that the order breaks down. A closer look at the beginning of the film demonstrates the initial suggestion of a method for transferring tanka to film:

1. The "Carpenter Town" tanka appears on-screen (as text).

   daiku-machi tera-machi kome-machi hotoke-machi rōba kau machi
   arazuya tsubame yo
   Carpenter Town, Temple Town, Rice Town, Buddha Town,
      The Town for Buying Old Mothers—
   Oh, sparrow, are there not such places?[24]

2. The same poem recited aloud (i.e., the sound of the text).
3. The pattern is repeated with the second poem (text, then sound of text).

   atarashiki butsudan kai ni yukishi mama yukue fumei no otōto to
   tori
   He went out to buy a new *butsudan* and never came back—
   my missing brother and a bird[25]

4. A blank screen appears with crows cawing (i.e., sound of the text's image).
5. A still image appears of children playing hide-and-seek (image of a third tanka).
6. Motion begins with diegetic sound (i.e., synthesis of image and sound).

In this first two-minute sequence, Terayama presents us with a condensed text-to-film evolution. This is, in effect, a tour of the technologies that were synthesized to produce this film: poem to theater to radio to photograph to motion picture. It would be dangerous to claim that Terayama is attempting to trace out the history of the medium, however; it is more likely that he is just dealing separately, and thereby conspicuously, with the constitutive elements of this particular sequence. As Garrett Stewart claims in his book on the relationship between film and photography, photographs on-screen and stop-motion images within a film serve to bring to consciousness the materiality of the film strip itself:

> The film medium owes a more *immediate*—rather than just histori-cal and mechanical—debt to the photograph than we can ever (quite) see on-screen.
> . . . The photogrammatic undertext of screen narrative may be (more or less implicitly) alluded to on-screen by "quoted" photos. Alternatively, this undertext may be obtruded in multiple dupli-cates on the strip in the form of the so-called stop-action image. This is the rapid fabrication of stasis that isolates a single visual moment, artificially lifted from the narrative space, and sets it apart from the real motion that invisibly spins it past in the form of sepa-rate (and now anomalously redoubled) imprints.[26]

Stewart wants to move film stills away from their diachronic referent (the photograph) toward their synchronic one (the film strip). The repeated presence of photographs in the film fit nicely with Stewart's comments on film as repetition of the static death image, since the people in those photos—dead relatives, mothers to be killed—are associated with death throughout this work. As the film periodically returns to bare tanka on-screen, the audience is brought back to these basic constitutive elements, from which the film continually rebuilds itself from scratch.

One element of the translation of this tanka collection from text to screen appears to be a linking of tanka with photographs and prose with moving images. The tanka collection moved from short-form poems into prose narrative, and within the film we find a similar juxtaposition of stills or photographs with images flowing smoothly (at least between the cuts). What is not clear is whether the visual cognates of tanka are photographs or single shots of moving images—Terayama's tanka were known for their narrativity, but we might argue that a single photographic image possesses narrative as well. It may be useful to consider a referent of the film's title in this regard. *Den'en ni shisu* is striking in its use of the classical form of the verb "to die," but another important modern text appeared with that same word in its title. Thomas Mann's *Death in Venice* was first translated into Japanese in 1939 as *Venisu ni shisu.*[27] There are almost no similar plot elements in the two texts, but there is a parallel in form: Mann dotted his prose with lines written in Homeric hexameter, much like Terayama's *sōshi* and this narrative film contain tanka.[28] Both authors weave classical poetic formations into otherwise modern texts, framing their immediate questions of aging and memory within the more gradual shifts of language over time.

The breaks in the flow of the film's narrative cited by Hariu may have more to do with the use of tanka aesthetics than he gives credit. His theory works well to explain why certain scenes may end when they do—at the moment that image and sound combine into something realistic and plotlike—but it neglects to theorize the juxtapositional schema at work between those individual scenes. At first glance, it may appear that there is little at all linking the scenes together—that the acting principle might be avoidance of linkage. This follows, as discussed previously, the conventional rules of linked verse that banned the continual treatment of the same subject matter. But that same tradition also encouraged poets to make some sort of associative link between poems, even as the main topic was varied, and on close examination of the film the same practice can be observed. In the opening sequence examined previously, the two tanka and the hide-and-seek segment do not form a coherent narrative. But by mentioning a sparrow in the first poem, a bird in the second, followed by the cawing of crows, images of dark birds associated with death appear immediately before the hide-and-seek game conspicuously placed in a cemetery. This practice continues throughout the film, as Terayama systematically utilizes features of the medium of film to link different scenes. Red tinted ponds and red suns link across scenes to red flowers. Discussions of escape by train carry through to itinerant circus scenes with the sound of a train whistle in the background.

Within individual scenes there is often a montage of images inserted that are loosely connected by theme to the primary narrative. Immediately following the hide-and-seek sequence is a series of four images and one tanka. Terayama's screenplay calls for the following list of images:

- Dirt floor of a dark house. From a gap in the doorway sunlight shines in.
- Photo of mother in her younger days. A thread ties the torn pieces together.

- Photo of two war-dead, a thread ties the torn pieces together.
- Photo of a young girl with a bob haircut, crumbled and torn.
  Above that a waka is superimposed and read aloud.

  hodokarete shōjo no kami o musubareshi sōgi no hana no hana kotoba kana

  Funeral flowers bound into a young girl's hair loosen and fall—
  oh, flower-words of funeral flowers!
- A single red flower dropped into a river and flowing away.[29]

The terse phrasing and intense imagery of these descriptions makes them physically resemble tanka in form and the links between them are tanka-like in their nonnarrative, but thematically clustered, content. Links back to the hide-and-seek image are formed with the young girl in the fourth image and one in the tanka. As mentioned previously, the photographs connect to the still image that begins the hide-and-seek sequence, as well as to the *butsudan* in the second tanka of the film's opening, since they would likely be found in the family shrine to ancestors. Stewart's claim that photographs signify death is quite literal in the Japanese cultural context, where photographs of dead ancestors are often placed inside the *butsudan* itself. The image of the single red flower that ends the montage series carries over into the following scene in which a boy pushes a cart carrying a dead (or perhaps scheduled to die) woman up Mt. Osore. The scene concludes with the following tanka:

naki haha no makka na kushi o ume ni yuku Osorezan ni wa kaze fuku bakari
Going to bury my dead mother's bright red comb—
the wind on Mt. Osore blows and blows[30]

The pretitle sequence of the film concludes with this fourth poem. The red comb links back to the red flower and the references to the girl's hair. The "dead mother" connects to the photo of a mother, the cemetery, the crows, and the *butsudan*.

If, however, this film is linked to the poetry collection as much by method as by content, then we should expect Terayama to use some of the same techniques to develop a recognizable narrative in spite of its apparent attempts to prevent plot from ever forming. The red comb image from the fourth tanka of the film serves as an interesting case for this sort of

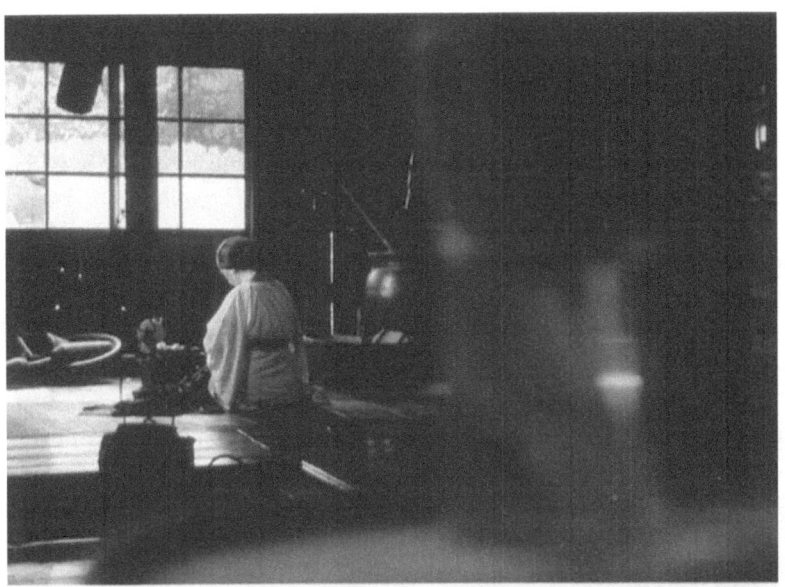

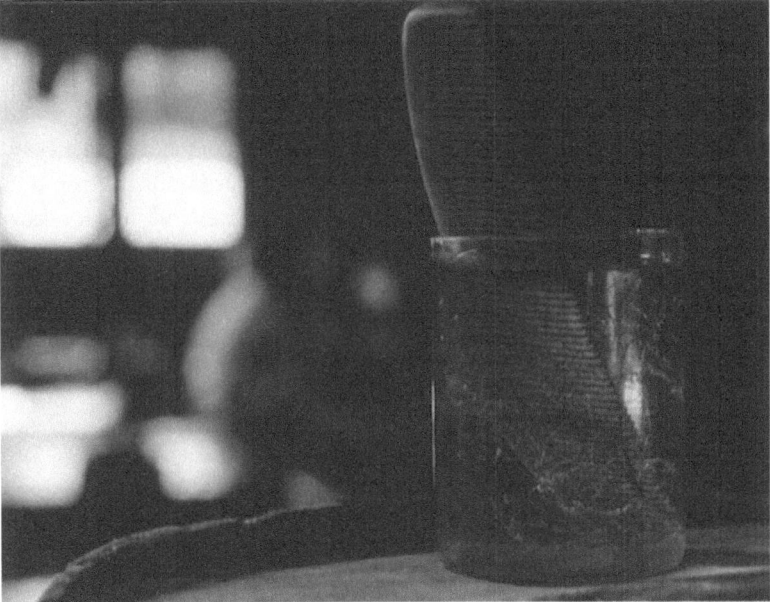

Figure 5.1. A shot of the protagonist's mother that draws its focus back with the same framing to link her to a red comb in the foreground near the beginning of Den'en ni shisu (Death in the country, 1974).

analysis. A few minutes after the tanka appears on-screen, the seventh scene opens with an image of the red comb: "Boy peering into the house from outside the kitchen window. Inside a cup placed on the shelf above the sink, mother's comb has been left to soak in water. Mother's hair, entangled in the comb, swims around in the water as if alive."[31] The comb is positioned in the extreme foreground and mother in the extreme background in this shot, which allows a shift in focal distance to move the viewer's attention from the hair-entangled comb to the mother without any camera movement— such a technique associates the two even more closely than might have been possible with montage (Figure 5.1). By this early point in the film, the comb has already been associated with death and the mother and has been treated as something uncannily organic—the same treatment of the wall clock in the tanka collection. The comb appears a third time in the tenth scene, this time in the lyrics of a song:

> Dusk falls, a temple bell rings
> My dead child's red comb[32]

This song is sung as background music to a scene in which the boy climbs Mt. Osore to contact his dead father through a medium to confess that he plans to leave his mother and run away from home. The background imagery consists of red skies, then a red moon on a dark sky, and a chrysanthemum dyed red. This imbrication of red images leads the comb to signify more than just the memory of a dead relative. The fourth occurrence of the red comb is in a montage sequence in the twenty-ninth scene that is described in the screenplay in the following way:

- Scarecrow wearing a girl's school uniform drenched in blood.
- Close-up of Ushi singing.
- "This Family in Mourning" sign on the back door of a poor farmer's house.
- A girl just raped passed out on a tatami floor, legs spread, flowing blood.
- Blood flowing between the teeth of a comb.
- Bleak-looking Mt. Osore.
- A straw doll nailed to the wall of a dirt-floored room.
- Clouds moving over Mt. Osore.
- Ushi singing on top of a rafter in the barn.

- Flying flock of crows.
- Blood dripping onto the paper mourning sign.
- A Jizō statue on Mt. Osore.
- Blood seeping through and spreading across white cloth.
- A Jizō statue on Mt. Osore.[33]

Here, the origin of the comb's color is finally disclosed as well as a partial explanation for why it seems to operate as the locus of so much abjection. By staining the comb in rape blood, this late in the film, Terayama has again used his technique of retrofitting horror onto seemingly everyday objects. Like the empty chair, the horror of the red comb is latent in its history, revealed only after we have become accustomed to it.

After making reference to the red comb in an on-screen tanka (text), a brief shot (image), a song (sound), and a montage (image plus meaning by juxtaposition), Terayama finally injects it into the narrative proper. In the thirty-fourth scene, Kachō, the married neighbor woman whom the boy plans to run away with, relates her memories of the war and postwar years:

Mother said she didn't want to sell. The money collector with
the black comb came by everyday advising her to sell the land;
she went half-crazy, saying that it would be against her husband's
wishes, that she couldn't let go of the land until he came back. But
she soon died. Then it was decided that the land would change
hands and I was brought to live with relatives in the next village.
I woke quietly in the middle of the night and buried my dead
mother's bright red comb in the wintry field that we had been
forced to sell.
    . . . At night that buried bright red comb sang a song: "Give
back my fields / Give back my land / Give back my mask from the
festival when I was fifteen and left this black hair entwined in the
comb / Give back my whistle / Give back my frown."
    . . . In my dreams I often returned to that field. Each time I dug
around in it and wherever I dug there was a bright red comb. Out
of that field in the middle of town I found a hundred, maybe two
hundred of my mother's bright red combs; bright red combs dyed
in blood. Then all of the combs said to me in unison, "I wasn't born
a woman," "I wasn't meant to be anyone's mother."[34]

Here the narrative hinted at in the previous montage is made explicit while the uncanniness of the comb is maintained and even extended. In much the same way as the wall clock narrative developed in the tanka collection, this narrative seems to end with its beginning—that is, the most basic facts surrounding the comb are saved for the last reference to it, at which point we are left to retroactively fit the pieces together to make sense of its earlier appearances. Backward time (into history) catalyzes horror.

This information about the origin of the comb's color was not hinted at anywhere in the tanka collection, in which bright red combs appear several times. The implication, then, to an audience familiar with both versions of *Den'en ni shisu* would be that the revealed horror of the blood-stained comb would stretch back through the film and then leap back between media and nine years of time to the tanka collection. Such linkage binds these two versions together as a single project and helps to make sense of the use of the same title for such seemingly different works. The standard direction of influence has been inverted. But the red comb can be traced back even further. The previous scene describing the red combs buried in the field is a reworking of part of the very first version of *Den'en ni shisu*, the television drama from 1962. The basic plot of the film version—a boy's jilted elope-ment to Tokyo with a married woman from rural Aomori—is sketched out first in this television version. The boy here is named Tsutomu and he plans to elope with Miki, who admits to him that she has just killed her husband:

MIKI: I didn't at all intend to kill him. And I . . . he was miserable, too, I think. Trying for his whole life to protect the field he inherited from his parents.

TSUTOMU: . . .

MIKI: His dead mother's red comb was buried in that field he was trying to protect. He always used to say, "Gather up the town for a game of *hana ichi-monme*."

TSUTOMU: . . .

MIKI: I'm not sure why, but he sang it.

TSUTOMU: So why did you kill him?

MIKI: When I got back last night he was picking through the car-rot seeds.[35]

The associations being drawn here are between infanticide (*mabiki* is the euphemism, referring to "weeding out" the weaker seedlings as is done with carrots, or nipping buds of chrysanthemums to enlarge one flower) and murdering someone for it and between the stewardship of this red comb (itself representative of the dead mother) and this children's game, *hana ichi-monme*, in which members of opposing teams are pulled out one at a time until one side completely absorbs the other.[36] The image suggests the comb, buried in fields weeded out to strengthen the crop, may have been stained in the blood of children weeded out of families too poor to support them. This link of the red comb to rural poverty is the direction literature scholar Kuritsubo Yoshiki takes in his analysis of the *Den'en ni shisu* film and poetry collection: "The 'red comb' is the 'red comb' of the 'winter night's field' which will almost certainly be pillaged, and it is the blood-spirit of the proletariat class. We can view this as Terayama Shūji scrupulously putting historical events he saw or heard about into the background as he executed his 'matricide.' And, to push further, they must be acknowledged as a symbolism only possible by imbricating postwar history [*sengoshi*] with personal history [*jibunshi*]."[37] Making sense of horrific children's songs and lullabies was at the center of the *Den'en ni shisu* project. Between the release of the tanka and film versions, Terayama explained his understanding of the purpose of lullabies in another television project called *Komoriuta yurai* (The origin of lullabies, 1967):

> Lullabies and nannies have certainly become rare over time. Yet, the sorrowful songs sung by these women—themselves sacrifices to quasi-feudal family-ism [*han-hōkenteki kazoku-shugi*]—did not take the form of lullabies, but rather shifted into another form deep within the hearts of the live-in clerks, factory girls, maids, nannies, waitresses, and prostitutes who sang them.
>
> Lullabies are songs about the philosophy of anonymous women. The song sung by a nanny on Mt. Tenjin as she pinches the behind of another's baby and the one sung by a mother pouring affection on her own lying in a cradle are ultimately the same. These are songs of blood that flows deeper than the rivers.
>
> These are songs for the women, they are not at all for the children. But one could say that these women only came to know love once they had songs for themselves and became independent.[38]

The bloodiness of these songs, as well as that of the red comb, is matched here by the gruesomeness of blood-based familial associations—both by actual blood links and the nannies who stand in by proxy. Earlier in the same drama, the character Shino, head of his village's "Modernity Study Group," discovers a comb buried under a conspicuously healthy camellia blossoming in the garden of Momo, a woman accused by the other villagers of killing her sixteen-year-old son Shinsaku:

> My, what a big camellia. Tall, slightly hunched, with a sturdy base, looks just like Shinsaku!
> (Begins digging with his bare hands. Something hard is entangled in the roots of the flower—realizes that it is Momo's comb)
> Hmmm, a comb.
> (Pulls it out and looks closely)
> It's Momo's comb. Must be some kind of a curse to keep Shinsaku monopolized for herself.[39]

The bright red camellia blossom feeds off of the buried comb and it is later suggested that the flower blooms brightly because Shinsaku himself is buried beneath it—invoking Kajii Motojirō's famous image of the beauty of cherry blossoms resulting from corpses buried below the trees. Shino digs up the camellia to replant it across the river, stopping as he crosses to toss the comb into the water—severing the tie between mother and son as well as linking by imagery the practice of *mabiki* with *mizuko* (lit., "water child"), the euphemism for both miscarriage and abortion. The bloody folk practices associated with backwardness and an impoverished past have not ended in this narrative—they carry on into modernity.

Terayama's use of this red comb image stretches across at least four texts between 1962 and 1974 in slight inflections, but it is always found buried in the soil and is always either red or linked otherwise to the blood of murder and rape. This seems a deeply poetic and symbolic, almost mythical, image, but there is a concrete, historical referent for it. The source is almost undoubtedly a set of red lacquered combs unearthed in an archeological dig near Terayama's hometown of Misawa. The Korekawa site near Hachinohe was first explored starting in 1920 by Izumiyama Iwajirō and his brother-in-law Izumiyama Ayajirō and is thought to represent Tōhoku's late Jōmon culture of approximately three thousand years in the past. The site was made a national historical dig in 1957, and then in 1962 (the same year as the first version of *Den'en ni shisu*), over six hundred items were designated important cultural properties (*jūyō bunkazai*) by the Japanese government. The red combs were among the most notable objects because they demonstrated an advanced lacquering technique and an aesthetic consciousness within what was otherwise believed to be a primitive preagricultural society.[40]

Terayama's narrative-based recreations of the history of his poetically buried red combs parallel, in some ways, the attempts of archeologists to describe the origins and uses of these historically buried red combs— both are by nature imaginative projects. But these combs also symbolized a broader association between Aomori and Tōhoku, in general, with the ancient Jōmon period. In 1962, the same year as the designation of these combs as treasures of the nation and the television broadcast of the first version of *Den'en ni shisu*, the painter and sculptor Okamoto Tarō toured Aomori and Yamagata to collect information for his "rediscovery of Japan" project, which focused on Jōmon figures and Okinawan folk art. That year, in many ways, saw the concretizing of an association between ancient Japan and the Tōhoku region, marking it as a site for research and sightseeing that it had not been before.[41] Okamoto's hand in Expo 70 in Osaka, with its one-liners on Japan's regions among the summaries of nations, corporations, and religions, likely further branded Aomori and Tōhoku, as did the Discover Japan campaign designed by Dentsū for Japan Railways immediately following the expo, which encouraged domestic travel to rural areas.[42]

Part of this transformation of Aomori into a tourist destination was the visualization of "Aomori" as its shape on a map. Aomori geography is distinctive, with two peninsulas, the Shimokita on the east and the Tsugaru on the west, both jutting north toward Hokkaidō (Figure 5.2). In notes written in preparation for the film version of *Den'en ni shisu*, Terayama writes of the axlike shape of the Shimokita peninsula being well suited to such a murderous region: "Looking at a map you'd immediately see that Aomori consists of the Shimokita Peninsula on the right, which is shaped like an ax raised to strike, and the Tsugaru Peninsula on the left that is like a head just about to be chopped off. The Tsugaru Kaikyō (straits) are the splatter of blood on the forehead after the blow—the form symbolizes the prefecture in our country with the most murders among kin."[43] The appearance of the ax in both the tanka collection and the film likely traces to the shape of the region Terayama was attempting to document through memory (the afterword to the tanka collection proclaims it to be a set of "recollections").[44] The decapitated sunflower image from the

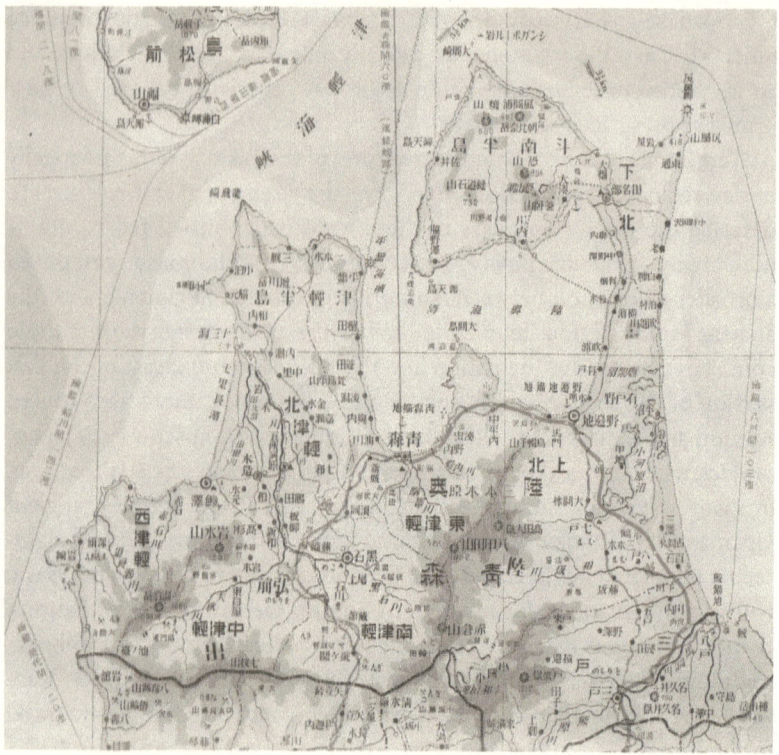

Figure 5.2. Map of Aomori prefecture showing the hatchet-shaped Shimokita peninsula to the east, home to Osore-zan (Mt. Fear), which Terayama visualizes as having just decapitated the Tsugaru region to the west. Image from Fuzanbō Henshūbu, Saishin Nihon chizu *(Tokyo: Fuzanbō, 1916).*

poem mentioned earlier in this chapter could then be linked to the shape of the Shimokita peninsula with three others that mention axes:

> *rōboku no nōten sakite kishi ono o kakumau gotoku idakineru beshi*
> Just back from splitting open the forehead of an aged tree—
>   probably cuddle up with that ax in bed, harboring it like a criminal[45]

This image appears in the film as well. The husband of the woman who plans to elope with the boy pulls away her covers as she sleeps and is shocked to find a sickle by her side (Figure 5.3). Immediately following the previous poem in the tanka collection is another on axes:

chūko no ono kai ni yuku haha no tame chōshi wa manabiori hōigaku
Goes out to buy a used ax, for the benefit of mother—
   the eldest son is studying forensic medicine[46]

Studying forensics so as to not leave a trace of the matricide he will commit with the ax: this image, too, appears in the film. Near the end, the filmmaker prepares to kill his mother in order to liberate the younger version of himself to escape from her. They both agreed that killing her is the only solution, so he prepares a rope to bind her with and carries a sickle (a visual match with the one in the neighbor woman's bed) into the house, only to lose his nerve and dutifully join her for dinner. A third poem in the collection also recalls the decapitated sunflower:

kyū-jinushi kaeritaru ato himawari wa ono no ichigeki matsu hodo no ki
After the former landlord returns home the sunflowers turn—
   as though waiting for the ax's blow—yellow[47]

This incessant return to the ax image—creating a literary topos deriving from the geographical (but just as fictional) link of the peninsula to the ax—parallels Terayama's constant return to the buried red comb. Both generate a neomythology for Aomori, not only rejuvenating the notion of regional literature but also parodying any concrete, determinative link between the content of that literature and the geography of the region. Most important for Terayama was the transformation within popular consciousness of the region of his childhood (his family moved often, but always within Aomori prefecture) toward a new set of images and meanings he did not grow up with. Nostalgia was faced with knowledge that a return home was now literally impossible—the Aomori he knew no longer existed, and bizarrely, it had with time come to represent not something more modern but something far older than before. The arrow of time, like the clock in the poems, seemed to point the wrong way.

    There is a strange glitch in the very beginning of the film version of *Den'en ni shisu* that engages another case of Aomori's transformation while Terayama was away. The first tanka printed on-screen—Carpenter Town, Temple Town, Rice Town (discussed previously)—is read aloud out of order.[48] The second two "towns," Temple Town and Rice Town, are reversed when read despite being printed on-screen in the original format. A glitch like this confronts a subtitler, for example, with a strange, almost

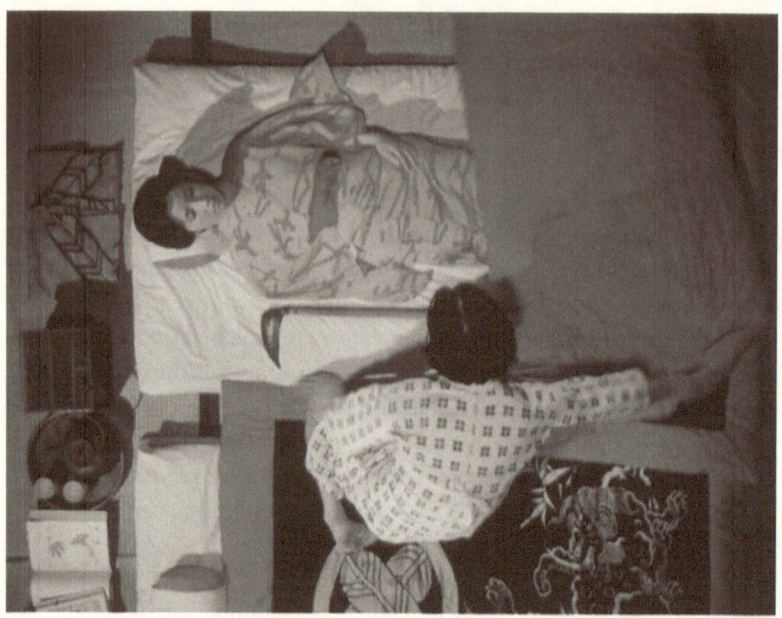

Figure 5.3. The neighbor in Den'en ni shisu *(Death in the country, 1974) discovers a sickle under his wife's bedcovers.*

Derridian dilemma: which should be privileged—written or spoken language? While this may have simply been an error, it would not be unlike Terayama to inject his work with this sort of willful slippage, and for it to punctuate, subtly, some sort of larger issue.

The Carpenter Town poem seems to speak abstractly about imagined villages in some idyllic fantasy, but they turn out to be actual districts in the center of Aomori City where Terayama spent his high school days. Aomori's downtown underwent redistricting, however, in 1968, which also involved renaming areas of the city. Traditional districts dating back to the Edo period, including Daiku-machi (Carpenter Town), Tera-machi (Temple Town), and Kome-machi (Rice Town) were split up and given bland new "modern" names such as Shinmachi (New Town), Chūōmachi (Central Town), and Honmachi (Main Town).[49] The question the poem poses, then—"Oh sparrow, are there not such towns?"—would have been accurately answered in the affirmative in 1965, at the time of the tanka collection's publication, but in the negative in 1974, when the poem reappeared (marked with the glitch) on film. The time gap between the texts had fictionalized the rhetorical question—a statement of fact at its initial appearance but either a fictional statement or a historically embedded quotation after 1968. The twisting of the truth status of a static statement by the flow of history is invoked here by this twist in the poem.

It was this type of time gap, or slippage in time, that had opened the film and earned it its title for foreign release—*Pastoral Hide-and-Seek* (or *Cache-cache pastoral* at Cannes). The young girl covers her eyes as her friends hide behind gravestones in a cemetery. She calls out to them, "Can I look yet?" (*mō ii kai?*), and they respond, "Not yet" (*mada da yo*). She calls again, "Can I look yet?" and this time they respond, "Go ahead" (*mō ii yo*), but they emerge from behind the graves as fully grown adults, the men in various uniforms, the women holding babies. The image comes from the tanka version of *Den'en ni shisu*—"The seeker in a game of hide-and-seek is never freed, left to grow old"—but the critical addition is this instantaneous and differential slippage in time. Time occurred at different speeds for these children, but we cannot be sure whether it had stood still for just one or been accelerated for the rest. The perspective here is identified with the young girl, but we distrust it, and are then forced to recognize the relativity of the experience of time. There is also an inversion here of typical commentary on differential development—slower development is associated with youth here whereas advanced, faster development is linked to not only adulthood and responsibility but also death. This link is further developed in an image later in the film in which a group of school-children in uniform cross a bridge but then return across the same bridge in the same uniforms in their old age (Figure 5.4). This sort of time slip may be a metaphor for the larger project at work here: Terayama representing memories of his childhood in Aomori. He needs to slip back thirty years to wartime Japan to recreate these images, memories he recognizes to have already become irrecoverable through distortion—"All individual memories are metaphors, events from foreign countries."[50]

The combination of time's relativity and time slippage comes up again midway through the film when it breaks out of the narrative and the director of the first half discusses his problems representing the past with a critic. The critic gives the director a puzzle to ponder: "If you rode a time machine back several hundred years and killed your great-great-great-grandmother, would you cease to exist in the present?"[51] This puzzle is called the grandmother paradox (or the grandfather paradox), and represents the standard logical critique of the possibility of time travel that

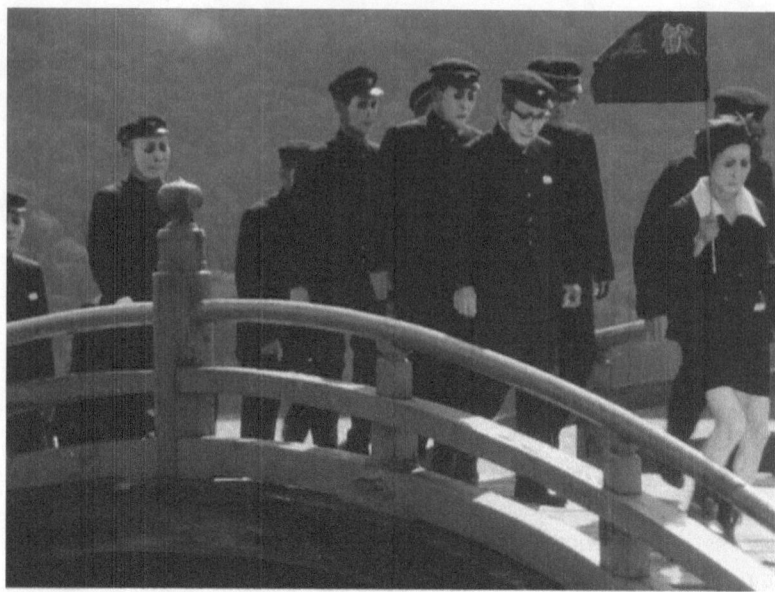

Figure 5.4. "Schoolchildren" on their way back from a field trip in Den'en ni shisu (Death in the country, 1974). Child actors in the same uniforms had walked across this bridge just moments before this shot.

Einstein's relativity equations seemed to suggest as possible.[52] For the narrative of Den'en ni shisu this reference serves two purposes: the first is to link the process of retelling even the most accessible, personal histories to the process, and likely impossibility, of time travel; and the second is to modernize our conception of historical time using Einstein's thesis of the space–time continuum. The closing image of the film finally makes sense when understood in these terms. When the director gives up on killing his mother and sits down to eat with her, we assume the setting must still be Aomori. The inside of the house as he enters has the same hearth and the same wall clock as it did when he was a boy, and his mother is still cleaning the same butsudan. But after they sit down to eat, the wall behind them suddenly falls to the ground, leaving them in the middle of a public square in the Shinjuku district of Tokyo with characters from the film walking by among the crowds as the credits roll. So the time slippage that opened the film (child to adult) is paired with a space slippage to finish it (Aomori to Tokyo), and the two are bridged by this self-reflexive intermezzo's reference to the space–time nexus of relativity theory (Figure 5.5).

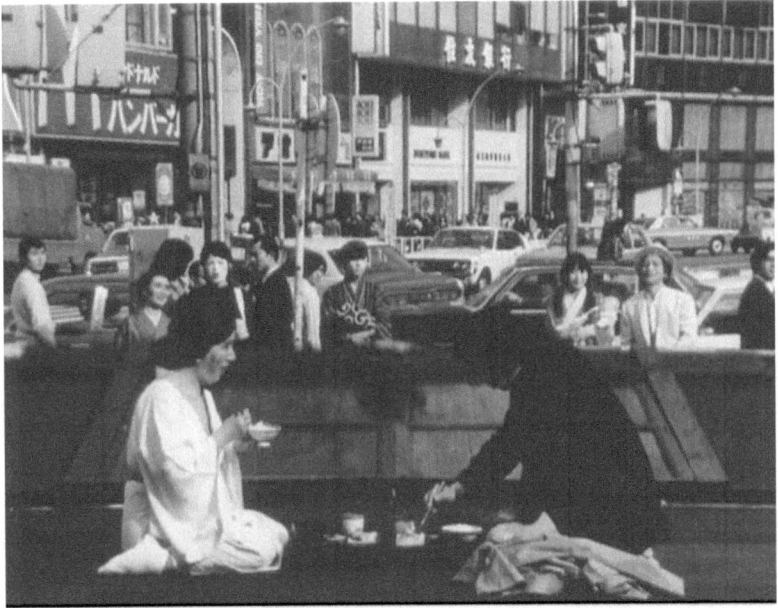

Figure 5.5. The walls of the world of his childhood to which the protagonist attempted to return fall at the end of Den'en ni shisu (Death in the country, 1974), revealing their location in the Shinjuku district of Tokyo.

Telling this history is impossible on film because the memories turn circuslike and even the landscape changes the moment it is selected for filming. This is a point made in the intermezzo by the director speaking to the critic: "I sit down to write, but the instant I objectify something—even myself or the landscape—they all turn vaudeville on me with everyone in thick makeup."[53] Awazu Kiyoshi, the graphic designer who did the artistic design for the film, worked with Terayama on this problem during the process of location hunting in Aomori:

Say you're location hunting for a film production. The landscape [*fūkei*] that you see out the window of the train or a car is somewhat vague, but it's as though a scene from the film has already been shot within that landscape. In the same way that a window in a house can be like the frame of a painting, the camera also plays a framing role. It's not exactly like contemplating a single picture, but the landscape that changes from one to the next in the window is similar to watching a film or television. The instant someone says, "How about here?" that location becomes a privatized image of the filmmaker ... the landscape ceases to be something you look at and becomes something you show.[54]

The landscape is only inscribed as natural or representative, beautiful or bleak, *after* its selection—it does not exist until that selection. This denaturalization of landscape was part of Terayama's stated attempt to "get beyond the landscape theories [*fūkeiron*] of the past," which he claimed, "historically have tended to emerge without fail after a setback for the antiestablishment movement."[55] One goal of the film was to explore the possibility of composing and editing landscape itself—exaggerating the impact of the artist on scenery chosen as a subject. This was particularly clear in the absurd, eclectic props added to a scene late in the film when the director is playing a game of shōji with the younger version of himself (Figure 5.6). They sit on tatami mats in the middle of a harvested rice paddy in a visual match to the final scene of dinner with mother. In the background, a young boy gets a haircut to the left, and Tora-san (from the popular film series) walks along the footpath near a giant book of matches (out of which will later emerge three women). There is no interaction between these layers of depth, which are visually reinforced by the row of utility poles fading toward a vanishing point perfectly centered in the frame. The teleology of this conspicuous single-point perspective is further paralleled by a discussion of fate between the director and the younger version of himself:

BOY: I'm thinking of going to a merchant marine academy when I
     grow up.
ME: You're too late. I went to a liberal arts university.
BOY: But maybe it would work to do it over.
ME: Impossible. Your turn.[56]

The director asks about a Turgenev novel he stole in middle school, but it turns out to be when he was a year older than the boy, to which the boy responds that he will buck his fate the following year and not steal the book (but we sense that his reaction against his fate may be just as deterministic as his fate itself). The director responds by saying, "I know everything about you, but you know nothing about me"—a concise critique of the problem of differential development in which the fate of the late bloomers is not only out of their control but also already known (and so predictable and exploitable) by their forebears.[57] The director speaks from the position of privileged knowledge about the future of the boy, meaning that their orientations toward time are opposite. This is reflected subtly in a comment ostensibly about the shōji game: "Move it left. Right to you. What's right to you is left to me."[58] They are mirrored images of each other, but it is a one-way mirror—a one-way dispossession of knowledge of the future of the boy, which will always be the past of the older director.

This confrontation with fate and determinism may have been the central problem of the *Den'en ni shisu* project. Awazu comments on the problem of deterministic causality in his conversation on landscape: "The causality between landscape and things is random. Randomness occurs once two causalities intersect, we usually call it an 'encounter' or a 'chance operation,' but new landscapes appear that have never existed before, and existing landscapes are destroyed. I think the only part humans see are the causalities— they are the most visible and they're the part we try to see."[59] This stance

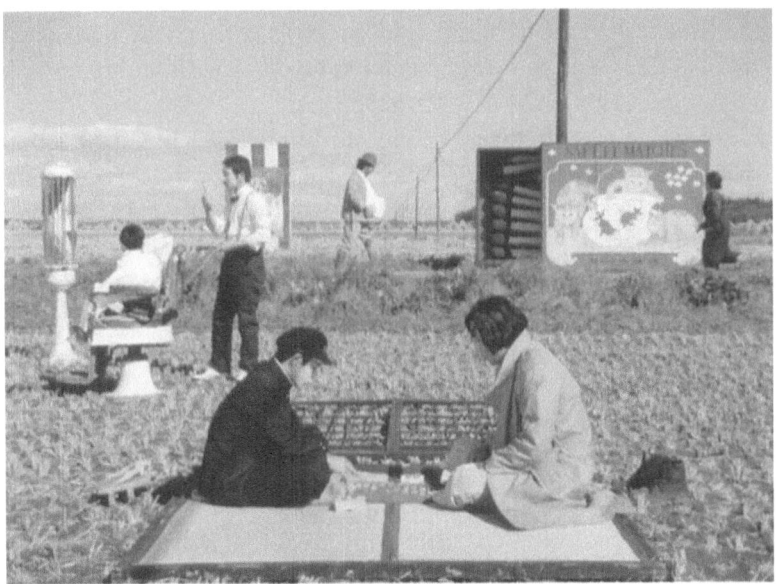

Figure 5.6. *The filmmaker challenges the boyhood version of himself to a game of shōgi within a landscape design by Awazu Kiyoshi near the conclusion of* Den'en ni shisu (Death in the country, 1974).

allows for the likelihood of materialism, but a materialism that is not predictable or fated. And if the modern, cohesive, subjective interiority is partially constructed in contradistinction to a similarly cohesive, but objective, exteriority in the form of landscape, then disrupting the stability of that notion of the external could help the internal into a new subjectivity. "Human beings will never be free until they can liberate themselves from their own memories," says the film critic during the intermezzo.[60] By denaturalizing both landscape and memory and exposing them as subjective constructs, Terayama opens the possibility of emancipation through self-fictionalization, that is, of self-determination within personal history itself. Thus the interior of a home and a barbershop placed in the landscape without houses or buildings is a breaking down of those borders between inside and out. This image pairs, then, with the image early in the film of Mt. Osore under the tatami mat in the house. Both were intended (according to Terayama's notes) to make a "labyrinth of interior and exterior": "The 'home' is dissembled, and its interior (furnishings, family, supplies) are placed at random in the field, while simultaneously the exterior (Mt. Osore, forests, rivers) is dragged inside of the 'home.'"[61] History, in parallel, is attacked as fluid and malleable—the director tells the younger version of himself, "There is no past which cannot be fixed."[62] Landscape is unnatural here, and history is fictional.

But this is an inversion, not a complete dissolution of reality. History is made fictional—open to manipulation and unbound by truth—but fiction is in turn bound and closed off to subjective control at the end of *Den'en ni shisu*. The director intends to kill his mother to liberate both himself from the present and the younger version of himself—not risking his own existence directly, since he would be killing her after his own birth, but altering history in a way that would certainly impact the present. But in the end he is not capable of killing her even though he recognizes that the murder would be within the fictional realm of film: "I could start everything over. Not just my mother but even I am nothing more than an actor in one little story I made up by myself. And this is just a film. Who am I if I can't even kill one little mother!?"[63] This stalemate in the narrative destroys the world of Aomori, the relationship with the mother, and the son's dutiful "return" to her, and the walls of this world literally come crashing down, revealing their rural home to be a construct. Outside that "fictional" world of the past are the members of the circus, now seen as enmeshed in the fabric of the city, welcoming the filmmaker back to his theater troupe, to his city, and to the present tense.

This delimitation of fiction's imaginative range coupled with the categorization of history as subjective within the thematics of this project parallels patterns in its form. The iterative form of reworking of the television and tanka collection versions of *Den'en ni shisu* into this film finds its imaginative core not in leaps into new territory but in the reworking of former work in a new medium and in the cutting up and reediting of memories and poems from the past. We see a commitment to collage techniques in this project similar to Terayama's own debut, but here he borrows the base material from himself—perhaps rather than cross-pollination here we find self-pollination. The incessant return to a stock set of images generates a lexicon of Terayama's own, the reshuffling of which might be conceived as attempts to speak in a fully individuated language. Translations of the tanka, then, onto the screen directly, into individual images or stretched into narratives, might best be understood as an experiment in modulating the length of the semantic unit translated: full narratives, single images, clusters of words used to describe an image, or individual sounds. The length of the cut and the editorial decisions regarding arrangement are the loci of creativity here. And yet the outcome is so far removed from the source that as readers of these versions of *Den'en ni shisu* we may be forced to acknowledge that repetition itself is impossible—that events, artifacts, and people are bound in a web of space–time such that the circumstances that created the context for meaning can never be reproduced.

"Japanese" Counterculture

I HAVE FORESTALLED DIRECTLY ADDRESSING JAPANESE counter-culture until this conclusion, partly to avoid the snare of conceiving a global, and explicitly antinationalist, movement through the category of the nation. Yet the category of "Japanese" counterculture still needs to be tackled because that was the frame within which Terayama's work was often received (and appraised) once it left Japan. It is not at all a stretch to claim that Terayama's projects *became* Japanese only once they left Japan—whereas within Japan they often seemed foreign. This foreignness could be certified by an award from a European festival, for example, and then reintroduced to Japan as international clout. So we find a pattern of move-ment from international into Japanese characterizing much of Terayama's work after about 1970. Still, this is not to deny the existence of a domestic countercultural discourse in Japan that spoke in Japanese to an audience mostly in Japan, which was particularly concerned with the response of the Japanese government and the people of Japan to the situation of the late 1950s into the mid-1970s. There are enough domestic referents within that discourse (among the many references to foreign or international issues) that Japan's national borders, to the extent that they coincide with its linguistic borders, do mark the maximum range of the assumed audi-ence of that conversation. But those borders are never what is meant by "Japan," even in the domestic discourse about the nation—the name of the nation always embodies a struggle over the meaning of history, a privi-leging of certain facets of culture, and efforts to control the future of the collective. I will sketch out, very briefly, some contours of this domestic discourse on counterculture before moving on to the slightly thornier issue of "Japanese" counterculture abroad.

Japan had a hippie movement, but it is reported to have been limited in scope—communes on small islands, a return to farming, the creation of a rice-growing and filmmaking collective in Yamagata by the radical documentary filmmaker Ogawa Shinsuke during the 1970s—but the ideas were very much in the air and alive in the media. Japan's own homegrown hippies, the *fūten-zoku* ("idler-tribe"), made news by lounging outside of Japan's busiest train station, Shinjuku, wearing oddball sunglasses and sedated on their drug of choice (possibly their only option): sleeping pills.[1] The popularization of the term traces to a *manga* called *Fūten* by Nagashima Shinji that was serialized in the magazine *COM* starting in the spring of 1967. Nagashima explains at the end of the first installment that the main characters of his *manga* are less Nagahima Hinji—Nagashima's alter ego, with plays on "spare time" (*hima*) and "poverty" (*hin*)—than the group of "*fūten*" friends he made over the previous years, including poets who do not write and jazz musicians who do not play.[2] Terayama comments on a group of about a dozen *fūten* who formed an ashram in Nagano where they built huts and grew vegetables:

> Looking at the fūten-zoku laying around on the greenhouse outside of Shinjuku station, I can't help thinking of Mark Twain's *Adventures of Tom Sawyer*, which I read as a kid. Tom Sawyer was a square from a bourgeois family, but Huckleberry Finn was hip. Huck was lazy and coarse, wore rags, and slept in a sugar barrel, but he was an idealist. The Shinjuku fūten have more ideals than they can manage—they talk of love, freedom, liberation from their chains. And with the clear blue sky for a roof, and the air for their furnishings, they dream of the return of a primordial society, when people could live as human beings. This group of fūten who have created their "bums' ashram" in the village of Kōdo in Nagano, which even includes the beat poet Gary Snyder, have surely out-done the Shinjuku fūten in the loftiness of their ideals.
>
> Yet, in dreaming of "human-ness" in the form of a return of primordial society, these young people who have chosen the fūten route seem to be reading from the book of life backwards. Me, I like pop music, the hustle and bustle of the city, the gossip rags and two-bit newspapers. I can't help loving the people who like deceiving people and being deceived themselves, the ones who focus all their energy on one side of a philosophical debate (even knowing that it's all relative in the end), or who gamble sometimes and lose, or get drunk on cheap hooch, or the ones who spend their time worrying and fretting about their lives. This love of dropping out is not going to be possible in every era.[3]

The critique here is not so much of separatism as it is of the ashram's assumptions about human history—this urge toward regressing to an idealized past was very much at odds with Terayama's notion of the synchronic time orientation of counterculture and its commitment to expanding the sensation of being in the present tense. Terayama was critical of the Japanese *fūten*, yet it was the common Japanese sleeping pill Broverin that Terayama would bring with him to Amsterdam to offer, as soup, to the audience of his 1972 play *Ahen sensō* (Opium War), perhaps giving the Dutch cannabis scene a sample of Tokyo-style hippiedom.[4]

It may be useful to think of Japanese counterculture as a set of particular spaces in Tokyo: the Sōgetsu Art Center as it moved from an emphasis on the family business of flower arranging toward support for collaborative experimentation, film, and debates on the role of art in culture; the Art Theater Guild's Shinjuku Bunka Art Theater cinema and the smaller Sasori-za (Scorpio) stage in the basement; and the nearby Fūgetsudō cafe, a hangout for student radicals, poets, and hipsters. Counterculture might be what happened in those spaces and under Kara Jūrō's red tent, Satō Makoto's black tent, or wherever Terayama's Tenjō Sajiki was performing. Counterculture as a space might be inscribed directly on the body in this period, both in terms of the sexual revolution, as well as in terms of the starkly visible in the development of "*ankoku butō*" (The dance of utter darkness) with Hijikata Tatsumi or in the "privileged-flesh" performance theory of Kara Jūrō. Counterculture might be in graphic design in this period, as figures like Yokoo Tadanori, Awazu Kiyoshi, and Uno Akira not only create a visual style for counterculture but also launch a journal to theorize the field of design called *Dezain hihyō* (The Design Review) in November 1966 that runs for four years, offering a way to periodize the heart of the era of counterculture and particularly its visual turn.

The significance of counterculture may not have been the radical newness of the ideas so much as the threat of their rapid massification. The term "underground," then, may be a misnomer, or at least anachronistic, since the core of the movement coincides with motion out of hiding and into public view. The nonchalance that marked this moment—in the presentation of nudity, of homosexuality, of anarchistic social organization, of loud music, and of the general disregard for state power as an authority—signals a minor subculture with momentum, moving toward becoming the representative ethos of a generation.

Politically, the rise of the New Left in Japan—in a broad nexus of protest against the situation of the cold war, administrative policy at the universities, the extension of contracts keeping U.S. military bases in Japan, the Vietnam War, technocracy, and the bureaucratization of society—was simultaneous with the student movements in Europe and North America. If we look at journal publishing, we find 1959 to have been a key year. The weekly news magazine *Asahi jānaru*, which would become emblematic of radical students by the late 1960s, was launched in March 1959 with a lead article on the state of intercontinental ballistic missiles, which had unified the world under an umbrella of potential annihilation and trapped Japan between the cold war powers. This stance of monitoring the cold war is clear in the set of dispatches that open each issue: a page each for Washington, London, and Moscow, a rotating fourth page for somewhere else (Bonn, Bangkok, Cairo), then Tokyo and Osaka. Two days after the first issue of *Asahi jānaru* would arrive the first issue of the *manga* weekly *Shōnen magajin*, filled with action comics (*gekiga*) but also peppered with news articles as well as anecdotes and political commentary in the margins of the stories. By 1970 the *manga* run alongside *Ashita no Jō*, for example, included a historical account of Kennedy's career and a series depicting the horrors of the Vietnam War. This pair of weekly magazines became emblematic of the late 1960s Zenkyōtō student radicals—"The *Journal* in their right hand, *Magazine* in their left"—but it is important to note that this pair had been available and was read by young, politicized intellectuals for the entire decade of the 1960s.[5]

The Japanese magazines most closely associated with the 1960s student movement arrived on the market several months before the launch of the emblematic English-language New Left publications. The United Kingdom's iconic *New Left Review*, the product of a merger between *New Reasoner* and *Universities and Left Review*, would publish their first issue in January–February 1960. A few months earlier, in the fall of 1959, the first issue of *Studies on the Left* would be published in Madison, Wisconsin, with greetings from earlier journals like *Dissent* (founded in 1954) and from the soon-to-launch *New Left Review*. Although the international flow of information was often unbalanced (pouring into Japan but often only trickling out), the space these groups were carving out between the old loyalties to the Comintern and the liberal, pluralist critique of the cold war, along with their emphasis on university students as a political force, was common across them all. The roots of each of these publications could be traced deeper into the 1950s (at least), but the point is that the transition to magazines emphasizing the student-led New Left occurred simultaneously in Japan and elsewhere—this was not the product of imitation.

The sociologist C. Wright Mills's "Letter to the New Left," published first in *New Left Review* in 1960 and reprinted in *Studies on the Left*, critiques both the liberal "end-of-ideology" ideology and the Soviet Union's whitewashed "socialist realism" before offering a definition of the Right as pro–status quo and the Left position as a humanist and secular, morally guided set of criticisms, demands, theories, and programs that "connect up cultural with political criticism."[6] This might sound too ambiguous to be effective, but there is a power in the flexibility Mills proposes here, as there would be in the Port Huron Statement's call for "participatory democracy" and in Terayama's cultural critique, so often misinterpreted as apolitical. Mills closes his letter by rebutting inevitable attacks on the New Left as a "moral upsurge," or the issues as too ambiguous, or the movement as "utopian," with "Tell it to the students of Japan. Tell it to the Negro sit-ins. Tell it to the Cuban Revolutionaries. Tell it to the people of the Hungry-nation bloc."[7] Japan, here, signals an international solidarity not yet achieved and a synchronic perspective that sees connections between Third World emancipation movements, civil rights, and student insurrection across the advanced industrial nations. The unfortunate reality is that these internationally minded beginnings of the New Left seem to have given way in scholarship on the era to a nation-bound conception of counterculture as fundamentally American—a pattern with the same contours as Terayama's shift from being understood first as international and only later as "Japanese."

It may be a stretch to proclaim counterculture a fully global phenomenon, and it is particularly hubristic to pair this sort of proclamation with a study of a figure from the counterculture of an always overdetermined "Japan." The cohort that Japan has historically functioned to internationalize would otherwise have been Euro-American, so this is, strictly speaking, a phenomenon among the advanced industrial economies (something the sociologists all point out). Japan's position within that group as an economic power goes unquestioned, and yet the emergence of cultural phenomena that parallel (and reject) economic power in Japan is often presented as an unexpected event or somehow imitative—and this accusation occurs at least as much within Japan as from outside. But if these "advanced economies" are synonymous with the nations that fought in

World War II, we might also note the way many of the border-crossing alliances that characterized counterculture were bridges across the former Axis–Allies divide: John and Yoko bridging the United Kingdom and Japan. Deleuze and Guattari bridging France and Italy. The Sozialistische Deutscher Studentenbund (SDS) and Students for a Democratic Society (SDS) bridging West Germany and the United States (perhaps mostly in spirit and by accident of acronym). Gary Snyder and the "bum ashram" *fūten* bridging the United States and Japan. British musician Julian Cope claims to have been "sustained" by krautrock in the years before punk, and his books—*Krautrocksampler* and *Japrocksampler*—are tellingly not on 1960s and 1970s American or British rock but rather that of West Germany and Japan.[8]

It may still be worth maintaining "global counterculture" as a framework, however, for the simple reason that those in the counterculture used this sort of "Whole Earth" paradigm to conceive themselves as citizens of the world, or as "Earthlings," to use Jim Haynes's preferred term. That the project was incomplete and that many of the borders crossed were on the same old cosmopolitan routes should not limit the scope of counterculture's aspirations. There is certainly more work to be done. Similarly, if it is possible for Japanese studies to enter a dialogue on the global in which Japan is recognized as an active, contributing participant rather than always as a marker of otherness—the contrasting case study, or the boundary that tests the range of a phenomenon—then we will have made some progress. It is as incumbent on Japanese studies to refuse a privileged position in the globalization discourse as it is for fields aspiring to be global, like visual culture, to avoid tokenizing the cultural products of Japan.

It is important to keep Terayama's contribution to a theory of counterculture within the realm of tactics and that this be a set of useful tools rather than a type of analysis that would prescribe a certain course of action. Terayama was consistent in calling for action rather than enaction (*kōi*, not *jissen*), particularly in the arts.[9] The poems themselves needed to perform an action, to cause something to happen, instead of documenting the past or being put to work in the service of a theory. The flexibility opened up by allowing for a disconnect between theory and practice, between words and action, is a useful kind of abstractness in Terayama's mind. He pushes this to the point of actively encouraging hypocrisy in certain instances, arguing that those who calcify their political position are destined for nothing other than the pointlessness of martyrdom (which functions only for the individual martyr, never for the cause).[10]

What ultimately is at stake, then, in an analysis of Terayama Shūji and counterculture? Something beyond just another dead "carpe diem" poet, one hopes. Terayama's work suggests an important cluster of proposals. A set of lateral-motion tactics for instigating an effective oppositional engagement with the times. A suggestion that we stand to see a great deal more by getting beyond the hegemony of diachronic time orientation to start focusing on synchrony and the present tense. A call for indeterminacy as the flexibility we need for an antiestablishment movement to survive over the long term and for the destabilization of meaning as a way to reinvigorate a discourse. But if any of Terayama's proposals are to be answered, perhaps the most important will be to do our half of the job as readers to complete the author's text and to do that with as much creative engagement as we assume the author (or authors) to have offered to us—to push our readings as far as they can go. I often felt as I wrote these chapters that I may have taken the analysis too far, that I overreached and overread, wandering into indefensible territory. But now I wonder if the opposite is the case—if taking a reading beyond the rational limit or past the range of possibility of authorial intent is precisely the task we are charged with, and so I am left wondering if this book did not go nearly far enough.

Acknowledgments

I AM GRATEFUL TO THE FOLLOWING mentors, informants, classmates, and colleagues for their generous guidance, shared memories,
and advice. Kathryn Sparling, my undergraduate advisor at Carleton
College, helped to start me down this path by supporting my proposal
to translate Terayama's 1960 debut play as part of a senior thesis project;
she then spent countless hours with me line editing my translation until
it was accurate. John Treat, my graduate advisor (first at the University
of Washington and later at Yale), saw this project through from beginning to end, pushing me to return to Terayama for my dissertation at a
time when my interests were getting too broad. Chiba Shunji, my advisor at Waseda University in Tokyo for a combined five years of research,
has steered me toward Japanese literary theorists and writers I would
never have found on my own. Carol Fisher Sorgenfrei, whose dissertation taught me who Terayama was, graciously made the introductions
I needed to arrange my first affiliation at Waseda—I am grateful for her
steady encouragement. My research in Tokyo was supported by grants
from the Japanese Ministry of Education (1996–98), Fulbright–Institute
of International Education (2002–4), and Fulbright-Hays (2008–9)—
I am indebted to these organizations for giving me the time and freedom to
complete the research needed to write this book. Edward Kamens generously helped with an early version of what would become chapter 5. Chris
Hill's demand for precision helped me rein it in somewhat when things
started spinning out of control. Jeff Brophy, archivist at the International
Boxing Hall of Fame, kindly mailed me copies of newspaper clippings on
Terayama's friend, "Fighting" Harada, the only Japanese boxer enshrined
in Canastota. Ozzie Rodriguez, Kaori Fujiyabu, and Ellen Stewart of
LaMama Experimental Theatre Club in New York integrated me into their
2002 retrospective of Terayama and Higashi Yutaka's LaMama plays. Jennifer Merin recounted her adventure to Tokyo to join Terayama's troupe,
including her shock when given a stack of pictures of Japanese men to
choose from after she asked where she would be staying (responses to a
personal ad they took on her behalf). Ritsaert ten Cate, director of the
Mickery Workshop in Amsterdam, generously opened his art studio to

me for an interview and made two particularly important comments on Terayama (whose troupe performed regularly at his theater through the 1970s): first, that looking to surrealism to understand Terayama "is a red herring; he was primarily interested in manipulation," and second, that "if you ever wanted a response to television, it was a Terayama show." On ten Cate's recommendation, I contacted Renate Klett in Berlin, who shared her recollections of seeing Terayama's troupe at the 1972 Munich Olympics. Hiroko Govaers, Terayama's film agent in Paris, shared her collection with me over several days and introduced me to Jim Haynes, an old friend of Terayama's, and Nicolas Bataille, Eugene Ionesco's stage director who spent several years in Tokyo in the late 1960s and early 1970s where he saw many of Terayama's plays. Kujō Kyōko, Terayama's ex-wife and producer for the troupe, brought me along to several performances and shared materials from her scrapbooks that helped especially with the Rikiishi Tōru funeral section of chapter 3. Hisao Mitsuko, producer for the troupe Tokyo Kid Brothers, shared a number of memories of time spent with Terayama, who she claims was actually rather shy. Sasame Hiroyuki, of Poster Hari's Company, helped me pin down dates using his incredible poster collection. Awazu Ken recalled translating for the American performances of *Directions to Servants* and introduced me to his father, the graphic designer Awazu Kiyoshi, who shared memories of his many collaborations with Terayama. Sasaki Shōichirō, the radio and TV documentary director from TV Man Union and Nippon Hōsō Kyōkai (NHK), told me about his collaboration with Terayama on the important stereo radio drama "Comet Ikeya." Kuwabara Shigeo, chief editor at Kamarusha, shared memories of the first stereo radio broadcasts in Japan during the 1950s (before FM), when you had to borrow a neighbor's radio to set up a two-receiver apparatus, one set to NHK 1, the other to NHK 2, to hear a half-hour stereo program. Members of my dissertation cohort—Jon Abel, Deborah Shamoon, Charles Exley, Ryan Holmberg, Mariko Schimmel, Allison Alexy, and Gavin Whitelaw—provided helpful suggestions and comic relief as this project took shape. I am grateful to my fellow organizers of the 2007–8 "Audio Culture in the Visual Era" Mellon Workshop at the University of Wisconsin–Madison—Nicole Huang, Michele Hilmes, Lee Blasius, Casey Lee, and Jill Casid—for creating a forum to think through issues in sound studies, the relation between the visual and the audio, aural, and oral, and the possibility of historicizing and culturalizing listening. My colleagues in the Department of East Asian Languages and Literatures, the Center for East Asian Studies, and in Japanese studies across UW–Madison have been wonderfully supportive. Thanks to Jason Weidemann, the manuscript readers, and University of Minnesota Press for advancing these ideas to print. I am grateful to my parents and sister for steady support over these years. Susan Ridgely has been my primary interlocutor since we met. This book is dedicated to her.

Notes

Introduction

1. Renate Klett, telephone interview, Berlin, July 2002.

2. Terayama writes about Jim Haynes in "Rondonkko nara dare demo Jimu Hēnzu o shitte iru," in *Yōroppa reinen* (Tokyo: Mainichi Shinbun Sha, 1970), 119–34.

3. Terayama recounts his visit to Algren in "Neon no kōya: Shikago," in *Chika sōzōryoku: Hyōronshū* (Tokyo: Kōdansha, 1971), 91–107.

4. Terayama's conversation with Michel Foucault is reprinted in several books, most recently in Terayama Shūji, *'70s Terayama Shūji* (Tokyo: Sekai Shoin, 2004), 25–40. The dialogue was first published in the April 1976 issue of the journal *Jōkyō*.

5. J. Milton Yinger, "Contraculture and Subculture," *American Sociological Review* 25, no. 2 (October 1960): 629. Yinger will later move toward seeing the culture–counterculture dialectic as the core force driving social change in "Countercultures and Social Change," *American Sociological Review* 42, no. 6 (December 1977), 833–53, and later expand those ideas to find this same dynamic in nearly all elements of life and across centuries of history in his book *Countercultures: The Promise and Peril of a World Turned Upside Down* (New York: Free Press, 1982).

6. Talcott Parsons, *The Social System* (Glencoe, Ill.: Free Press, 1951), 355, 522. Yinger, following up on Parsons's footnote, traces Lasswell's use of "counter-mores" back as far as 1935 (in *World Politics and Personal Insecurity* [New York: McGraw-Hill], 64) before dismissing as analytically unclear Lasswell's fairly apt description of "culture patterns which appeal mainly to the *id*" as seen in "revolutionists, prostitutes, prisoners, obscene and subversive talk." Yinger, "Contraculture and Subculture," 629n10.

7. Theodore Roszak, "The Counter Culture: Part I—Youth and the Great Refusal," *The Nation* 206, no. 13 (March 25, 1968): 400–407; "The Counter Culture: Part II—Politics of the Nervous System," *The Nation* 206, no. 14 (April 1, 1968): 439–43; "Counter Culture: Part III—Capsules of Salvation," *The Nation* 206, no. 15 (April 8, 1968): 466–71; "Counter Culture: Part IV—The Future as Community," *The Nation* 206, no. 16 (April 15, 1968): 497–503.

8. Theodore Roszak, *The Making of a Counter Culture* (Berkeley: University of California Press, 1969), 5–22.

9. Takahashi Akira, "Amerika no shin-sayoku to wa nani ka: Tenkanki ni okeru chishikijin," *Sekai* 254 (January 1967): 106–7. Takahashi is engaging Ronald

Aronson's "The Movement and its Critics," *Studies on the Left* 6, no. 1 (January–February 1966): 3–19 here directly, using Aronson's term "counter-style" to describe the antihierarchy position taken by the bulk of the New Left organizers.

10. Terayama Shūji, *Sengoshi* (Tokyo: Kinokuniya Shoten, 1965), 71–87.

11. Ibid., 77–78.

12. This film was shot in 1962 but not edited or publicly screened until 1969. The date listed in the title sequence, 1964, has been repudiated by Hagiwara Sakumi, who is credited with editing the film in 1969. Nakajima Takashi, ed., *Terayama Shūji: Seishōjo no tame no eiga-nyūmon* (Tokyo: Dagereo Shuppan, 1993), 120.

13. Norman Mailer, "The White Negro: Superficial Reflections on the Hipster," *Dissent* 4, no. 3 (Summer 1957): 278. The first Japanese translation (by Ōhashi Kichinosuke) of "The White Negro" was available by February 1960 in the journal *Mita bungaku*. This version would be included in an anthology compiled by Saeki Shōichi and published in 1961 on the topic of "new literature," which included a chapter on the United Kingdom's "Angry Young Men" (another interest of Terayama's). Terayama quotes from Mailer's essay in his critique of postwar poetry, *Sengoshi*, mentioned previously. Terayama playfully refers to himself as a jazz-obsessed "Yellow Negro" in "Ierō niguro datta koro," in *Ōgon jidai: Terayama Shūji hyōronshū* (Tokyo: Kyūgei Shuppan, 1978), 260–62.

14. Yomota Inuhiko, *Haisukūru 1968* (Tokyo: Shinchōsha, 2004), 128.

15. The early biographical information is primarily drawn from Ogawa Tarō's *Terayama Shūji, sono shirazaru seishun: Uta no genryū o sagutte* (Tokyo: San'ichi Shobō, 1997), the result of a thorough series of interviews Ogawa conducted with Terayama's family and acquaintances to fact-check the details of Terayama's two dubiously autobiographical works, *Keshigomu*, which was first serialized in *Yomiuri shinbun* between November 10, 1976, and December 3, 1976, and was later reprinted in *Ōgon jidai*, cited previously, and *Tareka kokyō o omowazaru*, first serialized in the journal *Shinpyō* between July 1967 and April 1968 and later published as a book in 1968 by Haga Shoten (Tokyo). I have cross-referenced as many of these details as possible with other sources, such as Takatori Ei's recent *Terayama Shūji: Kageki naru shissō* (Tokyo: Chūsekisha, 2008), and the time lines and publication lists in books like Terayama Henriku, ed., *Terayama Shūji engeki bijutsukan* (Tokyo: Paruko Shuppan, 2008); and Terayama Shūji, *Terayama Shūji zen shiikaku* (Tokyo: Shichōsha, 1986). I have been more cautious about the biographical details in books like Kuritsubo Yoshiki, ed., *Terayama Shūji*, vol. 56 in the series *Shinchō Nihon bungaku arubamu* (Tokyo: Shichōsha, 1993), because it relies so heavily on biographical detail from Terayama's own "autobiographies," which were demonstrated to be embellished in some places and incorrect in others by later work like Ogawa's.

16. Tanikawa Shuntarō, "'Watakushi-sei' no hinin," in *Terayama Shūji no sekai*, ed. Fūba no Kai (Tokyo: Jōkyō Shuppan, 1993), 11. This was originally a presentation given in December 1992 within a series of ten presentations set up by Ogawa

Tarō and the Fūba no Kai (The Nonchalant Society), a group of devotees of Ter-ayama's work, particularly his tanka poetry. Tanikawa confesses that he and the other members of his poetry circle, Kai (Oar), survived during the 1950s and early 1960s by writing dramas for commercial radio.

17. The newspaper serialization, titled "Narayama nijūshi-kō" (Twenty-four thoughts on Narayama) is a play on Fukazawa Shichirō's 1956 story "Narayama bushikō" (The ballad of Narayama), made famous by Kinoshita Keisuke's 1958 film version. This initial set was expanded and published as a paperback in April 1963. See Terayama Shūji, *Gendai no seishunron: Kazoku-tachi, kedamono-tachi* (Tokyo: San'ichi Shobō, 1963).

18. This novel shares its title with the Japanese translation of Eugene O'Neill's 1933 play *Ah, Wilderness!* but the connection between the two seems to go no further.

19. "Hankōteki kijin o atsumeta Terayama Shūji-shi no jikken-seikatsu," *Hei-bon panchi* 4, no. 21 (May 29, 1967): 38.

20. Takatori, *Kageki naru shissō*, 201–2.

21. Terayama Hatsu, *Haha no hotaru: Terayama Shūji no iru fūkei* (Tokyo: Shin-shokan, 1985), 9.

22. Terayama Shūji, "Jijoden rashiku naku: Tareka kokyō o omowazaru," *Shinpyō* 14, no. 7 (July 1967): 144. This caveat appears near the beginning of the first install-ment of this serialization, a clear warning about the unreliability of the narrator.

23. The one earlier reference to a 1935 birth year came as a side note in the bio-graphical sketch at the end of a poetry collection from the *For Ladies* series called *Sayonara no shiro* (Tokyo: Shinshokan, 1966), 176: "A Short Terayama Shūji Dic-tionary: Born January 10, 1936 (according to public records, but he was actually born on December 10, 1935). His star is the Centaur, and his sign is Sagittarius." This aside, almost whispered into the ear of his reader, combined with a horse-racing fan's sudden move into a zodiac sign with a half-man, half-horse icon, has led some critics (Sugiyama Seijū, for example) to question the legitimacy of Terayama's claim.

24. Ogawa suspects a letter may have arrived in the mid-1960s from Teraya-ma's maternal grandfather, Sakamoto Shigetarō (who ran the Kabuki-za cinema in Aomori), explaining the history of the cinema as well as Hatsu's complex childhood. If such a letter was in fact sent to Shūji at that time, it may also have included information about the two birthdays. Alternatively, he could have sim-ply asked his mother around the same time. In any case, Terayama would have been collecting information about his past in preparation for publishing "Tareka kokyō" starting in mid-1967.

1. Poetic Kleptomania and Pseudo-Lyricism

1. Akimoto Fujio, "Tanka to haiku no aida," *Tanka* 2, no. 5 (May 1955): 22.

2. Terayama Shūji, "Tōsaku," *Hōseki* 15, no. 1 (January 1960): 192–94.

3. Terayama Shūji, "Tōsaku-byō," *Gendaishi* 8, no. 9 (September 1961): 16.

4. Terayama, "Tōsaku-byō," 17.

5. Terayama Shūji, "Ryōjū-on," *Tanka kenkyū* 13, no. 4 (April 1956): 24. This first appearance was in Terayama's fourth published tanka sequence. It was reprinted in his first book, *Ware ni gogatsu o* [Give me May] (1957), in a section called "Sokoku sōshitsu" [Loss of my homeland]—probably a nod to Nakajō Fumiko's set of tanka, "Chibusa sōshitsu" [Loss of my breasts], for which she won *Tanka kenkyū*'s prize half a year before Terayama would win it. His first formal tanka collection, *Sora ni wa hon* [A book up in the sky] (1958), contained the same "Sokoku sōshitsu" section, so the poem was reprinted here, too. His second tanka collection, *Chi to mugi* [Blood and wheat] (1962), also includes the poem, this time in a section called "Waga toki, sono hajimari" [My time and its beginning]. Three of Terayama's first four poetry collections, then, all contain this poem. It also serves as an epigraph to the first chapter of his only full-length novel, *Aa, kōya* [Ah, wilderness] (1966).

6. Raymond Williams's *The Country and the City* (New York: Oxford University Press, 1973) compares well. The linguistic slippage around both "country" and *kuni* is similar, but the difference in usage may also inflect the relationship of *kuni* to both "nation" and "city." *Kuni* may map better to the slippage around the American usage of "state," since both can signify either a geographical unit that makes up the nation or the collective of those units, the national government itself.

7. Terayama Shūji, *Terayama Shūji haiku zenshū* (Tokyo: Anzudō, 1999), 28. This collection cites the poem's original publication as being in the coterie journal *Aoi mori* 3, no. 11 (August 1953).

8. Tomizawa Kakio, *Teihon Tomizawa Kakio kushū* (Tokyo: Teihon Tomizawa Kakio Kushū Hakkōkai, 1965), 39. The poem was first published in *Kikan* 7, no. 2 (February 1940).

9. Ibid., 18. The poem was first published as part of a collection called *Ten no ōkami* (Todashi, Saitama prefecture: Ten no Ōkami Kankōkai, 1941). Nagao Saburō points out the similarity in *Kyokō jigoku: Terayama Shūji* (Tokyo: Kōdansha, 1997), 102.

10. Ishikawa Takuboku, "Ichiaku no suna," in *Gendai Nihon bungaku taikei* (Tokyo: Chikuma Shobō, 1972), 26: 219. Line breaks are included here following Takuboku's characteristic three-line format for his tanka.

11. Nagao, *Kyokō jigoku*, 78.

12. Ibid.

13. Dialogue is quoted from Julius Epstein, Philip Epstein, and Howard Koch, *Kasaburanka* (Tokyo: Magazine House, 1994), 224–30.

14. It is unclear whether the songs were subtitled during the first screenings. The songs are not subtitled in copies of the film circulating now, but the contest of patriotisms is clear enough in the scene.

15. Sugiyama recalls his first assignment upon entering Nihon Tanka Sha, the company that owns *Tanka kenkyū*, to be memorizing the family trees of masters and their students posted on the wall of the editing division. See his *Terayama Shūji: Yūgi no hito* (Tokyo: Shinchōsha, 2000), 36.

16. Nakai Hideo, *Teihon: Kokui no tankashi* (Tokyo: Waizu Shuppan, 1993; Tokyo: Ushio Shuppan, 1971), 11. Citations are to the Waizu Shuppan edition.

17. See Nakai's "Nijūdai ni tsuite" in his *Kokui no tankashi*, 11–13. Originally published in *Nihon tanka*, another monthly published by Nihon Tanka Sha, in August 1949.

18. Sugiyama, *Yūgi no hito*, 37.

19. Terayama Shūji, "Hi no chūkei," *Tanka kenkyū* 11, no. 11 (November 1954): 118.

20. Terayama Shūji, "Chehofu-sai," *Tanka kenkyū* 11, no. 11 (November 1954): 7.

21. Ōno Nobuo, Yamashita Mutsu, and Maekawa Samio, "Kadan no hankyō: Dainikai gojūshu nyūsen sakuhin," *Tanka kenkyū* 11, no. 12 (December 1954): 122–23.

22. Terayama, "Chehofu-sai," 7, 9.

23. Shino Hiroshi's three-volume history of modern tanka is the best survey of the phenomenon. The entire second volume traces "The Avant-Garde Tanka Era." See Shino Hiroshi, *Gendai tankashi*, 3 vols. (Tokyo: Tanka Kenkyū Sha, 1983–94).

24. Kuwabara Takeo, "Daini geijutsu: Gendai haiku ni tsuite," in *Kuwabara Takeo zenshū* (Tokyo: Asahi Shinbun Sha, 1969), 5:13–29. It was originally published in *Sekai* 9 (September 1946).

25. Kusamoto Kenkichi, "Aru 'jūdai': Tanka haiku ni okeru junsuisei no mondai," *Haiku kenkyū* 12, no. 2 (February 1955): 33.

26. Wakatsuki Akira, "Haiku to tanka no aida," *Haiku kenkyū* 12, no. 2 (February 1955): 25.

27. Saitō Shōji, "Sōzō to sōi: Yori konponteki na kanten kara," *Tanka kenkyū* 12, no. 1 (January 1955): 44.

28. Ibid.

29. Terayama, "Chehofu-sai," 10.

30. Hishikawa Yoshio, "Nani ga owarō to shite iru ka, nani ga hajimarō to shite iru ka," *Tanka kenkyū* 12, no. 1 (January 1955): 36.

31. Terayama, "Chehofu-sai," 8.

32. Nakamura Kusatao, "Bokyōkō," in *Nakamura Kusatao zenshū* (Tokyo: Misuzu Shobō, 1989), 3:192. The poem is dated 1954 and was published as part of a collection in 1956.

33. Teika is clearest on this point in his preface to *Eiga taigai*: "In composing a new poem by taking an old one, using as many as three lines out of the five is using far too many, for there would be no effect of novelty. However, it is permissible to use two lines and three or four syllables of a third." Fujiwara Teika, *Fujiwara Teika's Superior Poems of Our Time: A Thirteenth-Century Poetic Treatise and*

Sequence, trans. Robert H. Brower and Earl Miner (Tokyo: University of Tokyo Press, 1967), 44n10.

34. Nakamura Kusatao, "Hi no shima," in *Nakamura Kusatao zenshū,* 1:42. The poem is dated 1937 and was published as part of a collection in 1939.

35. Terayama, "Chehofu-sai," 7.

36. Saitō Sanki, *Saitō Sanki zenkushū* (Tokyo: Chūsekisha, 2001), 152. This haiku was first published in *Tenrō* 7, no. 4–5 (April–May 1954).

37. Terayama, "Chehofu-sai," 6.

38. Saitō, *Saitō Sanki zenkushū,* 117. This poem was first published in *Tenrō* 4, no. 3 (March 1951).

39. Terayama, "Chehofu-sai," 9.

40. Peter Bürger, *Theory of the Avant-Garde* (Minneapolis: University of Minnesota Press, 1984), 22.

41. Edward Kamens, "Waking the Dead: Fujiwara no Teika's *Sotoba kuyō* Poems," *Journal of Japanese Studies* 28, no. 2 (Summer 2002): 379–406.

42. Nakamura Kusatao in particular seems to have been a poetic hero to Terayama. After several years heading the literature club at his high school, Terayama contributed an essay on Kusatao's work to a volume of commemorative writings for his graduating class, which was published several months before his tanka debut. See Terayama Shūji, "Ringo no tame ni hiraita mado: Gendai no kikō nōto," in *Seitokai shi: Shōwa nijū-hachi nendo,* ed. Aomori Kenritsu Aomori Kōtō Gakkō Seitokai (Aomori: Kenritsu Aomori Kōtō Gakkō, 1954), 29–34.

43. Asanuma Keiji, *Utsuroi to tawamure: Teika o yomu* (Tokyo: Ozawa Shoten, 1978), 130–31. The notion of words in a mirror (or perhaps a "looking glass") is one the literary critic Miura Masashi will use again later in his essay on Terayama's use of appropriation, his relationship with words (i.e., they come before ideas, even before the idea of the self), and his transition from haiku to tanka. Miura Masashi, "Kagami no naka no kotoba," in *Terayama Shūji: Kagami no naka no kotoba* (Tokyo: Shinshokan, 1992), 17–64.

44. Terayama Shūji, *Terayama Shūji haiku zenshū,* 27. Kamens argues that the time span between Teika's poems and their *honka* may not be as great as it seems, since the classic poems were in constant circulation during Teika's time: "The chronological span across which Teika reaches for reference may be sizable, but as suggested above, Teika is not really reaching all that far, if we recognize that the poems he chooses to build on as foundations were readily accessible in the matrix of potential points of reference, already kinetically charged by prior use and in active circulation, and therefore susceptible to temporary seizure and deployment in the construction of new referential schemes as this one." Kamens, "Waking the Dead," 396.

45. Okamoto Tarō, "Gabunshū avangyarudo," in *Okamoto Tarō chosakushū* (Tokyo: Kōdansha, 1979), 1:373.

46. Terayama, "Chehofu-sai," 7.

47. Edgar Allen Poe, "The Premature Burial," in *The Complete Tales and Poems of Edgar Allan Poe* (London: Penguin, 1982), 258.

48. Ibid.

49. Ibid.

50. Ibid., 262.

51. Ibid., 263.

52. Terayama, "Chehofu-sai," 8.

53. Tsubota Jōji, "Mahō," in *Tsubota Jōji zenshū* (Tokyo: Shinchōsha, 1977), 7:149. Originally published in *Akai tori* 9, no. 1 (January 1935). My thanks to Professor Chiba Shunji of Waseda University for pointing out the reference to Tsubota's story in Terayama's poem.

54. Ibid., 149.

55. Terayama, "Chehofu-sai," 6.

56. Terayama admitted fabricating the quotation in a letter to theater critic Dōmoto Masaki. See Ogawa Tarō, *Terayama Shūji, sono shirazaru seishun: Uta no genryū o sagutte* (Tokyo: San'ichi Shobō, 1997), 98–100.

57. Premodern *waka* may not have been read as lyrical, but since its renewal by Masaoka Shiki, and especially after Takuboku, reading modern tanka as genuine expressions of emotion from the poet seems to have become normative.

58. The Signet Classic edition includes the following caveat by the translator, Lloyd C. Parks: "Most of the epigraphs in *The Red and the Black* are imaginary, and so are their ascriptions. They serve chiefly to supply a thematic gloss for each chapter." Stendhal, *The Red and The Black* (New York: Signet Classic, 1970), 11.

59. While I realize that notions of "authenticity" have been so completely deconstructed now that we risk seeming naïve by not bracketing the term, I use it mostly without irony in the next section in order to follow Terayama's argument that faithfulness to a fictionalized version of oneself is "honest."

60. This essay is available from *Haiku kenkyū* 12, no. 2 (February 1955): 39.

61. Nakai Hideo, "Kaisetsu," in *Terayama Shūji seishun kashū* (Tokyo: Kadokawa Shoten, 1972), 189.

62. Terayama, "Hi no chūkei," 118–19. He refers here to Gérard de Nerval (penname of Gérard Labrunie), a French author in the forefront of nineteenth century romanticism.

63. Terayama, "Chehofu-sai," 6.

64. Nakai Hideo, Terayama Shūji, Kitamura Mitsuyoshi, Ōzawa Kiyotsugu, Nagai Kiyūko, Ishikawa Fujiko, "Asu o hiraku uta: Kizu no nai wakasa no tame ni," *Tanka kenkyū* 12, no. 1 (January 1955): 73–74.

65. Alain Robbe-Grillet, "A Future for the Novel," in *For a New Novel: Essays on Fiction*, trans. by Richard Howard (New York: Grove Press, 1965), 18. The essay was originally published in 1956. Terayama makes direct reference to Robbe-Grillet in an essay published in 1962: "I think that what these so-called *anti-roman*

writers like Robbe-Grillet and Michel Butor were after was rebellion against the inclination of everything to move toward poetry." See "Kōi to sono hokori: minato no gendaishi to Action-poem no mondai," in *Chi to mugi* (Tokyo: Shiratama Shobō, 1962), 106.

66. André Bazin, "The Evolution of the Language of Cinema," in *What Is Cinema?* trans. Hugh Gray (Berkeley: University of California Press, 1967), 37.

67. Terayama, "Hi no chūkei," 119.

68. Kishigami Daisaku, *Kishigami Daisaku zenshū* (Tokyo: Shichōsha, 1980), 13.

69. Terayama Shūji, "Keshigomu," in *Ōgon jidai: Terayama Shūji hyōronshū* (Tokyo: Kyūgei Shuppan, 1978), 267–70.

70. Kishigami Daisaku, "Terayama Shūji ron," in *Kishigami Daisaku zenshū* (Tokyo: Shichōsha, 1980), 160.

71. Kishigami Daisaku, "Boku no tame no nōto," in *Kishigami Daisaku zenshū*, 303–4.

72. Terayama Shūji, "Buta—1960," *Bungakukai* 14, no. 8 (August 1960): 113–14.

73. Terayama Shūji, "Jūkyū-sai no burūsu: Atogaki," *Shinario* 16, no. 8 (August 1960): 106.

74. Terayama Henriku, ed., "Nenpu," in *Terayama Shūji kinenkan* (Tokyo: Terayama World, 2000), 1:109.

75. *Nuhikun*, the Tenjō Sajiki's version of Swift's *Directions to Servants*, operates on this theme. On a small wooden model used to choreograph the performance in Amsterdam, Terayama wrote a simple slogan for the play: "The world awaits the absence of all masters." The model is in the archives of DasArts, a performing arts institute in Amsterdam.

2. Radio Drama in the Age of Television

1. Nagai Jun, "Ōdio no ayumi," in *Ōdio 50-nenshi*, ed. Nihon Ōdio Kyōkai (Tokyo: Nihon Ōdio Kyōkai, 1986), 23.

2. Ibid., 20–21.

3. See Nishizawa Minoru's *Rajio dorama no ōgon jidai* (Tokyo: Kawade Shobō Shinsha), 2002. Although written in 2002, Nishizawa, a radio drama scenarist, carries his history only through 1964, citing the years from 1925 through 1965 as the era of the radio drama, with the twenty years after the war being its "most lively period" (*hyakka sōmei no jidai*). The most tangible marker of the end of the era was less the advent of television than the demolition in 1965 of the "Broadcasting Hall" (Hōsō Kaikan) in Uchisaiwaichō, which had been the headquarters for NHK's radio production since 1926. Fellow scenarist Ima Harube assembled a group to gather rubble from the site in commemoration of its cultural importance.

4. Rudolph Arnheim, "In Praise of Blindness," in *Radio: The Art of Sound* (London: Faber & Faber, 1936), 133–203.

5. Irit Rogoff, "Studying Visual Culture," in *The Visual Culture Reader*, 2nd ed., ed. Nicholas Mirzoeff (New York: Routledge, 2002), 28.

6. Walter Benjamin, "The Work of Art in the Epoch of Mechanical Reproduction," trans. H. H. Gerth and Don Martindale, *Studies on the Left* 1, no. 2 (Winter 1960): 31. This early English version comes via Pierre Klossowski's 1936 French translation but was adjusted after feedback from Adorno and review of the German. A translation of Benjamin's 1936 essay by Takagi Hisao and Takahara Kōhei (from the original German) was published in 1965 by Kinokuniya Shoten.

7. Yamada Taichi, afterword to *Jiono, tobanakatta otoko: Terayama Shūji dorama shinario shū*, by Terayama Shūji, ed. Yamada Taichi (Tokyo: Chikuma Shobō, 1994), 275–76.

8. Moriyasu Toshihisa, "Fukuoka sōdō tenmatsuki: Rajio dorama 'Otonagari,'" in *Barokku no Nihon* (Tokyo: Kokusho Kankōkai, 2003), 113.

9. Ueda Bin's posthumous poetry collection *Bokuyōshin* (Tokyo: Kanao Bunendō, 1920) is another possible source for the title of the teen haiku journal, but titling his first radio drama *Giono* suggests an awareness of the French writer.

10. Terayama Shūji, "Jiono, tobanakatta otoko," 24.

11. Ibid., 26–31.

12. Ibid., 32.

13. Terayama Shūji, "Keshigomu," in *Sakka no jiden, 40: Terayama Shūji*, ed. Kuritsubo Yoshiki (Tokyo: Nihon Zusho Sentā, 1995), 174. The chronology is wrong for this to be the actual derivation of the idea for the plot, since *Nakamura Ichirō* aired in February 1959, two months before the imperial wedding. The reversal of logic (*gyakusetsu*) he writes of in this "autobiography" may be less a reversal of the incident seen on television than a reversal of the time relationship between it and his radio drama.

14. Oiwake Hideko, "Hatsu no idō TV chūkei to tōseki shōnen: Kōtaishi seikon," in *60-nen Anpo, Miike tōsō: Ishihara Yūjirō no jidai, 1957–1960*, ed. Nishii Kazuo (Tokyo: Mainichi Shinbunsha, 2000), 98.

15. Ibid., 98.

16. Terayama, "Keshigomu," 173.

17. Terayama Shūji, "Nakamura Ichirō," in *Jiono, tobanakatta otoko*, 9.

18. Ibid., 10.

19. Ibid., 13.

20. This was one year after *Nakamura Ichirō*, during which time Terayama had also begun a serialized radio drama collaboration with Tanikawa Shuntarō called *Oshaberi danchi* (Chatty apartment building) and released, in December 1959, another radio drama called *Kanoke-jima* (Caja de Muertos Island), the "coffin

island" that served as the model for Robert Louis Stevenson's *Treasure Island*. Scripts for both are in *Jiono, tobanakatta otoko*, 79–90, 237–69.

21. These first screenings at Sōgetsu were followed by a month at the Sasori-za under Shinjuku Bunka (October 1970) and then two more weeks in January 1971 in the basement of the Tenjō Sajiki-kan, which functioned as Terayama's office, café, and rehearsal space in Shibuya. See Moriyasu Toshihisa, "Gekiga to akumu: Eiga 'Tomato kechappu kōtei,'" in *Barokku no Nihon* (Tokyo: Kokusho Kankōkai, 2003), 131.

22. The script for this radio drama is reprinted as "A Forgotten Interlude" in Ronald A. Knox, *Essays in Satire* (New York: E. P. Dutton, 1930), 279–87.

23. Terayama Shūji, "Otona-gari," *Tanka* 7, no. 5 (May 1960): 155.

24. Moriyasu Toshihisa, "Fukuoka sōdō tenmatsuki," in *Barokku no Nihon*, 116–23.

25. "Kodomo ga kakumei o okoshita: Hōsōgeki 'Otona-gari' no tōjita hamon," *Shūkan bunshun*, April 18, 1960, 67–69.

26. Terayama Shūji, "Sakuhin nōto: *Otona-gari*," in *Terayama Shūji no gikyoku* (Tokyo: Shichōsha, 1984), 4:403.

27. Moriyasu, "Fukuoka sōdō tenmatsuki," 115.

28. Terayama, "Otona-gari," 152–53.

29. Ibid., 153.

30. Ibid., 156.

31. Moriyasu, "Fukuoka sōdō tenmatsuki," 125.

32. Takatori Ei, *Terayama Shūji: Kageki naru shissō* (Tokyo: Heibonsha Shinsho, 2006), 20–21.

33. Minami Yōichirō, *Soromon-tō tanken* (Tokyo: Kaiseisha, 1941), 1.

34. Ikeda Nobumasa, *Hittorā* (Tokyo: Kaiseisha, 1941), 2–3. This book is conspicuously left out of the biographical timeline in his volume of *Shōnen shōsetsu taikei* (Tokyo: San'ichi Shobō, 1988), 6:547–53.

35. Terayama Shūji, "Ningen jikkenshitsu," *Bungakukai* 14, no. 12 (December 1960): 95–96. Publishing on right-wing youth in December 1960 in this way must have invoked, and was likely a response to, the televised stabbing to death of Asanuma Inejirō, chairman of the Japan Socialist Party, on October 12, 1960. Ōe Kenzaburō would respond to this incident with his short stories "Sevuntiin" (Seventeen) and "Seiji-shōnen shisu" (A political youth dies) in the January and February 1961 issues of the same literary journal Terayama published in, which would mark him for attack by right-wing groups. Terayama's essay is released the same month as Fukazawa Shichirō's infamous short story "Furyū-mutan," (The story of a dream of courtly elegance), with its episode of decapitating the Japanese emperor, which would spark an attack on the publisher in his home, killing a maid and sending Fukazawa into hiding.

36. My translation of these intertitles and the voiceovers from the film is available in *Review of Japanese Culture and Society* 17 (2005): 89–97.

37. Moriyasu notes that the 1.3 million yen was taken from royalties Terayama had earned from writing the lyrics for a hit pop song called "Toki ni wa haha no nai ko no yō ni" (Sometimes, like a motherless child), sung by Carmen Maki. "Gekiga to akumu," in *Barokku no Nihon*, 140.

38. Stereo television would come much later, but earlier in Japan than anywhere else. Experiments began in September and October of 1978 and quickly spread to all the domestic networks. See Tomura Eiko and Nishino Yasushi, *Terebi media no sekai* (Tokyo: Surugadai Shuppansha, 1999), 223.

39. See Sasaki's account of working with Terayama on this project in Sasaki Shōichirō, *Tsukuru to iu koto* (Tokyo: JICC Shuppankyoku, 1982), 72–79. *Kometto Ikeya* was the third collaboration between Sasaki and Terayama (after the prize-winning 1965 *Ohayō India* [Good morning, India] and early 1966 *Nijussai* [Twenty years old], which starred a young Yoshinaga Sayuri), as well as Sasaki's final piece for radio before he moved to producing for television.

40. This was Ikeya's first comet discovery, but he would go on to spot several more over the next forty years. He is now a legend among stargazers. See "Japan's Famous Kaoru Ikeya Bags Another One," *Stella* 174 (April 2002): 1.

41. Terayama Shūji, "Kometto Ikeya," *Terayama Shūji no gikyoku* (Tokyo: Shichōsha, 1983), 1:227.

42. Sound in motion through the sound field would not require conditioning to be experienced as stereo. But does this more material stereo experience bolster or hinder the conditioned experience of hearing voices centered between the speakers? It could negate that coaching by seeming more positioned relative to the unmoving voice. Does pure stereo sound, then, require motion? The scenes in *Kometto Ikeya* are often bridged by sound in conspicuous motion (e.g., trains, demos, street sounds with voices crossing left and right), which may reassert the stereo space but risks making the dialogue sound even flatter and more monaural than without the juxtaposition.

43. Kuwabara Shigeo, in discussion with the author, Tokyo, February 17, 2004.

44. An exhibition of the *rittai hōsō* technology at an audio fair earlier that month, December 5 through 7, had been very popular. Nihon Hōsō Kyōkai, ed., *NHK nenkan 6: April 1952-March 1953* (Tokyo: Yumani Shobō, 1999), 27–28.

45. Ibid.

46. NHK claims that this was the world's first regularly scheduled stereo radio program. Nihon Hōsō Kyōkai, ed., *NHK nenkan 8: April 1954-March 1955* (Tokyo: Yumani Shobō, 1999), 131.

47. Nagai, "Ōdio no ayumi," 21.

48. The Prix Italia is an international contest for radio and television programs that was founded in 1949—it is essentially the Cannes for broadcast media.

Terayama won the top award for radio dramas in 1964 with *Yamanba*, an amalgamation of the Bluebeard myth and the quasi-mythical practice of *obasute*, sending the elderly of a village to die in the mountains to reduce the number of mouths to feed. A Japanese radio drama had won once at the Prix Italia before Terayama's awards with a version of Inoue Yasushi's *Hi no yama* (Mountain of fire) in 1962 (also a stereo production). Nihon Hōsō Kyōkai, ed., *NHK nenkan '63* (Tokyo: Nihon Hōsō Kyōkai, 1963), 139.

49. "Terayama Shūji no kūsōgeki: Itaria-shō no sanka-sakuhin," *Yomiuri shinbun* August 31, 1966, 7. The radio programming listings on the same page show the drama scheduled from 9:15 to 10:00 P.M.

50. "NHK no ni-sakuhin ni 'Itaria-shō': Kokusai hōsō konkūru," *Yomiuri shinbun* September 27, 1966, 14; and "Rajio shūhyō: Sukēru ōkii hōsōgeki, 'Kometto Ikeya,'" *Yomiuri shinbun* October 8, 1966, 10. The radio programming listings on October 2 show the AM two-channel broadcast of *Kometto Ikeya* scheduled from 10:15 to 11:00 P.M. The installation of stereo FM broadcasting equipment throughout the country was completed in November 1963. Broadcasting began in Tokyo that December, and in Osaka and Nagoya in February 1964. See Nihon Hōsō Kyōkai, ed., *NHK nenkan '67* (Tokyo: Nihon Hōsō Kyōkai, 1967), 139, 555.

51. Terayama, "Kometto Ikeya," 232.

52. Benedict Anderson, *Imagined Communities: Reflections on the Origin and Spread of Nationalism*, rev. ed. (London: Verso, 1991), 33.

53. Ibid., 25, 26.

54. Terayama, "Kometto Ikeya," 230.

55. Terayama Shūji, "Yamanba," in *Jiono, tobanakatta otoko*, 124.

56. Terayama Shūji, "Mōjin shokan," in *Terayama Shūji no gikyoku* (Tokyo: Shinchōsha, 1986), 6:64.

57. Terayama, "Kometto Ikeya," 231.

58. Cicero, *Tusculan Disputations*, in *The Loeb Classical Library: Cicero*, trans. J. E. King (London: William Heinemann, 1927), 18:51, 53. There is a related invocation of Terayama's fellow Tōhoku poet Miyazawa Kenji earlier in the drama when the blind narrator speaks of the stars being people's eyes: "I'm blind, so mine are both shining up in the sky. The twin stars are my eyes." "Kometto Ikeya," 244. The reference is to Miyazawa's "Futago no hoshi" (1918), a short fairy tale about the adventures of twin stars during the day (when they are free to move around). See Miyazawa Kenji, *Kōhon Miyazawa Kenji zenshū* (Tokyo: Chikuma Shobō, 1973), 7:19–37. Miyazawa would later use the stars' names from that story ("Chunse" and "Pōse") in a short public letter written to mourn the untimely departure of his younger sister's soul in 1922. See *Kōhon Miyazawa Kenji zenshū* (Tokyo: Chikuma Shobō, 1974), 11:319–21. The star becomes the missing human soul in Miyazawa's writings, whereas Terayama's script and Cicero's piece imply that it is the missing human soul that has become the new star.

59. Terayama, "Kometto Ikeya," 230.

60. It may be helpful to consider her narrating position in regard to either Kamei Hideo's discussion of "non-person narration" (*muninshō*) in *Kansei no henkaku* (Tokyo: Kōdansha, 1983) or the beat poet Lawrence Ferlinghetti's notion of "fourth-person singular" as the disembodied voice of the poet, one which creates, rather than represents, poetic consciousness.

61. Terayama, "Kometto Ikeya," 231.

62. Ibid.

63. Ibid., 236.

64. Sasaki Shōichirō, in discussion with the author, Tokyo, June 16, 2004.

65. Nishii Kazuo, ed., *Kōdō seichō, Biitoruzu no jidai: 1961–1967* (Tokyo: Mainichi Shinbunsha, 2000), 84–85.

66. "Taiheiyō o koeru sho no TV denpa," *Asahi shinbun*, November 20, 1963, 1.

67. "Kenedi ansatsu to Nichi-Bei TV chūkei," in *Kōdō-seichō, Biitoruzu no jidai: 1961–1967*, ed. Nishii Kazuo (Tokyo: Mainichi Shinbunsha, 2000), 84.

68. "Terestā kichi," *Mainichi shinbun*, January 1, 1963, 1.

69. Tanikawa Shuntarō, "Ningen no ie," *Mainichi shinbun*, January 1, 1963, 1.

70. *Asahi shinbun*, January 1, 1963, 34.

71. "Gorin mezashi kensetsu isogu," *Asahi shinbun*, January 6, 1963, 13.

72. Terayama, "Kometto Ikeya," 246–47.

73. See Kazuo Kinoshita, "27P/Crommelin: Past, Present, and Future Orbits," *Gary W. Kronk's Cometography*, http://cometography.com/pcomets/027p.html (accessed September 18, 2010).

74. Moriyasu Torihisa, "Terayama Shūji ni okeru mōsha no shisen," *Shōwa bungaku kenkyū* 40 (March 2000): 97.

75. Tomura and Nishino, *Terebi media no sekai*, 177.

76. Denis Diderot, "The Letter on the Blind for the Use of Those Who See," in *Diderot's Early Philosophical Works*, ed. Margaret Jourdain (1749; New York: AMS Press, 1973), 109.

77. Terayama, "Kometto Ikeya," 237–38. The radio drama includes some lines not in the script, so I have transcribed them from the compact disc release (which was the longest edit of the drama). See "Kometto Ikeya" in *Terayama Shūji no rajio dorama: CD senshū* (Tokyo: Nikkan Supōtsu Shinbunsha, 1993). This "touching the stars" image invokes *Le Petit Prince*, which is referred to directly in the text by the blind narrator.

78. See Shirley Wajda, "A Room with a Viewer: The Parlor Stereoscope, Comic Stereographs, and the Psychic Role of Play in Victorian America," in *Hard at Play: Leisure in America, 1840–1940*, ed. Kathryn Grover (Amherst: University of Massachusetts Press, 1992), 112–38.

79. Sasaki Shōichirō, in discussion with the author, Tokyo, June 16, 2004. Sasaki and the staff ignored the standard flourishes of a stereo radio drama, such

as recording a door opening and closing at one side of the space, then footsteps moving toward the center—the gimmicks of the genre had become restrictive, so they worked to push stereo in directions it had not been before (forward and back, up and down).

80. Nihon Hōsō Kyōkai, ed., "Rittai-hōsō kotohajime," in *Zoku hōsō yawa: Zadankai ni yoru hōsōshi* (Tokyo: Nihon Hōsō Shuppan Kyōkai, 1970), 264.

81. Terayama, "Kometto Ikeya," 246.

3. Boxing—Stuttering—Graffiti

1. See Joyce Carol Oates, *On Boxing* (Hopewell, N.J.: Ecco Press, 1994), 4.

2. Terayama Shūji, *Jūkyūsai no burūsu* (Tokyo: Shinshokan, 1980), 7. Although this screenplay was never made into a film, it was published in the August 1960 edition of *Shinario* magazine.

3. While not a title bout, the death of collegiate boxer Charlie Mohr in April 1960 led to the end of the University of Wisconsin boxing team and to the National Collegiate Athletic Association dropping its sponsorship of college boxing later that year. It may be this death of a university athlete that should be credited with fueling the boxing-ban and death-in-the-ring discourse, although Norman Mailer will later credit the live television broadcast. Deadliness was certainly not new to boxing in the 1960s. Nat Fleischer, the former editor of *Ring Magazine*, tallied around 450 boxing deaths between 1900 and 1962—and a rate of around ten deaths per year during the 1950s—with blood clots in the brain accounting for three quarters of the deaths in New York over a thirty-year period. Amateurs faired no better than professionals, with twelve pros and ten amateurs dying in 1953 worldwide. See Robert L. Teague, "Many Fatalities Listed for Boxing," *New York Times*, April 3, 1962, reprinted in Gene Brown, ed., *The New York Times Encyclopedia of Sports, Volume 7: Boxing* (New York: Arno Press, 1979), 144.

4. "Igaku de wa yogen dekinu: Kyanberu jiken no kyōkun," *Asahi shinbun*, May 27, 1961, 11.

5. "Bokushingu wa 'satsujin kyōgi' ka: Ijō na hankyō yonda Paretto jiken," *Shūkan asahi*, April 13, 1962, 104–6.

6. "Bokushingu no kikendo," *Asahi jānaru*, April 15, 1962, 48. When the American Medical Association recommended banning the sport in 1984, it acknowledged these statistics but condemned the sport for making damaging an opponent's brain an objective. See Ira R. Casson, "Brain Damage in Modern Boxers," *Journal of the American Medical Association* 251, no. 20 (1984): 2663–67.

7. Norman Mailer, "Ten Thousand Words a Minute," *Esquire* 57, no. 2 (February 1963): 116.

8. Ibid.

9. "Sugao: Terayama Shūji-shi," *Asahi jānaru*, December 6, 1964, 85.

10. The Harada–Jofre rematch in May 1966 ranked highest at number 5 (63.7 percent viewership), and the other bouts ranked 8, 12, 21, 22, and 24. The most-watched programs above Harada's rematch were the 1963 New Year's Eve singing contest (*Kōhaku uta-kassen*) (81.4 percent), the 1964 Japan–USSR women's volleyball Olympic final (66.8 percent), the 2002 Japan–Russia World Cup soccer match (66.1 percent), and the 1963 World Wrestling Association (WWA) professional wrestling title match between The Destroyer and Rikidōzan (64.0 percent). See Video Research Ltd., "Zenkyoku kōshichōritsu bangumi 50," http://www.videor.co.jp/data/ratedata/all50.htm (accessed September 18, 2010).

11. See Harada's autobiography: Harada Masahiko, *Boku Faitingu Harada desu* (Tokyo: Hinode Shuppan, 1984).

12. Terayama Shūji, "Bokushingu o miru," *Asahi jānaru*, July 10, 1965, 33.

13. Terayama Shūji, *Terayama Shūji zenkashū* (Tokyo: Chūsekisha, 1982), 43. This collection is analyzed in greater depth in chapter 5.

14. Nelson Algren, *Never Come Morning* (New York: Avon Publishing, 1948), 181. Terayama and Algren began writing to each other in the early 1960s. Algren spent two weeks in Tokyo with Terayama in December 1968 on his way to Saigon (as a reporter). Algren comments briefly on the Tokyo stopover in a piece called "No Cumshaw, No Rickshaw" in *The Last Carousel* (1973; Seven Stories Press, 1997): 125–30.

15. Harada Masahiko, "Jofure datte ningen: Dōryoku sureba kateru to omotta," in *Kyūkyoku no eikō*, ed. Ikeda Tetsuo (Tokyo: Bēsubōru Magajin Sha, 2000), 8.

16. I am using this term "reality effect" somewhat more broadly than Barthes does in the essay in which he coined the term. His comments are mainly limited to elements in a narrative that seem superfluous but, for that reason, generate the reality of the text by not serving as communicative signs for the reader. See "The Reality Effect," in *The Rustle of Language*, trans. Richard Howard (New York: Hill and Wang, 1986), 141–48.

17. Nat Fleischer and Sam Andre, *An Illustrated History of Boxing*, 6th ed. (New York: Citadel Press, 2001), 63–70.

18. Fuji TV, which broadcast all of "Fighting" Harada's title matches, only started color broadcasts in 1967, well into Harada's career.

19. See Gilles Deleuze, "Coldness and Cruelty" in *Masochism* (New York: Zone Books, 1991): 76–77. I will engage more extensively with Deleuze's work on sadism and masochism in chapter 4. In Roland Barthes's essay on professional wrestling, he specifically denies this sadism—"It is not true that wrestling is a sadistic spectacle: it is only an intelligible spectacle"—but then goes on to admit that "the crowd is jubilant at seeing the rules broken for the sake of a deserved punishment." See Barthes's "The World of Wrestling," in *A Barthes Reader*, ed. Susan Sontag (New York: Hill and Wang, 1982), 24–25. Wrestling is the opposite of sadism, in his account, because its sadism is conspicuously faked, meant to be

a representation of commitment to the greater contract binding heroes to uphold laws of justice, which require the violation of lesser rules.

20. Terayama Shūji, "Kaneda Morio to iu na no bokusā," *Taiyō* 4, no. 1 (December 1965), 141.

21. Barikan ("hair clippers") is the nickname used to refer to him throughout the text, since he is an itinerant barber—the word itself derives from "Bariquand et Marre," a brand of French hair clippers. Barikan's real name is Futaki Kenji.

22. Terayama Shūji, *Aa, kōya* (Kawade Bunko: Tokyo, 1993), 87. The emphasis in the original is boldface.

23. Ibid., 89.

24. Ibid., 207.

25. It was published in German as . . . *Vor meinen Augen . . . eine Wildnis . . .* (Frankfurt am Main: S. Fischer, 1971). The translator was Manfred Hubricht, who had previously translated *Kometto Ikeya* and who later helped arrange for Terayama's theater troupe to perform at a festival in Frankfurt in 1969. The French translation by Alain Colas and Yuriko Kaneda was *Devant mes yeux le desert . . .* (Paris: Calmann-Lévy, 1973). Parco rereleased the original Japanese novel in 2005, intercut with Moriyama Daidō's grainy photographs of Shinjuku and Kabukichō.

26. Terayama, *Aa, kōya*, 335. This was not the first linking of boxing and modern musical forms within the realm of postwar fiction in Japan. Mishima Yukio wrote a radio drama in 1954 called "Bokushingu" (Boxing), which he later described as something he designed according to the compositional method of "musique concrète" (see Mishima Yukio, "'Bokushingu' ni tsuite," *Mishima Yukio zenshū*, vol. 22 [Tokyo: Shinchōsha, 1975]) and which, like *Aa, kōya*, includes a boxer's girlfriend named Yoshiko. Ishihara Shintarō would win the Akutagawa Prize the following year, in 1955, with a boxing-themed short story called "Taiyō no kisetsu" (Season of the sun), which led to a string of "sun tribe" (*taiyōzoku*) films starring his younger brother Yūjirō, including one in which Yūjirō plays a jazz drummer— *Arashi o yobu otoko* (The man who causes storms, 1957). The pairing of boxing and jazz, then, may have been almost normative by the time Terayama wrote his novel in the mid-1960s.

27. Terayama Shūji and Takemitsu Tōru, "Hizuke no aru hyōgen e," in *Takemitsu Tōru no sekai*, ed. Saitō Shinji and Takemitsu Maki (Tokyo: Shūeisha, 1997), 239. The interview was first published in the monthly *Yuriika* in January 1976.

28. Terayama Shūji, "Bokushingu: Nikutairon no adoribu," *Shisō no kagaku* no. 24 (March 1964): 72–76. The essay is more Terayama ad-libbing his thoughts on physicality than a careful thesis on the improvisational nature of the sport, but the link is there.

29. Terayama, "Chehofu-sai," *Tanka kenkyū* 11, no. 11 (November 1954): 9. "Barracks" is a difficult term here because it referred to both military barracks and the

military-like temporary shelters that much of the population lived in during the immediate postwar period.

30. Terayama Shūji, "Keshigomu," in *Sakka no jiden 40: Terayama Shūji,* ed. *Kuritsubo Yoshiki* (Tokyo: Nihon Tosho Sentā, 1995), 169–71.

31. Terayama Shūji, "Kōi to sono hokori: Minato no gendaishi to action-poem no mondai," in *Chi to mugi* (Tokyo: Shiratama Shobō, 1962), 101.

32. Uno Akira, in discussion with the author, Tokyo, January 17, 2004.

33. Terayama and Takemitsu, "Hizuke no aru hyōgen e," 242.

34. Terayama, *Aa, kōya,* 96. Terayama would later rework this theme of the suicide machine into a mock suicide manual called *Seishōnen no tame no jisatsu nyūmon* [The young person's guide to suicide] (Tokyo: Doyō Bijutsu Sha, 1979). The manual demands so much preparation for a proper suicide—construct an original suicide machine, write a formal suicide note, check for adequate motivation, choose the perfect location, apply for a suicide license—that a suicidal reader who made it all the way through the text would probably have already reconsidered, which was likely Terayama's goal. Suicide machines also show up in an "epic poem" Terayama wrote in 1970 called *Jigokuhen* (The inferno). See Terayama Shūji, *Jigokuhen* (Tokyo: Shichōsha, 1983), 15–20.

35. Terayama, *Aa, kōya,* 96–97.

36. The word is too formal and archaic to be used to mean "suicide" in Terayama's novel (he uses *jisatsu*), but the juxtaposition of the ideas of taking possession of one's fate and suicide is conspicuous here.

37. Terayama, *Aa, kōya,* 180.

38. Ibid., 52.

39. Ibid., 14.

40. Terayama Shūji, "Sho o suteyo machi e deyō," in *Terayama Shūji zen shinario* (Tokyo: Firumu Āto Sha, 1993), 1:214.

41. Takemitsu Tōru, "Kitsuon sengen: Domori no manifesuto," in *Takemitsu Tōru chosakushū,* ed. Tanikawa Shuntarō and Funayama Takashi (Tokyo: Shinchōsha, 2000), 1:69. This piece was originally published in the fourth issue of *SAC* (July 1960), the monthly publication of the Sōgetsu Art Center, which extended beyond ikebana in the 1960s to host avant-garde events in many formats.

42. Takemitsu, "Kitsuon sengen," 70.

43. Terayama, *Aa, kōya,* 111. Barikan's loneliness in the ring and his sensation of being "millions of light-years away" was likely a nod to Terayama's friend and fellow poet Tanikawa Shuntarō, who debuted in 1952 with a collection called *Nijūoku-kōnen no kodoku* [Two billion light-years of loneliness] (Tokyo: Sōgensha, 1952).

44. Terayama, *Aa, kōya,* 122.

45. Ibid., 111.

46. Ibid., 36–37.

47. Ibid., 153.

48. Ibid., 19.

49. Ibid., 167.

50. This celebration of "challenging one's star" could be taken as still more reason for suspicion regarding Terayama's sudden shift to Sagittarius in 1966, around the same time this passage was first published.

51. Terayama, *Aa, kōya*, 253–54.

52. Ibid., 271.

53. Ibid., 232. The connection of Miyagi to the rest of the narrative is conspicuously stretched, willfully mocking the convention dictating that all characters appearing in a novel be part of a gradually revealed web of interconnectivity: "To add a bit of novel-esque causality here let's have One-Eye, who opened the gym in Kabukichō, be the brother-in-law of Miyagi Taichi" (24).

54. Terayama Shūji, *Bōryoku toshite no gengo: Shiron made jisoku 100-kiro* (Tokyo: Shichōsha, 1983), 9.

55. Terayama, *Aa, kōya*, 199, 268.

56. Ibid., 82, 291.

57. Terayama, *Bōryoku toshite no gengo*, 155. This is obviously the inverse of other trends in graffiti writing, that is, toward conspicuous stylizations of the writer's nickname. See Susan Stewart's analysis on this form of signature writing in her *Crimes of Writing: Problems in the Containment of Representation* (Durham, N.C.: Duke University Press, 1994), 206–33.

58. Terayama, *Bōryoku toshite no gengo*, 180.

59. Terayama, *Aa, kōya*, 324.

60. Ibid., 327.

61. Ibid., 296.

62. Terayama Shūji, "Dare ga Rikiishi o koroshita ka," in *Ashita no Jō no dai-himitsu: Yabuki Jō to sono jidai*, ed. Takatori Ei (Tokyo: Shōbunkan, 1993), 147. Originally published in the *Nihon dokusho shinbun* on February 16, 1970.

63. Terayama, "Rikiishi," 147.

64. "Kimyō na o-sōshiki," *Mainichi shinbun*, March 21, 1970.

65. Hisao Mitsuko, in discussion with the author, Tokyo, April 3, 2004.

66. "Rikiishi o naze koroshita: Hen na sōshiki ni nekkyō no 700 nin," *Tōkyō chūnichi shinbun*, March 25, 1970.

67. Takatori, *Ashita no Jō no dai-himitsu*, 153.

4. Deinstitutionalizing Theater and Film

1. Gilles Deleuze, "Coldness and Cruelty," in *Masochism* (New York: Zone Books, 1989), 40–42, 76–79. The original essay, "Le froid et le cruel," was published in 1967, the same year that Terayama's play *Kegawa no Marii* was first performed.

2. The play was performed twice between June 3 and 4, 1969, for a festival called Experimenta 3 at Theater am Turm (TAT). Posters advertised the title of the play to be *La Marie Vison*, the French chanson from which Marie got her name and a song featured in the play, which was the title used in foreign performances of the play as well as a subtitle for the Japanese version. But the title used in the German reviews of the play, articles in *Theater Heute* for example, used *Marie im Pelz*, following Manfred Hubricht's translation of the script. See Hans Schwab-Felisch, "Fernost-Aggression," *Theater Heute* 10, no. 12 (December 1969): 10.

3. Terayama must only have heard about or read a description of the play. It does not seem to have been translated until 1982. See Satō Tomoko's translation in Shimura Masao, ed., *Beikoku goshikku sakuhinshū* (Tokyo: Kokusho Kankōkai, 1982).

4. Arthur Kopit, "Oh Dad, Poor Dad, Mamma's Hung You in the Closet and I'm Feelin' So Sad," in *Three Plays* (New York: Hill and Wang, 1997), 31.

5. Ibid., 61–62.

6. Ibid., 77.

7. Terayama Shūji, *Gendai no seishunron: Kazoku-tachi, kedamono-tachi* (Tokyo: San'ichi Shobō, 1963), 20. Terayama extends this description for the release of this text as a paperback in the early 1970s, adding (falsely) that in Kopit's play the boy is kept busy chasing butterflies around the Havana hotel room. This is a detail from Terayama's *Kegawa no Marii* not seen in Kopit. A reader of Terayama's paperback familiar with Terayama's play would be led to believe that it was even *more* indebted to Kopit that it actually was, perhaps another moment of false "kleptomaniac" plagiarism willfully cultivated. See Terayama Shūji, *Iede no susume* (Tokyo: Kadokawa Shoten, 1972), 13–14.

8. Terayama, *Iede*, 73.

9. Deleuze, "Coldness," 20.

10. Ibid., 77.

11. I use "transvestism" rather than "transgender" here in following Miwa Akihiro, who speaks of the time when he started wearing women's clothes rather than the time he reconceived himself to be a woman (it is noteworthy that he changes his family name but maintains his clearly male given name "Akihiro"). Yet if Marie is struggling to alter the "furs" of her own male skin in the play, then it may be useful to this as a play about the way transgender undermines the male–female binary social institution.

12. Terayama Shūji, "Kegawa no Marii," in *Terayama Shūji no gikyoku* (Tokyo: Shichōsha, 1983), 1:127–28.

13. Erving Goffman, "On the Characteristics of Total Institutions," in *Asylums: Essays on the Social Situation of Mental Patients and other Inmates* (New York: Anchor Books, 1961), 5–6.

14. Ibid., 6.

15. Ibid., 12.

16. *The Sexual Revolution* was released in Japanese in December 1969, after Terayama's play, but the ideas were certainly part of counterculture discourse much earlier. Reich published the first German edition in 1936, which was released in English in 1945. Terayama summarizes Reich's principles in a roundtable transcription called "Seiyokuron: Sekkusu reborūshon," in Terayama Shūji, *Byakuya tōron* (Tokyo: Kōdansha, 1970), 9–40.

17. See Wilhelm Reich, *The Sexual Revolution: Toward a Self-Regulating Character Structure* (New York: Farrar, Straus and Giroux, 1974), especially 6–7 regarding rape and pedophilia, 20 for fascism, and 34–39 on the problems of compulsory marriage. The entire second half of the book treats the early successes and later failings of the Soviet Union's attempt to revolutionize sexuality.

18. Terayama, "Kegawa," 155–56. Nicolas Bataille, who met Terayama in Tokyo in 1967 while there to direct Ionesco's plays (as he had done in Paris since the first performances and as he continued to do until is death in 2008), directed a translated version of *Kegawa* in Paris. Bataille reports that audiences were often deeply disturbed by the subtle cruelty in the play. Nicolas Bataille, in discussion with the author, Paris, July 20, 2002.

19. Terayama, "Kegawa," 134.

20. Terayama Shūji, "Rekishi," in *Bungei bekkan: Nagayama Norio*, ed. Abe Harumasa (Tokyo: Kawade Shobō Shinsha, 1998), 133. The essay originally appeared in Terayama's *Kōfukuron* (Theory of happiness) essays serialized in the journal *Shisō no kagaku* starting in January 1968, which were released as a book by Chikuma Shobō in 1969. This critique of Nagayama also appears in a piece Terayama wrote for the *Mainichi shinbun* on April 14, 1969, that makes this same point. Terayama would revisit Nagayama's shooting spree in a short story published in December 1976 (in the magazine *Gendai no me*) called "Nagayama Norio no hanzai" (The crime of Nagayama Norio), which would spark a long response from Nagayama himself, his "Han-Terayama Shūji ron" (Against Terayama Shūji), published in August 1977 (also in *Gendai no me*).

21. Hariu Ichirō, "Terayama Shūji ron," in *Hariu Ichirō hyōron 1: Geijutsu no hanran* (Tokyo: Tabata Shoten, 1969), 63. Originally published in the monthly *Eiga geijutsu* in June 1969.

22. Kujō Kyōko, interview with Kuwabara Shigeo, Tokyo, February 17, 2004.

23. Mori Kōta's *Kawa: Ano uragiri ga omoku* (*The River: Betrayal runs deep*) was on at ATG during the Shinjuku Bunka premier of *Kegawa no Marii*, which ran from September 1 through 7, 1967. The troupe did an encore performance about a month later, from October 12 through 14, which would have followed the 1950 talkie version of Eisenstein's *The Battleship Potemkin*. The year 1967 was an important one for ATG and Japanese cinema. Ōshima's feature-length film of the *manga* by Shirato Sanpei, *Ninja bugeichō* (*Ninja arts manual*), was screened in February

and ATG's first trial coproduction, Imamura Shōhei's *Ningen jōhatsu (A Man Vanishes)*, opened in July. *Kegawa no Marii* was not, however, the Tenjō Sajiki's first performance at Shinjuku Bunka—they did an encore performance of their first play, *Aomori-ken no semushi otoko*, at Shinjuku Bunka from May 13 through 15 after the April performances at Sōgetsu Hall.

24. Ōshima Nagisa and Matsumoto Toshio had a particularly interesting debate on collaboration in the wake of Matsumoto's participation (alongside Yokoo Tadanori, Teshigahara Hiroshi, Abe Kōbō, and others) in experimental film for a pavilion at Expo 70 in Osaka. Ōshima attacked Matsumoto for hypocritically denouncing formalistic conservatism while offering his support to the existing form of film and profit distribution. Matsumoto retorted with the claim that too much political film maintained a core structure inherited from that which it opposed with only its surface content. Both were making coproductions with the ATG, however, apparently without any collaborationist consciousness. See Ōshima Nagisa, "Matsumoto Toshio: Shura to shutai," *Eiga hihyō* 2, no. 11 (November 1971): 35; and Matsumoto Toshio, *Eiga no henkaku: Geijutsuteki rajik-arizumu to wa nani ka* (Tokyo: San'ichi Shobō, 1972): 265–66.

25. Terayama Shūji, *Sho o suteyo machi e deyō* (Tokyo: Haga Shoten, 1971).

26. Terayama Shūji, "Sakuhin nōto: *Sho o suteyo machi e deyō*," in *Terayama Shūji no gikyoku* (Tokyo: Shichōsha, 1984), 3:326–28.

27. Terayama Shūji, "Dokumentaru rebyū: Sho o suteyo machi e deyō," *Terayama Shūji no gikyoku* (Tokyo: Shichōsha, 1984), 3:15.

28. Hubert Niogret, "Shuji Terayama," *Positif* 148 (March 1973): 44–50.

29. This resonates somewhat with the opening scene of Ōshima's *Tōkyō sensō sengo hiwa* (The battle of Tokyo, 1970) in which the voice-over on a handheld camera's image scolds, "You should have brought it back this morning," suggesting a renegade filmmaker and jarring the audience with camera motion. The camera following Eimei down the railroad tracks in the early scenes of the film uses a similar effect, and it would not be unlike Terayama to reference Ōshima's work in a combination of homage and parody. See Maureen Turim, *The Films of Oshima Nagisa: Images of a Japanese Iconoclast* (Berkeley: University of California Press, 1998), 96–99.

30. Terayama Shūji, "Sho o suteyo machi e deyō," in *Terayama Shūji zen shinario* (Tokyo: Firumu Āto Sha, 1993), 1:189.

31. See, for example, Terayama's comments in his dialogue with the designer Awazu Kiyoshi, "Fūkei o tsukurikaeru tanoshimi," in *Dezain junyū* (Tokyo: Gendai Kikakushitsu, 1982), 202–10.

32. There are several options for translating "Rōra." It is listed in Film Index International as "Rolla," and ships from the Image Forum in Tokyo with that spelling. The theater scholar Shimizu Yoshikazu, in his recent *Terayama Shūji: Kaigai firumu dorama* (Tokyo: Bunka Shobō Hakubunsha, 2007), suggests that the title

of Terayama's film probably comes from Alfred de Musset's 1833 poem "Rolla," citing that this poem is mentioned in *Poesies* by Comte de Lautreamont, an author we know Terayama read (at least his *Maldoror*). The content of Musset's poem, about a man who has spent his last remaining money on a prostitute who falls asleep on him, is somewhat difficult to link to the film (unless the film likewise fails to deliver its sexual promise). Another possible source for "Rolla" (if that is correct) is Rolla France, one of the stars of René Clair's 1931 film *À nous la liberté*, a comic jailbreak (and a possible example of deinstitutionalization). I long thought the title might come from "Lola," the Kinks song about a well-disguised transvestite picking up an unsuspecting man in a bar, fitting as it does with the gender games of so many Terayama projects from this era. One also finds "Roller" in places like Joshua McDermott's master's thesis, "Terayama Shuji and *The Emperor Tomato Ketchup*: The Children's Revolution of 1970" (University of Hawai'i, 2005), but without explanation. A strong case can be made for "Laura," however, as a reference to the unconsummated affair between Laura and Alec in the 1945 film *Brief Encounter*. Lines of dialogue between Laura (Rōra) and Alec (Arekku) are quoted in an exchange of letters between Terayama and Yamada Taichi reprinted in Terayama's *Hadashi no koiuta* (Tokyo: Shishokan, 1967), 66. Yamada quotes the lines and notes that he also saw the script on Terayama's bookshelf. Terayama's experimental short film may be a representation of the consummation of the "forbidden romance" between actress and audience in literally allowing the viewer into the film. *Brief Encounter* may have been on Terayama's mind in 1974 if he had heard that Sophia Lauren, an actress he liked, was in the process of shooting her remake.

33. See the interview on this topic in the first issue of Image Forum's monthly: "Sukurēn no uragawa de eizō o kiita," *Imeiji fōramu* 1, no. 1 (November 1980): 8–18.

34. Terayama, "Sho o suteyo machi e deyō," 189. The published script includes a line not in the film: "Hold hands. Try up the skirt, and if things go right, all the way into the panties." Eimei may have just left it out, but it may not have been dropped for being too scandalous. The skirt comment genders the audience members, or at least the target of their actions. With the skirt left out of Eimei's suggestion in the final cut of the film, it could more interestingly apply to men or women targeting either men or women.

35. Ibid., 189–90.

36. Ibid., 233.

37. See Terayama's report of this trip, including descriptions of kibbutz, in *Yōroppa reinen* (Tokyo: Mainichi Shinbun Sha, 1970), 189–201.

38. Minami Yōichirō, *Soromon-tō tanken* (Tokyo: Kaiseisha, 1941), 157–62.

39. Terayama, "Jinriki hikōki," 7.

40. Terayama Shūji, "'Ichi mētā shihō ichijikan kokka' no tatoi," in *Zōki kōkan josetsu* (Tokyo: Farao Kaikaku, 1992), 138–40.

41. The full line in notes to the script is "What's the point of doing revolutionary theatre? We should be using theatre to find interconnections between our illusions; we should theatricalize every kind of revolution." Terayama Shūji, "Jashūmon," in *Terayama Shūji no gikyoku* (Tokyo: Shichōsha, 1986), 6:126. This note is labeled a January 1972 addition to the script of this play.

42. See Robert Brustein, *Revolution as Theatre: Notes on the New Radical Style* (New York: Liveright, 1971). Terayama was well-connected enough with the New York underground theater scene by 1970 to have direct knowledge of this book, so there is a chance that by advocating "dramatized revolution" he was directly targeting Brustein's position (and therefore somewhat less in conflict with Satoh's of "theater of the revolution"). My thanks to David Goodman for suggesting consideration of Brustein.

43. Yoshimi Shun'ya, *Toshi no doramaturugii: Tōkyō, sakariba no shakaishi* (Tokyo: Kōbundō, 1987), 299. For a detailed history of the founding of Parco within its larger Seibu–Saison context, see Thomas R. H. Havens, *Architects of Affluence: The Tsutsumi Family and the Seibu–Saison Enterprises in Twentieth-Century Japan* (Cambridge, Mass.: Council on East Asian Studies, Harvard University, 1994).

44. Sasame Hiroyuki, in discussion with the author, Tokyo, June 11, 2004. Tenjō Sajiki's two Bartok opera remakes, *Chūgoku no fushigi na yakunin* (The miraculous Mandarin, 1977) and *Aohigekō no shiro* (Duke Bluebeard's castle, 1979), the tribute series of Tenjō Sajiki plays the year after Terayama's death, and occasional revival performances of *Kegawa no Marii* (with Miwa as Marie) have all been performed at Parco's theater.

45. Terayama is spoofing the BBC's television series *A Young Person's Guide to the Orchestra*, which was released in Japan as *Seishōnen no tame no kangengaku nyūmon*. He uses this template a number of times such as in his 1979 book, *Seishonen no tame no jisatsu nyūmon* (The young person's guide to suicide), or elsewhere in the film *Sho o suteyo machi e deyō* where a girl is learning to smoke marijuana with the phrase "The young person's guide to drugs" (Seishōnen no tame no mayaku-nyūmon) written in chalk on the street in front of her.

46. Terayama, "Sho o suteyo," 235.

47. Ibid., 228–29.

48. Ibid., 235.

49. Articles on this event from various sources are collected in a volume on the Sōgetsu Art Center during the 1960s called *Kagayake 60 nendai: Sōgetsu Āto Sentā no zenkiroku*, ed. "Sōgetsu Āto Sentā no kiroku" Kankō Iinkai (Tokyo: Firumu Āto Sha, 2002).

50. Matsumoto Toshio, "'Eiga' ni totte ima nani ga hitsuyō ka: 'Ba' wa akumademo baitai," in *Kagayake 60 nendai*, 402–3. Originally published on November 17, 1969, in *Shūkan dokushojin*.

51. Ishiko Junzō, "*Ba* wa *baitai* dewa nai," in *Kagayake 60 nendai*, 403–4. Originally published in the January 1970 issue of the magazine *SD*.

52. Kawanaka Nobuhiro, "Puraibēto sukuriin: Sen-kyūhyaku nanajūnen to sono fukin no nōto," in *Kagayake 60 nendai*, 404. Originally published in his book, *Eiga: Nichijō no jikken* (Tokyo: Firumu Āto Sha, 1975).

53. Kawanaka Nobuhiro, "Yonen sankagetsu no taizai," *Imēji fōramu* 36 (September 1983): 52–54.

5. The Impossibility of History

1. Terayama Shūji, "Den'en ni shisu," in *Jiono, tobanakatta otoko: Terayama Shūji dorama shinario shū* (Tokyo: Chikuma Shobō, 1994), 107.

2. Inaga Shigemi, "The Impossible Avant-Garde in Japan," trans. Margaret J. Flynn, *Comparative and General Literature* 41 (1993): 69. The article was first published in French as "L'impossible avant-garde au Japon" in *Connaissance et réciprocité*, ed. Alain Le Pichon (Louvain-la-Neuve, Belgium: Presses universitaires de Louvain, 1988): 197–208.

3. The film was released in France under the title *Cache-cache pastoral* (Pastoral hide-and-seek).

4. Terayama uses the term "*waka*" rather than tanka in his screenplay for the film, giving them a medieval flavor. The *sōshi* here are plays on two twelfth-century *emaki* (narrative picture scrolls): the *Yamai no sōshi* (Diseases scroll) and *Gaki no sōshi* (Scroll of hungry ghosts).

5. The opening line, "Chikagoro otoko arikeri," is a direct play on the standard opening line to chapters of *Ise monogatari*, which typically begin with "Mukashi otoko arikeri." Terayama's use of *apāto* here within classical Japanese text invokes the effect of the word "hotel" (*hoteru*) in the opening lines of Mori Ōgai's "Maihime" (The dancing girl, 1890).

6. Inaga, "The Impossible Avant-Garde," 68.

7. Terayama Shūji, "Den'en ni shisu," in *Terayama Shūji seishun kashū* (Tokyo: Kadokawa Bunko, 1992), 121.

8. Terayama, "Den'en ni shisu" in *Terayama Shūji seishun kashū*, 116.

9. Ibid., 117.

10. Isoda Kōichi, "Kokyō no niritsu haihan," *Kokubungaku: Kaishaku to kyōzai no kenkyū* 21, no. 1 (1976): 36.

11. Terayama, "Den'en ni shisu," in *Terayama Shūji seishun kashū*, 116.

12. Ibid., 126.

13. Janine Beichman, *Masaoka Shiki* (Boston: Twayne Publishers, 1982), 87. Beichman is quoting from Shiki's "Nana-tabi utayomi ni atauru sho" (Letters to a tanka poet #7), dated February 28, 1898.

14. Terayama, "Den'en ni shisu," in *Terayama Shūji seishun kashū*, 115.

15. Ibid., 125.

16. Ibid.

17. Terayama announced in an early essay following his debut that the first of his four compositional methods for tanka was to write them as "modern renga." See Terayama Shūji, "Romii no daiben," *Haiku kenkyū* 12, no. 2 (February 1955): 41.

18. Isoda, "Kokyō," 36.

19. Terayama, "Den'en ni shisu," in *Terayama Shūji seishun kashū*, 124.

20. Isoda, "Kokyō," 37.

21. Terayama, "Den'en ni shisu," in *Terayama Shūji seishun kashū*, 116, 139, 143.

22. Hariu Ichirō, "*Den'en ni shisu*," *Kokubungaku: Kaishaku to kyōzai no kenkyū* 21, no. 1 (1976): 152.

23. This strategy resonates with descriptions of the organizational structure of student groups during the Zenkyōtō ("All-Campus Joint Struggle Committees"— a collection of groups that sought to unify factions of student political groups and independents for direct action between 1968 and 1969) movement's occupation of university campuses. According to Kuroko Kazuo, literary scholar and former radical who has written about fiction from the period, leaders and hierarchy would inevitably emerge within the groups, especially during fights for territory behind the barricades, but that hierarchy would then be disassembled, by force if necessary, after each mission was complete. Kuroko Kazuo, in discussion with the author, Seattle, spring 2000.

24. Terayama, "Den'en ni shisu," in *Terayama Shūji zen shinario* (Tokyo: Firumu Āto Sha, 1993), 1:115. "Old mother" is glossed with the reading *rōba* here, rather than the standard *rōbo*, possibly as a dialect-variant from the Tōhoku region.

25. Ibid.

26. Garrett Stewart, *Between Film and Screen: Modernism's Photo Synthesis* (Chicago: University of Chicago Press, 1999), 4, 9.

27. This was Saneyoshi Hanao's translation (Tokyo: Iwanami Shoten, 1939).

28. See Clayton Koelb's translation of *Death in Venice* (New York: W. W. Norton, 1994), 25n6, 34n1, 36n5, 41n2–3.

29. Terayama Shūji, "Den'en ni shisu," in *Terayama Shūji zen shinario*, 1:239.

30. Ibid., 240

31. Ibid., 241.

32. Ibid., 244.

33. Ibid., 256.

34. Ibid., 260–61.

35. Terayama Shūji, "Den'en ni shisu," in *Jiono, tobanakatta otoko*, 113.

36. *Hana ichi-monme* (One bunch of flowers) is a children's game in which two groups win or lose members with rounds of rock-paper-scissors and is played

while singing a song that starts with the line "Gather up the town for a game of *hana ichi-monme*."

37. Kuritsubo Yoshiki, "Terayama Shūji—Tankateki-eizō, eizōteki-tanka: Kashū oyobi eiga *Den'en ni shisu* ni tsuite," in *Terayama Shūji ron* (Tokyo: Suna-goya Shobō, 2003), 152.

38. Terayama Shūji, "Komoriuta yurai," in *Terayama Shūji no gikyoku* (Tokyo: Shichōsha, 1983), 2:234–35.

39. Ibid.

40. See Hachinohe-shi Hakubutsukan, ed., *Hachinohe-shi Jōmon Gakushūkan, Korekawa Kōkokan, Rekishi Minzoku Shiryōkan: Tenji annai* (Hachinohe: Hachinohe-shi Hakubutsukan, 1995), i, 2, 28; and Hosaka Saburō, ed., *Korekawa iseki shutsudo ibutsu hōkokusho* (Hachinohe: Hachinohe-shi Kyōiku Iinkai, 1972), 85–86.

41. Kusumoto Aki, ed., "Okamoto Tarō satsuei ryokō, shuzai nenpyō," *Tarō Museum*, http://www.taromuseum.jp (accessed December 17, 2004).

42. See Marilyn Ivy's *Discourses of the Vanishing: Modernity, Phantasm, Japan* (Chicago: University of Chicago Press, 1995), 29–65.

43. Terayama Shūji, "Sakuhin nōto: *Den'en ni shisu*," *Terayama Shūji no gikyoku* (Tokyo: Shichōsha, 1986), 6:360.

44. Terayama, "Den'en ni shisu," in *Terayama Shūji seishun kashū*, 158.

45. Ibid., 117.

46. Ibid.

47. Ibid., 122.

48. Moriyasu Toshihisa makes note of this discrepancy in a footnote to his essay on the film version of *Den'en ni shisu* but does not attempt to theorize it. See his "Terayama Shūji no eiga *Den'en ni shisu*: Sei to han to no montāju," *Utsunomiya Daigaku Kyōiku Gakubu kiyō* 46, no. 1 (1996): 32.

49. "Daiku-machi," "Tera-machi," and "Kome-machi," in *Aomori-ken*, vol. 2 of "Kadokawa Nihon chimei daijiten" Hensan-iinkai, *Kadokawa Nihon chimei daijiten* (Tokyo: Kadokawa Shoten, 1985), 520, 609–10, 382–83.

50. Terayama, "Sakuhin nōto: *Den'en ni shisu*," in *Terayama Shūji no gikyoku*, 6:357.

51. Terayama, "Den'en ni shisu," in *Terayama Shūji zen shinario*, 1:255.

52. The grandfather paradox traces to Hugo Gernsback, the original publisher of *Amazing Stories* and a major figure in promoting serious discourse regarding the propositions of Wells's *The Time Machine*. Gernsback published the following puzzle in an editorial called "The Question of Time-Traveling," part of the December 1929 issue of his *Science Wonder Stories*: "Suppose I can travel back into time, let me say 200 years; and I visit the homestead of my great great great grandfather, and am able to take part in the life of his time. I am thus enabled to shoot him, while he is still a young man and as yet unmarried. From this it will be noted that I could have prevented my own birth; because the line of propagation

would have ceased right there. Consequently, it would seem that the idea of time traveling into a past where the time traveler can freely participate in activities of a former age becomes an absurdity. The editor wishes to receive letters from our readers on this point; the best of which will be published in a special section." This was reprinted in Paul Nahin, *Time Machines: Time Travel in Physics, Metaphysics, and Science Fiction* (New York: American Institute of Physics, 1993), 172.

53. Terayama, "Den'en ni shisu," in *Terayama Shūji zen shinario*, 1:254.

54. Awazu Kiyoshi and Terayama Shūji, "Fūkei no tsukuri-kaeru tanoshimi," in Awazu Kiyoshi, *Dezain junyū* (Tokyo: Gendai Kaikakushitsu, 1982), 203.

55. Ibid., 202.

56. Terayama, "Den'en ni shisu," in *Terayama Shūji zen shinario*, 1:267–68.

57. Ibid., 268.

58. It is likely that the political nuance of this line was also intended. See Oguma Eiji's history of post–World War II Rightist tendencies within the Japanese Left and Leftist tendencies within the Japanese Right in *"Minshu" to "aikoku": Sengo Nihon no nashonarizumu to kōkyōsei* (Tokyo: Shinyōsha, 2002). Terayama links politics with shōji elsewhere as well: "I started thinking about the way the knight moves. It dawned on me that it's a very postwar sort of motion. After taking two steps forward it turns either right or left for one more step. Whether you choose right or left depends on your situation in the game. Such an essential problem as 'right or left' is not an ideological problem in shōji, it's no more than a reaction to the opponent's move, giving it an interesting and almost Machiavellian feel. The knight can never make three steps of foreward progress." Terayama Shūji, "Tareka kokyō o omowazaru," in *Sakka no jiden 40: Terayama Shūji*, ed. Kuritsubo Yoshiki (Tokyo: Nihon Tosho Sentā, 1995), 90.

59. Awazu and Terayama, "Fūkei," 205–6.

60. Terayama, "Den'en ni shisu," in *Terayama Shūji zen shinario*, 1:254.

61. Terayama, "Sakuhin nōto: *Den'en ni shisu*," 364.

62. Terayama, "Den'en ni shisu," in *Terayama Shūji zen shinario*, 1:269.

63. Ibid., 273.

Conclusion

1. This is at least how the *fūten-zoku* are described in "Shinjuku fūten konchūki: Negura mo shokuji mo sono hi no kaze ni makase—fūzoku rupo," *Shūkan Asahi*, August 8, 1967, 22–27. See also Yamada Kaiya, *Ai amu hippii: Nihon no hippii mūvumento '60-'90* (Tokyo: Daisan Shokan, 1990).

2. Nagashima Shinji, *Fūten* (Tokyo: Mandarake Shuppanbu, 2008), 27.

3. Terayama Shūji, "Ushiro kara yomu hon," *Asahi jānaru*, October 8, 1967, 84.

4. I analyzed this play in more detail in "Terayama in Amsterdam and the Internationalization of Experimental Theatre," in *Modern Japanese Theatre and Performance*, ed. David Jortner, Keiko McDonald, and Kevin J. Wetmore Jr. (Lanham, Md.: Lexington Books, 2006), 109–21.

5. Sharon Kinsella, *Adult Manga* (Honolulu: University of Hawai'i Press, 2000), 32.

6. C. Wright Mills, "On the New Left," *Studies on the Left* 1, no. 4 (Winter 1961): 63–65.

7. Ibid., 67, 72.

8. Julian Cope, *Japrocksampler* (London: Bloomsbury, 2008), 9. This survey includes a chapter on the music and sound designer for Terayama's troupe, J. A. Seazer. See also Cope's *Krautrocksampler* (Wiltshire, United Kingdom: Head Heritage, 1995).

9. Terayama Shūji, "Kōi to sono hokori: Minato no gendaishi to Action-poem no mondai," *Gendaishi* 7, no. 9 (September 1960): 100, 107.

10. See, for instance, Terayama Shūji, "Akkan-shigan," in *Gendai no seishunron: Kazoku-tachi, kedamono-tachi* (Tokyo: San'ichi Shobō, 1963), 89–93.

Index

STEVEN C. RIDGELY is assistant professor of Japanese at the University of Wisconsin–Madison.